PAY ATTENTION AND REMEMBER

EARLY TEACHINGS

PAY ATTENTION AND REMEMBER

EARLY TEACHINGS

Lee Lozowick

Compiled and Edited by Karuna and Vijaya Fedorschak

HOHM PRESS
Chino Valley, Arizona

Cover Design: Hohm Press

Interior Design and Layout: Kubera Book Design, Prescott, Arizona

Library of Congress Control Number: 2021942214

ISBN: 978-1-942493-69-3

Hohm Press
P.O. Box 4410
Chino Valley, AZ 86323
800-381-2700
http://www.hohmpress.com

This book was printed in the U.S.A. on recycled, acid-free paper using soy ink.

Dedicated to all those who have in any way been touched,
or will ever be touched, by Lee Lozowick's Work

...and to Lee, Yogi Ramsuratkumar, and Karuna,
whose love left a wound that surely only God can heal.

ACKNOWLEDGMENTS

The editors are thankful to all those who provided support in bringing transcripts of Lee Lozowick's early teachings into publication. We are particularly grateful to Nicola Maessen, without whom the project would not have moved forward. Brother Juniper Abeles, who recorded the original talks in New Jersey, New York, and Arizona, offered ongoing help in gathering tapes and information about them. The Hohm Press staff including Regina Sara Ryan, Dasya Zuccarello, Bala Zuccarello and Becky Fulker brought the manuscript to press. We want to thank the following sangha members of the Hohm Community for transcribing Lee's words: Nicola Maessen, Rogayeh Tabrizi, Ted Violini, Nancy Estrada, Mandy McFarlan, Lesley Ball, Linda Hitson, Eli Francovitch, Chris McMaster, Fernanda Brunet, Shanthi Vairavan, and Shinay Tredeau. Finally, we would like to thank all those who have participated in this unreasonable, life-changing work, which has given all of us the opportunity to pass on, in our own way, something of what we have received.

CONTENTS

Satsang, 1975

INTRODUCTION

There is only God. There is nothing outside of God, there is nothing inside of God, there is no relationship that takes place in terms of God. There is only God.[1]

—Lee Lozowick

During the latter part of 1975, a buzz surged through the New York spiritual scene about a new guru who had "woken up" in New Jersey. People began to flock to check out this Westerner, Lee Lozowick, and his unique style, intensity, and irreverent humor. Many seemed to come with an interest in confirming their own conceptual understanding of traditional spiritual teaching and did not stay long. Some had a need to look more deeply into the existential dilemma we all face in a more vital way. All were met with an offering that utterly challenged a worldview in which we assume ourselves to be separate individuals at a cellular level despite philosophical truisms of oneness. This book is a compilation of some of the early talks that Lee Lozowick gave and made available to those who were drawn to consider his enigmatic teaching during the first ten years of his teaching Work.

Lee was the son of Louis Lozowick, the eminent painter and printmaker, and Adele Lozowick, a woman of character who dedicated herself to supporting her husband's work throughout her life. He described his early years as having been pretty ordinary. Then, as a young man, Lee unexpectedly became absorbed in the Silva Method, a course that taught processes to access higher powers of the mind. He quickly took on the role of New Jersey State Director of the program. Inevitably,

1 "The Assumptive Dilemma" (recorded talk), July 31, 1977.

in his enthusiasm for the field, Lee encountered information about traditional spiritual teaching—of the Sufis, yogis, mystics, and the Indian scripture. He came upon ideas of spiritual transformation, reading and assimilating material about those who had been "lost in God" and had realized the always present condition of union with all of existence.

Lee went to see most of the teachers who came through the New York area in the early 1970s. One night in July 1975, after being immersed in prayer, he fell asleep chanting the "Om Sri Ram Jai Ram Jai Jai Ram" mantra. Next morning, everything was different. Though his practice and need for God had intensified to the degree that he began to "live God," he said that enlightenment was a fluke that could not be attained. Years later, he attributed his realization, awakening, or "shift in context"[2] to the non-linear Influence [transformative power embodied by a spiritual Master] of the Indian Beggar-Saint, Yogi Ramsuratkumar, whom he did not meet in the flesh until early 1977. Interestingly, the same mantra had catalyzed Yogi Ramsuratkumar into spiritual freedom seven days after he had received it from his guru, Swami Papa Ramdas.

From the morning of his transformation in 1975, Lee appeared as a man on fire with devotion to God, which showed up as sacrifice to the endless process of universal unfoldment in myriad ways. This continued until his last breath and *mahasamadhi* [Hindi term for a realized being's conscious departure from the physical body at death] in the early morning on November 16, 2010. There were many different chapters of his teaching Work, and this book is intended to present a glimpse into the foundational part of it.

Part I of the book includes transcripts of talks used as part of a twelve-week Study Course through which new students learned about

---

2 A phrase Lee used to describe the event that precipitated his teaching Work, which he preferred to "enlightenment" given his perspective that enlightenment is already present for everyone.

basic principles of traditional spiritual work, communicated in ways familiar to those who had grown up in Western culture. In particular, the Study Course opened the door to work with Lee and the Hohm Community—the organization of students that he established. This gave individuals who approached the school a sense of what they were getting into. Though the essential material in the Study Course addresses the basic dilemma of life in any time and place, some of the information about the particular circumstances in the Community around 1976 has not been included due to its lack of current relevance.

Following the Study Course material, contained in Part I, are transcripts of recorded talks that Lee referred to as "commercial tapes." Part II includes teaching given from 1976 until July 1978, while Lee lived in eastern New Jersey and traveled regularly into New York City to give public talks. Part III contains teaching that he gave to students from July 1978 until July 1980 in a more concentrated setting after moving to the rural town of Johnsonburg in northwestern New Jersey. Part IV consists of talks he made available during the first six years after moving with the Community to an ashram in Arizona in July 1980. The Arizona talks were given to the students who had moved with Lee from the East Coast, and to others who found their way to him, who were involved most directly with him and with the practices that he recommended. Some of these practices—meditation, study, exercise, diet, right relationship, and tithing—were known as the life-level "conditions" through which students could work with the undisciplined mind and optimally access the spiritual Influence that flowed through Lee.

A number of the early commercial tape talks, or parts of them, are not included in this volume as they have already been published in other books by Lee Lozowick, including *In the Fire*, *Laughter of the Stones*, *Acting God*, *The Alchemy of Love and Sex*, and *Conscious Parenting*. There is a list of these talks and references to where they have been published in an Appendix.

Lee related to those who came to see him in very different ways, based on what they needed in the moment. He seemed to know that those who were drawn to access the Influence that came through him would find him. Lee was available to those who stumbled upon the Community in an ordinary way that was uncommon for spiritual masters—sometimes answering the phone or sitting in a bookstore (*Mind of Man* in New Jersey, or *Mudra* in Arizona) when someone first approached the school, or looking up from behind his desk where he was doing crossword puzzles in the ashram office to the surprise of someone who had been invited to visit.

At the same time, Lee always kept the Community small so that he could be personally involved with practitioners and not have their focus distracted from their own work by having to manage a stream of people with casual interest in the path. When he gave public talks, his unique presentation often seemed to dissuade visitors. Strong reactions could be provoked by Lee's use of earthy language and humor, which required an ability to see beneath the surface presentation and look honestly at oneself and one's inner experience. It was not an infrequent occurrence for visitors who had reactions to his style to walk out of public talk spaces. But regularly, as soon as the room cleared out, Lee would give sublime teachings—including some of the talks that have been transcribed for this book. Perhaps Lee's style was a gesture of compassion for those whose lives might be turned upside down if they were not ready for the work with ego that would be encountered on a genuine spiritual path.

Talks that Lee gave could be a wild ride in which one was faced with a variety of "higher" and "lower" experiential states all in one night. He could appear arrogant, capricious, boring, puerile, sexist, self-deprecating, or dumb; and then radiant, regal, and omniscient, with people being drawn into higher mystical states. To be around Lee, or any real master, there had to be an inner understanding of the need to work, to look beyond intellectual understanding into assumptions we make about ourselves, spiritual work, and a guru. Though ego resists with everything it has, there is something essential we all have that draws us to lose ourselves in the condition of freedom, love, and sacrifice for the creation—which Lee expressed in an abiding and completely functional way. Sometimes the talks—which have been edited to maintain Lee's essential communication and hopefully something of his unique style of delivery—went on for many hours. It was as if, in the early years of his teaching, it was useful for students to be in the spiritual master's physical presence for extended periods of time. This seemed to loosen one's armor and foster attachment to the guru, who shows the way through the confusion of the survival-oriented mind. Later in *sadhana* [the discipline of spiritual practice including an outer form and inner work], there would be a weaning process and a recognition of the need to find the guru as direct experience, beyond physical form and individuated personality.

Over the years, Lee communicated practices for students to use in going deeper as they developed greater maturity and resonance with the Work.[3] These were always integrated on the ground of the basics that continued to inform one's practice. Lee expressed great respect for other genuine masters who provided a fully transformational Influence, which he referred to as Grace or Gift, in other traditions. Yet, he said, it was important to recognize that every real guru is unique and offers a path that is not available anywhere else.

---

3 "Work" or "The Work" is a term that Lee used at times to refer to the transformational process that was engaged through relationship to the Influence that came through him. Sometimes he alluded to the Work as a broader transformational process that was accessed through any real tradition, teacher, or practice. He also used the term at times to indicate the system of ideas that the Russian mystic George Gurdjieff developed and called "The Work."

This book is offered to anyone who has inner necessity to unravel the dilemma of life, death, and identification, in appreciation for the sacrifice made by the true guru and specifically by Lee Lozowick. Lee's life of surrender to the Divine was extremely rare, and was expressed in his relationship to his master, Yogi Ramsuratkumar. Lee became an ardent advocate for the use of *Nama*, the divine name of Yogi Ramsuratkumar, after his third trip to India in 1986, when the blessing power of the name was communicated. Lee said that when a name or a mantra is empowered by a master, it activates the living presence of the master who has activated the mantra and brings divine help to anyone who uses it.

As with other masters throughout history, Lee's Influence is still available in the teachings and artifacts he left behind. Many students fortunate enough to have been introduced to the Work through him feel a responsibility to pass along what has been received. The material in this volume is presented with the wish that anyone with a true yearning to traverse the path will find Lee's words useful.

EDITOR'S NOTE ON TERMINOLOGY

Throughout his life, Lee's presentation and use of language challenged Western cultural norms and kindled a need to look more deeply into assumptions about self and the spiritual path. For the first few years of his teaching Work, Lee referred to those rare beings who embodied the promise of real spiritual life and who were instruments for enlivening it as "Godmen" and "Godwomen." These have been people whose longing for God led them to surrender to the life process, what Lee later termed "The Great Process of Divine Evolution," and to live the truth of nonduality or God-life—moved by, identified and aligned with the oneness of creation rather than the dictates of an assumed separate self. Such transformed individuals have always existed as a sacrifice for others who suffer under the illusion of separation from God or All that exists.

The term "Godman" has historical relevance in India, which has been home to many great Realizers throughout time. But it had a rub and was a very provocative term to use in America where theistic beliefs are mostly static given the overriding cultural perspective of God as a separate all-powerful being. It served to bring stark attention to the shift in context Lee had undergone and was a call for others to consider the spiritual possibility of human life and the obstacles to living from a prior condition that is everyone's true nature. Early on, Lee referred to his students as "the Enlightened Community," given the truth that enlightenment is always present even if we are asleep to it and especially with the access to Grace that exists when there is the living Influence of a Godman or Godwoman. This Influence continues after his or her death.

As Lee's teaching Work evolved, the terms "Godman," "God-life," and even "enlightenment" fell into disuse. By 1980, Lee employed this language much less frequently. Reference was more commonly made to masters, gurus, or teachers—and to the need to recognize that there are different levels of teachers ranging from those who have the ability to articulate the teaching to those who actually live, embody and have become the teaching.

With students in New Jersey, 1976

PART I

BASICS

STUDY COURSE 1976-1978

SURVIVAL

When a baby is in the womb, there is no such thing as survival because everything is taken care of. You don't get hungry because you are hooked up to mommy's blood system. You are part of the mechanism, part of the machine. You grow, you get arms and legs, and you are just floating around in amniotic fluid. It's like a samadhi tank.[1] You react to loud noise because a baby responds to sensory input, but there is no thought around that. There are no survival issues when you are in the womb.

Then at nine months and three weeks, baby begins to descend the birth canal. Mommy's body is saying, "Hey kid, it's time to come out." Mommy's body starts the process in coordination with the fetus. In an average birth, baby goes head-first down the birth canal. Baby doesn't know it's a birth canal; all baby knows is tactile sensation. Baby is floating in the womb, feeling pretty good, eyes closed. Suddenly, baby feels the pressure of the contractions of labor. Baby is interested, curious. There's no concept involved. Baby is not thinking, "Oh, this is a tight space." The experience is completely non-conceptual, simply tactile. Baby is feeling a sense of movement and begins to slip down the canal. Baby is still connected by the umbilical cord to mommy. Baby is still one with mommy. There is no separation. When baby crowns, there is a very interesting sensation. There is a sudden temperature change of

---

1 A dark, soundproof tank, filled with a foot or less of salt water, which allows an individual to float effortlessly on the surface of the water. The intent is to produce a state of meditative absorption or samadhi (a term used in various Eastern traditions).

probably twenty degrees. That's uncomfortable. Still, survival is not an issue. The reaction to that is just discomfort. Baby still doesn't have likes and dislikes.

The birth process goes on and baby's body comes all the way out. There are bright lights. Baby's eyes have never seen such bright light. Until now all light has been filtered through mommy's body. Baby's mechanism is saying, "This is going to be hard to adjust to." Every sensory receptor in the child is at a loss as to what to do with all the sensations. And just that quick, within minutes after birth, as soon as baby loses mommy, the first concept is impressed at a deeper level than any other concept will ever be impressed as long as the child lives: survival. Baby doesn't think in a temporal framework. There are only two things that go on for baby: mommy and not mommy. When baby comes out of the womb, he or she is not mommy. Survival—Concept One—kicks in. Every other concept from that point on—friendship, sex, family, love, marriage, politics, religion—is laid on top of Concept One.

The context of life, regardless of the form, is survival. What do you do about that? There is only one thing that can possibly be done. It's called God-life, awakening, realization, enlightenment, illumination, transcendence. It's the only answer to being a total machine.[2] When every concept is built on top of survival and you don't know that, you are a machine. When you were three years old, Uncle George picked you up and you disliked it. He smelled like a beer hall and he was wearing a red shirt. Now you are twenty-five years old. You walk down the street and see someone wearing a red shirt and *wham*! It doesn't matter that you were in a great mood. Like a machine, fifteen minutes later, you find yourself feeling down.

Any one of seventeen billion stimuli could lift you up or bring you down in an instant. You have spent years getting a million impressions

---

2 Study of the human being as a machine is a principle of the Gurdjieff Work.

a minute all on top of Concept One, survival. How can you deal with something like that? You can't ever understand it; you can't ever work it all out. Why are you down one minute and sailing the next? Is it God? Is it your mantra? Or that you saw a green shirt and you have a very good impression of green shirts? There is no great meaning behind it. Red shirt–green shirt is all there is. We generally do not have the least bit of awareness of the unconscious patterns that move us. What we're doing is winning, surviving.

Most of us have a cultural bias toward thinking that God is judgmental. We don't get that from our religious upbringing. We actually get that much earlier. Because mommy is God to babies. Who is everything to the child—warmth, love, food? Mommy. Baby grows up thinking that mommy is God. Because what does God do for you? God gives you whatever you need to survive. That's why people pray to God—to give them what they need to survive. We are more sophisticated; we pray for enlightenment, but it's no different.

We grow up thinking that God is judgmental, because as a baby we were hungry and mommy was busy. She had water boiling on the stove, and we were spitting and crying, and mommy wasn't there when we needed her. When a little child cries, he or she is not unhappy—they are hungry or maybe they miss mommy. If mommy's got to do something for a minute before she can pick up baby, the whole organism is impressed with the sensation of hunger and the gap of time before that hunger[3] is satisfied. Because the organism has been impressed with certain information as a child, we grow up with one shoulder a little higher than the other, the left leg shorter than the right, a muscle twitch in our chest, and maybe knee problems. All of that affects our opinion about God and life.

Everyone is brought up with different interests and a particular form of survival that is unique to that individual. Some people survive

---

[3] This may include hunger for contact.

through their talent—the expression of their music, art, writing, athletic activity, or intellect. Some people can only survive through emotional interaction. It doesn't matter if that interaction is positive or negative—they may survive through fighting with people they live with. Ego says that's the way to survive. Some people can only survive through activity. They have to be working—at anything. If it's cooking, they survive by cooking. When they are not working with their hands, they work with their heads. All their energy is about working. Every individual has a different form of ego that says, "This is what you need to survive," and when it comes down to the wire, that is the most important thing in their lives. Higher principle is not more important to the individual than survival.

We stumble upon God and we say, "That's what's missing. It must be God!" When we stumble across Truth it impresses us, and what we do is interpret God in some way. Some of us say, "I should start eating better food and get my body straight." Others say, "It's a terrible thing that's going on down South, so I am going there to march and get involved in social action." Some people say, "There's an Indian guru coming to America and he says not to worry about social action. First become enlightened and pray and then you'll know what to do." So, we go to the ashram and we practice. We get healthier, we stop doing dope and alcohol and cigarettes, and stop being bummed out so much. But we still have a concept of God that is strictly limited by what is impressed here [*Lee thumps his chest*]. This whole thing—the body and the mind—has an impression of God and that's what we are limited by. The traditions all say that to truly understand who or what God is, it is necessary to transcend, to experience revelation. But to transcend what? The Eastern traditions talk about *maya*,[4] the play of the worlds. Ramana Maharshi talked about the world being just another dream. At

[4] In Vedic literature, *maya* is the power that creates the illusion of separate manifestations within the one reality.

night you sleep and dream, but when you wake up you are still in the dream—just a different one.

We are not identified with self as Self. We are identified with this body/mind as self. We really think that we are going to die someday. What is necessary, the traditions say, is to recognize self as Self. That can't take place in the context of mental activity. People expect God to be intelligent and compassionate. God is not any of that. God is not a being. It's a *process*, an intelligence.

The most anyone can do is just give it up to the process. That's always the way it has worked and that's the way it will always work because there is only one process. So, as a spiritual student, you have to make yourself available to Grace. The more you make yourself available, the more you get the payoff. It is paradoxical. The biggest payoff is waking up, but the only way to get the biggest payoff is not to have *you* anymore! Because when you wake up, *you* aren't. You are still flesh and blood. You can get hurt or catch God-knows-what awful disease, but when you totally give up you, who is it that needs to survive?

COMMITMENT

Before anyone can consider real God-life they first have to realize that reputation is a killer—any reputation. You can't even begin to conceive of God-life until you are not concerned at all with reputation. If you try to explain to your friends and family that you are involved in real God-life, they will establish prayer groups for you or try to kidnap and deprogram you. People are really concerned about anybody who is involved in doing anything real. You are not going to get support except from others who are doing the same thing, and they are a very small minority. That does not mean that you should stop doing what you are doing that is service-oriented. Living God-life doesn't mean leaving the world and studying all day. It would be absurd to leave the world because the best form of recognizing God-life is *in* the world anyway. I am not suggesting the form your life should take; what I am suggesting is that you recognize what's true and cop to that. It is easy to recognize what is true but being able to cop to that is a different story.

God-life is not just something you do when you are comfortable and have a full belly and your lover is by your side. Anyone can live God-life when they are relatively satisfied. Then it's easy to be devoted and meditate together. God-life is when the biggest chance you've had since you've been working for a sales company is coming up, you've got an appointment with an important client at ten o'clock, and your car gets a flat tire. You get out, take your jacket off and fix it, and when you're done you are covered in grease. Then you get back in the car and the other tire goes flat. That's when God comes up. Not when you are comfortable. What do you do? You need to make a commitment.

Remembering God when you are comfortable is what everyone does. Hilda[5] is a real nice lady, and people call her all day long with the most absurd questions. She puts up with it, and she answers their questions, but the stuff that people ask her is absurd because people don't think about God when they are upset. They think about God when it's nice. They come to Hilda's and she is wearing a beautiful sari and they chant "Om" and it's all peachy-keen. But when things aren't going so well, they call her and say, "I am having a terrible day. I forgot last week's lesson." Hilda has been giving a lesson every week for years. One day she asked, "Who can tell me what the lesson was from last week?" There were four hundred people there and not more than five people could remember what she said a week ago. That's what people do, and that's not good enough. That's not God-life.

When I started teaching, the world seemed very absurd because I saw that people were not using their capacity. Everyone has the capacity to be available, full, happy, pleasurable, and infinitely more talented

---

5 Hilda Charlton was a spiritual teacher and mystic who taught classes in New York City for over twenty years. Lee attended some of her meetings in the early 1970s.

than they are, and nobody uses this capacity. When I looked at all my friends—at everybody actually, even the people I didn't know—I saw the same thing. There isn't one person in this room who wouldn't be okay without any of this stuff [spiritual life]. Just look at your families. They've gotten along just fine, and you can do the same thing. But getting along is not good enough from my perspective. You have to really cop to what you know, and that means living it. It doesn't mean living it when you are comfortable and not living it when you are not comfortable.

Question: When I first walked in, I saw some of your students wearing white-face make-up.[6] What is the meaning or significance of this?

Lee: There are a couple of reasons for the make-up. One is that we've all got a face on, whether we think we do or not. I include myself in that. I have a face on too, but you have to realize it's not "Lee" talking if anything valuable is going to happen. The other reason for doing things like this, and the postering campaign we're currently doing in New York City, is that people think I am just like other teachers. "Oh, Bubba Free John, Rajneesh, Trungpa, or Gurdjieff did that." I don't care, because I know who I am; but we are going to achieve some distinction at whatever cost. Not for me, but for my students, because it does them a great disservice to have to approach people who already think they know what I'm about. I don't know if certain teachers are who they say they are. But if anyone is a focal point for Grace manifest, they can't be like anybody else.

---

6 Lee asked students to wear white-face during this public talk that was given in New York City.

SPIRITUAL COMMUNITY

Community life, with or without a specific leader, serves a very important function. The fact is that we are living in the world and relating to people every day. Whether it be at our job, speaking to the waiter or waitress at a restaurant, getting gas, going through a toll booth, or meeting people in various social situations, we are always relating to people and responding at a certain level. We typically have our own kingdom that we can go back to rather than learn how to relate to others. We establish that particular territory as a kind of inviolate space that we can go to whenever we need nurturing—to escape from any kind of tension or any situation that may not sit too well with us.

Our capacity to live life rather than suffocate life has a significant amount to do with our ability to relate to and enjoy other people. If we have an inviolate territory or kingdom we can go to whenever anyone shakes us up a little bit, we never really need to learn to enjoy people. Why should we want to learn to enjoy other people when we have our own little space with our own little fireplace that we can throw a few logs in and sit and look at the flames and get absorbed in? We forget about who we are supposed to be working with, playing with, and relating to.

If you are sixty-five years old living alone in New York City, you can go into your own little territory with multiple locks on the door and make sure the windows are locked, the gas isn't on, and that there is enough food in the refrigerator for the weekend. You can use that inviolate space as an excuse for not getting involved in any situation that requires availability from you. People grow up learning to create a space that is safe and secure from any kind of attack, including attacks through pleasure, spiritual life, or understanding. Community serves a very valuable function. It enables us to be in a situation where the kinds of attacks that we guard against—that relate to understanding people and our lives better and to expanding our capacity for pleasure, enjoyment, and celebration of all the things that God has so gracefully presented us with—can occur.

Community provides us with an environment where we are forced to recognize how contracted, constricted, and limited our lives are. Once we see that, we can take whatever steps are necessary to expand and increase our capacity for enjoyment and pleasure. As a result of our upbringing, we all have developed habits that reinforce self-meditation[7] rather than relationship with others. We've got eccentricities. We like the toothpaste tube rolled up or we don't like it rolled up; we like the dishes washed right away or we pile them in the sink and start washing when we are out of clean dishes. These eccentricities reinforce the negative habit of closing off to other people's input and relationship. One of the valuable things that community serves is the capacity to recognize how our habits can separate us from others. Another thing that community—whether it be spiritual community or just an extended family sharing economic resources, responsibilities, child rearing and so on—is very valuable for is that it can establish a supportive environment for personal growth and recognition of who we are essentially.

It's true that there are communities that support the kind of environment that is abrasive to the personality because their belief system suggests that what they need to do is to tear down the personality and then re-establish something more positive. Even that is a supportive environment, because the people that become involved in that environment are looking for that kind of support. So, any community supplies a supportive environment surrounding the belief system that brings people to that particular situation. It's very helpful if we are working on something and have a need for what we are working on to be supported by others of like mind.

---

7 Lee used this term to describe a chronic unexamined focus on ourselves and what we want or need to the exclusion of people and situations around us.

When we belong to a group or community of people with similar interests, we are going to get feedback on our interests and ideas from people that are more experienced than us, who can teach or supply us with the tools that we need to pursue those interests. If our interest happens to be God-life, we could get involved in a community that surrounds a Godman. There we would find an environment provided to make God the focus of our attention. We can get involved in conventional community—join a chess club or the local bowling league—to pursue an interest in basically the same way that our interests are supported in spiritual community. But spiritual community is an environment in which we can pursue what is real instead of what is illusionary.

Another very important service that community provides is to support and reinforce the philosophy of a particular culture. In a group like Montessori, there is a philosophy about how children should be educated. For adults looking for that kind of culture, they find in Montessori a community where children are educated in a fashion that will reinforce that philosophy. If we don't become involved in a community that supports the culture of our choice then not only our lives, but the lives of our children, will be totally dependent on the culture that is expressed in the world at large—which trains people to be self-centered and competitive. Even the best conventional schools teach children to be cutthroat. It is the law of the jungle under the guise of education.

If there is a particular form of life that we think is more real than another form of life, we need a community that supports that kind of culture and philosophy. Without a community making a statement in terms of our belief systems, more often than not we will simply get ostracized from the conventional community that we're in. A spiritual community offers an alternative culture that can really make a statement about the texture of life in the world. If we aren't involved in a spiritual community that makes that kind of statement, the texture of our lives is basically at the effect of the world culture, which is infinitely more dehumanizing than humanizing.

In a spiritual community, we are given a genuine space in which to work on ourselves spiritually. The emphasis of the environment in the world is on survival and security. Work on oneself in the world has to do with establishing a nest-egg of money and territory, like the houses in Hollywood with electrified fences, a guardhouse, and dogs. What a community offers, particularly a spiritual community, is a place to work on the higher principles beyond day-to-day survival through money, food, and sex. Spiritual community offers the possibility to work on principles such as service, attitude, compassion, and the texture rather than the form of relationship. In the world, if we give a party and forty people show up, it's a successful party. If we are having a spiritual party, we're more interested in the texture of the relationship of the people who show up, not in how many people come and if the neighbors notice how popular or unpopular we are by how many cars are parked in front of our house.

THE GODMAN AND HIS FUNCTION

There are living yogis and spiritual teachers in the world. A lot of communities surround people who have something to offer in terms of knowledge, culture, teaching, and education. The spiritual community that surrounds Hohm is involved with what we call "the Godman." Hohm is not so much interested in offering education, knowledge, attainment, or service, but rather with making something available in the world that's always been here but is extremely rare.

Why the Godman? What function does the Godman serve? Why not any spiritual community where people have a spiritual goal and an ecstatic culture in mind and are interested in freedom, relationship, and the texture of life? Why is the Godman necessary to real community? Without one unified focal point in a community that is powerful enough, real enough, and true enough to transcend the illusion of survival, no community can function for any great length of time. Without this major focal point, when the community starts to become real, each individual is going to have their survival mechanism triggered. Whatever ego thinks they need to survive is going to become stronger than the group intention.

Even if the initial concept of the community is valid—a higher culture, an ecstatic form of life, a prayerful, devotional, and religious environment for adults and children—without that one focal point, the survival mechanism is going to get triggered when the community starts to get real. One person is going to compulsively cook without regard for anyone who has suggestions in the kitchen. Another person is going to compulsively work and is not going to take suggestions from anyone who that work may interfere with. Another individual is going to compulsively play music. Another person is going to run around the community wiping everybody out with manic-depressive activity, regardless of anything else that is going on. That's what happens when there's no focal point. Ego triggers and survival is more real than any ideal, philosophy, culture, or way of life—except for that which is offered by the Godman.

The Godman serves the most important function in a community that is really a community, not simply a bunch of people living together. The Godman serves the function of the focal point which, regardless of people's differences, solidifies the group intention in relationship to a prayerful life and in relationship to what is true. The main function the Godman serves is to embody Gift, the only thing in the entire universe that can obviate the egoic mechanism of survival. Grace is what we refer to when we use the word "Gift." Gift is literally Divine possibility —not human or egotistical possibility. Gift is not a form, an energy, a texture, or an attitude. It is inclusive context[8] that is always present, available, and optimally made manifest in the physical world that we live in through the presence of the Godman.

---

[8] "Context" refers to the matrix or field in which all specific events, objects, and forms arise. It may also refer to the texture of any given manifestation. Context may be distinguished from content—all of the specific forms and events that arise in creation.

For any real community to survive and to manifest its ideal—culturally, spiritually, and physically—it must have that focal point. If that focal point does not embody Gift, then the community can survive for a period of time, but it's ultimately doomed to failure. If that focal point, the Godman, embodies Gift, then the enlightened community becomes an assumed reality. Otherwise it's simply a dream and no more real than a dream. So, why Godman? Because Godman is a need, not simply a nice guy to have around. The Godman or Godwoman is a necessity in any kind of true, ultimate, and transcendent culture.

There is another function that the Godman serves. The seeker approaching spiritual life needs to obviate ego, and the Godman serves to bring this about. There are only two true forms of life: God-life and the search.[9] Paradoxically, both forms of life are true. The search is true, and God-life is true. God-life encompasses and is inclusive of the search. The search excludes God-life; there is only the search unless there is God-life. The spiritual student that approaches the community involved in the search cannot help but have a concept of God and the spiritual master—the ideal human being, "real man" as Gurdjieff talked about. This concept may be nebulous or very exact. Perhaps the spiritual student believes the realized human being is always pure, gentle, and compassionate. Maybe the spiritual student believes the enlightened being is a fire that's hot and cathartic. Whatever the spiritual student's concept is of the enlightened human being, cosmic consciousness, or the great myth, nobody who enters the spiritual community is free of the expectation of a payoff—at least initially—because everybody is seeking. You are either seeking or awake. There is nothing in between. Everybody that enters the spiritual community enters seeking a particular dream and expecting a particular response. We all expect something in return for our heartfelt devotion and mindfulness.

---

9 In the early days of his teaching, Lee often referred to "the search" as the underlying context of the mind's drive to survive by trying to reach or attain mundane or spiritual goals.

It is very important to recognize that the Godman is not a teacher. The Godman made manifest in his or her physical form can teach and can serve as an example. But for us to ideally get the most that we can from Gift, we must recognize that the Godman is not here to be a teacher. The Godman is simply present to offer Gift. For no other reason—not as a teacher, an example, a spiritual ideal, an end result of spiritual practice, a fulfillment of devotional life—none of these. Simply to offer Gift.

When you enter a spiritual community, what is the implied payoff? The living promise is the Godman. "If I do my sadhana right—exercise, meditate, and study—I am going to get to be that guy. Oh boy! I will be in heaven, and never have to come back to this dirty round of birth and death or worry about being reincarnated as a dog." So, the Godman serves a function that is total illusion and yet is necessary to draw people to this Work. The Godman is the promise, the ideal, the ultimate fulfillment of spiritual life or spiritual practice. That is one of the functions that the Godman serves in form.

We come to a spiritual community ostensibly to love God, to wake up, to become enlightened, to own who we are, to be responsible for the fact that our nature is the nature of the Lord. We make a commitment that this guy is a Godman, but we don't know it. As deeply as we want to believe, the Godman is also flesh and blood. He gets a cold occasionally. If somebody drops a rock on his foot, it bleeds. He gets black and blue when he gets punched in martial arts. He is just a guy like us. We can say that we believe it, we can want to believe it, we can have faith in it, but somewhere deep down inside of us we don't believe that the Godman is who he says he is. We think of Jesus or Buddha or Krishna being Godmen. Because they are dead. They are myth.

The Godman is the spiritual ideal, Gift manifest, and at the same time he is perfectly ordinary—paradox embodied. Paradox is something that the rational mind finds impossible to understand. The rational mind—which is ego—can learn to recognize it, dance around it, and try to accept it, but it cannot understand paradox under any circumstance. Paradox, however, can be perfectly understood prior to mind. The Godman can serve the function of presenting paradox in a way that can be grasped prior to mind, but not in a way that can be logically or rationally explained under any circumstance. We can develop a concept around the nature of paradox, but we can only *know* it prior to mind. [The particular individualized expression of the Godman] serves that function.

Everybody who comes to the Godman starts out with one rule, a principle that is inviolate: Do as I say, not as I do. We may ask, "Why is that?" You are told that the Godman will often behave in a way that is inconsistent with spiritual principles. After all, the Community is supposed to be considerate, gentle, and understanding. One is supposed to have a particular diet, to exercise and meditate every day. Sometimes the Godman is not gentle, and you wonder, "How can he be that way? He is so heartless." My students respond, "Don't you understand the paradox of the Godman? Sometimes he is supposed to work with somebody in a fashion that breaks down their resistance to expressing their real God nature, and the only way that he can do that is by manifesting a form that is not consistent with what he teaches."

Another function the Godman serves is that, over time, he can become a real force for spiritual life in the world. There are spiritual teachers in the past who were recognized by their students as the embodiment of Gift and became so exclusive that they were useless to spiritual students around the world except as a picture to pray to. If the guru is so exclusive that he is only an icon, a picture, or a name to use with prayer beads, that guru loses his or her function and does not serve any purpose. You need the real thing in flesh and blood.[10]

---

[10] The Influence of the guru or Godman is alive, and also available, to students who never met him physically. His availability is through the Community or sangha, artifacts, and Work that he communicated.

The Godman also serves the function of reminding us that we're flesh and blood, living in the streets. It doesn't matter where our home is—that's who we are: street people. We are ordinary. We can't transcend the world by developing bodies of light and floating around in some heavenly nirvana [freedom from suffering, in Hinduism and Buddhism]. We are going to be in the streets whether we like it or not. When somebody gets too spiritual and stops being real, the Godman reminds them, "Hey, look, you are real and spiritual too." Spiritual life is not some dream where perfection is attained by abstaining from coffee ice cream. That's not spiritual life.

Spiritual life is fulfilling the "Law of Sacrifice." You don't fulfill the Law of Sacrifice in a cave in the Himalayas or by giving everything up. You fulfill the Law of Sacrifice by being available to who needs you. The root of the word "sacrifice" is sacred. What is sacred? To give is sacred. To give up is oftentimes stupid, not sacred. The function that the Godman serves is to get us to recognize the Law of Sacrifice, which is giving. Sometimes we give things up in the process of learning to recognize real spiritual life, but it's not necessary to give things up. To *give* is necessary. We can't be real without giving. But we can be perfectly real without giving up. The Godman reminds us of that.

[The form and personality of the particular individual] serves the function of being perfectly human *and* the Godman. He is literally the world *and* just another guy hanging out—a human. Most of us think we are humans, but we are machines. We begin as machines, all of us. From machines, if we are lucky, we become human. It takes a tremendous amount of work, consciousness, and strength to become human. Then where do we go? Study of the teaching is designed to get you to recognize how necessary it is to become human and what you can do to become human. It can give you an intuition of what you can do after you become human.

The Godman serves the function of being a teacher. He can be an example, if you want. He can impart lessons, knowledge, teachings. He can create examples in which you can recognize spiritual principles. The Godman can create an environment in which you can recognize knowledge of Self—see what you're up to, who you are and how you function. He can help you understand the workings of the mind, the functions of the body, and emotional relationships. The Godman can do all of that. He can express the *dharma* [spiritual teaching] so that your questions are answered, and your brain is satisfied. He can initiate you in particular forms of physical activities so that your body can be purified, and your chakras can be cleansed. He can engage you in a particular form of emotional interaction so that the emotional poisons that you have allowed to infect your whole being can be expelled. But that is not the function of Godman. What the community ideally makes available is not all that juicy stuff. It offers Gift.

THERE IS NOTHING TO ATTAIN

Attainment—developing yourself so you are healthier, stronger, smarter, more centered, and in fact better than other human beings—is not what the Godman's community offers. It is founded upon the ideal of non-dualism. A Godman wakes up and realizes non-dualistic life. There is nothing to attain. At the same time, when we look at the state of the world, we see some people that seem to be better off than other people. Certainly, for us as individuals it is better to be healthy than sick. It is preferable for us to be economically comfortable so that we don't have to worry so much about getting food that we can't pray. It's fine to be comfortable, although all forms of attainment are illusionary. Because survival is not an issue, we cannot *not* survive. We are going to survive whether we live or die.

At the same time, one of the things that can manifest in the Godman's company is attainment. You can become a great yogi if you spend a few years with the Godman. That's not the point. Many great yogis are not awake. They haven't realized the Self or God, but they are great yogis. We don't want to ridicule attainment, but we want to recognize that attainment is not necessarily God-life. God-life can encompass attainment or not. There are people who have lived God-life who don't have any particular degree of attainment. They work hard all their lives and are not particularly intelligent. They never make a mark in the world, they don't write books, paint beautiful paintings, or sculpt exquisite statues. Nobody knows their names or remembers them, but they live God-life for forty or fifty years. So, attainment is fine in its place, but we should never identify attainment as realization. Realization is always present whether we have heard of the word or not. God-life is inclusive of realization and attainment, but attainment does not necessarily indicate God-life.

TRYING TO SURVIVE IN MORE SOPHISTICATED WAYS

It is important to recognize that one's approach to spiritual life is founded on the same dilemma that motivates the worldly search for attainment, survival, and fulfillment. It is not the love of God or the desire to do spiritual work that is the motivation. It is the same dilemma that has motivated your pursuit of a particular job, level of schooling, personal relationship, financial security, or the fulfillment of a talent: the need to secure survival. An artist, musician, or author will write a book or do a work of art that lasts a hundred years, thereby ensuring the survival of the identity even after the body leaves. But as people come to realize the emptiness of that kind of survival, they do not look for an alternate to the dilemma, they look for a more sophisticated way of surviving, which is spiritual life.

In spiritual life, the implication is that one can obtain eternal life either in this body or in another kind of astral or ethereal body. That kind of survival is not threatened by disease or old age. On the spiritual path, survival is seen as more than simply bodily survival. We all know that this body is going to die because none of us have known anyone that has lived more than one hundred years. So, in spiritual life we have a more sophisticated motive to attain the kind of body that is immortal.

DEVOTION TO A LIFETIME OF DISCIPLINE

We approach the spiritual community thinking that we are special, that we are going to be able to see in the Godman what others have not seen. We're absolutely convinced of it. We realize, at least intellectually, that we are entering into a lifetime relationship of discipline. "Oh yes, of course, I realize that I have to work for a lifetime, and I'm looking for something like that," says the novice approaching a community. Yet in truth, no individual is looking for that. No individual expects to spend a lifetime doing sadhana. Most people truthfully expect to spend two or three months in the Community, and in that period of time to have gotten whatever result they were looking for.

If you look at yourselves honestly, in the privacy of your own little mind—which is not as private as you think it is—you can decide what presumptions you have about attainment, enlightenment, awakening, and what goes on after that. We all have a very definite conceptual framework about what it means to be enlightened, and what we as an individual are going to do after we become enlightened. We want to begin to examine that in ourselves so that we can be open to what is being offered, rather than taking a sliver of what is being offered that happens to coincide with our conceptual framework of spiritual life and doing a little bit of work with that.

We want to be open to what has been said about traditional spiritual life in every real community in recorded history, which is that spiritual life is a matter of a lifetime of sadhana. At this stage, we are not even going to consider sadhana in any kind of temporal framework. Our perspective is an ongoing matter of discipline and heartfelt commitment without consideration of the future. If the future holds forty years of doing basic student sadhana, that's what the future holds. If the future holds some other kind of sadhana, then that's what the future holds. But we can't put a time frame on that and say that in one year we will be here, and in another year we will be somewhere else. We must simply work without any concept of how long it's going to take us to get somewhere.

If we don't recognize that our perceptions have literally kept us in the mental attitude of children all our lives regardless of how old we are, then what will happen is that we're not going to be open to what is being offered for optimizing our availability to Grace. The way to optimize our availability to Grace is not by sitting on our ass and looking at the Godman with misty eyes. The only way to optimize the possibility that our lives will be gracefully consumed, in the way the lives of Godmen and Godwomen throughout history have been consumed, is by being truly and deeply attentive to what is being spoken. Because what is being spoken is giving us the clearest framework and ideology about what we have to do in our lives, practically and functionally, to optimize that possibility. All of the traditional literature says that it's a matter of many years just to fulfill basic sadhana. If that is said in all the traditional literature, how could we imagine that we are going to advance in spiritual sadhana in a matter of months?

Because we are alive and have survived up to this point, we believe subconsciously that we are experts on survival. Ego interprets everything that we have ever done as substantiating survival. We have convinced ourselves, subconsciously, that we are unique because we are experts at survival. We assume that anything that we undertake will be completed perfectly in a record amount of time, including spiritual life. But if we recognize that this concept is founded in the fear of death, or extinction—which is an impossibility, but nonetheless we fear it anyway—then we can begin to approach the spiritual community from a position of openness, possibility, attention, and gratitude. That is the way we must approach in order to be able to use what is made available.

We say Grace is made available, but that doesn't mean much to us because we don't know what Grace is. We don't know what the Godman is, we don't know what or who God is. We have concepts about all these things, but we absolutely do not know. So, we must approach openly and with attention, so that we become impressed with the idea that spiritual life is really a matter of a lifetime of discipline, devotion, and sacrifice. If that point is made with us, we can become responsible for that recognition being implemented in our lives and prepare to engage that kind of discipline.

When we don't have attention, instead of recognizing, embracing, and being responsible for Truth when it begins to make a point with us, we *pretend* that the Truth has made a point with us. That is the way ego works. It's not that those who are weak will do it and those who are strong will overcome it. Regardless of how strong your will is, how intelligent or attained you are—the response will be identical. We will give our lives to what is in fact a fantasy and turn our backs on the Truth. We will forget. We will swear that we don't know what is going on. We must approach the teaching and the Community with gratitude and the willingness to receive what is being offered.

GATHERING MOMENTUM

We typically lay expectancies, crystallized concepts, and presumptions on our spiritual life and then feel the pain of disappointment that arises when these expectancies, concepts, and presumptions are undermined. We must pierce the root of the disappointment, not simply cover it over with another emotion that is more pleasant. This whole process is like starting a small snowball rolling down a hill. The snowball gathers more and more snow on its way to the bottom of the hill, until it is not only many times larger but is also traveling at a rate of speed that is infinitely greater than when it first started rolling at the top of the hill.

Initial or primary sadhana in any spiritual process is very much like that snowball: we begin small and slow. We begin with a concept that is limited by whatever education we've had about spiritual life prior to entering it. Any education offered in society is absolutely empty of any kind of real spiritual culture. When we enter spiritual life, our ability to appreciate what is being offered is very limited. So, we start off slow like a small snowball at the top of the hill. We begin examining the functional activities that we're given, the life-level conditions or practices that we're asked to participate in. No one approaches with the ability to fulfill all the conditions as the natural form of what is arising in their lives. If we force ourselves to follow all the conditions that relate to meditation, diet, sexuality, money, and exercise, we find that we have resistance to all of them. This resistance is analogous to the slowness of the snowball when it is starts down the hill.

As we start to recognize the benefits that we derive from following the life-level conditions, we also begin to develop more trust in what's being offered, more trust in the word of the Godman. If the Godman suggests we meditate an hour a day, instead of resisting that, we meditate even if our legs are aching. Because of the degree of trust that we are developing and because we have seen that basic sadhana does work in our lives, we begin to move faster and faster. After a couple of years of life as active members in the Community, our snowballs are rolling at a tremendous rate of speed.

Then we find what is arising naturally is appropriate diet, exercise, work, and so on. In initial sadhana it is important to recognize that the more our philosophy or our image of ourselves is threatened, the more identified we are with our expectations, the more intense the suffering or disappointment will be when one of those expectations is undermined. Ego reacts as if it is the final death. The closer we get to the root of the actual dilemma, the more grossly exaggerated becomes the suffering and the more dramatic the response is to the undermining. The highs are higher, and the lows are lower because we are approaching the core knot, the basic dilemma of the search.

RETURNING TO THE NON-DUALISTIC DHARMA

We must always come back to the recognition, at least rhetorically, of the non-dualistic dharma. We are doing spiritual practices, engaging certain conditions that surround the Work, making the teaching available, etc. At the base of all of that must be a recognition of the non-dualistic realization of God and not the dualistic recognition of any kind of attainment. In an average spiritual community, the implied and stated assumption is that when you reach the highest position in the hierarchy you will be realized or awakened. Although there is certainly a hierarchy with students at different levels of maturity, the present assumption prior to all form is that we are always already enlightened. It's not a matter of attaining enlightenment. All of the Work is simply fulfilling the Law of Sacrifice. Enlightenment is already present.

The work of self-observation, recognizing what arises with clarity as our very self, or owning the position of already-present enlightenment, is a matter of synthesizing or corresponding what is arising to the Law of Sacrifice—willfully and with celebration. Corresponding the natural conditions of our lives to the Law of Sacrifice is fully feeling the Law, as designed, in every moment. It's not resisting the Law by supporting the illusion of a separate self or individual who can attain various states of consciousness over and against any other individual. We tend to see ourselves, our friends, families, and community over and against other selves—friends, families, communities, races, countries. We tend to be patriotic about our particular territory, which encompasses not only ourselves but others of similar mind. In fact, there is nothing to be patriotic or nationalistic about because we are not separate from others. We are not other than or separate from other human beings, animals, plants, rocks, etc. We should always be able to rhetorically bring our situation back to the non-dualistic perspective. We must recognize that disappointment at its root is not disappointment because there is no such thing as disappointment. Who is there to be disappointed? What is there to be disappointed in relation to? If you feel upset, depressed, hurt, angry, in pain—in short, if you feel that you are suffering—who is it that is suffering? What is it that is suffering? Is God suffering? Is God conscious of an individual that suffers?

AUTONOMIC RESPONSE OF THE UNIVERSE

If your body has any kind of illness—it can be a cut, it can be a tumor—your body or intelligence as a whole is not typically aware of that cell that has the illness. Instead, there is a response from the autonomic nervous system to either eliminate that cell or send antibodies to the cell, so the illness is automatically taken care of in the natural process or flow of life. Our body is constantly in the midst of dissolution. There are always areas in our body that are not at optimum health that we are totally unconscious of. Yet, the autonomic nervous system is not unconscious of these areas. The autonomic nervous system automatically inputs what is necessary to either heal, isolate, or otherwise respond appropriately to that cell.

The same analogy holds very clearly in basic sadhana. In a sense, we are the cells of God's body. God is also not intelligently or consciously aware every time that a cell is suffering. But every time there is a cell that needs a particular response, there is an automatic input of the universal forces of manifestation. Whatever is necessary to respond appropriately to the aberration is directed to that cell or individual. Our being in an aberrated condition draws an autonomic response from the process that is life. There's no conscious being up there somewhere, or down here somewhere, that pays attention to an aberrant cell. There is an autonomic response and whatever is necessary to heal that cell is offered and given—even a response of more suffering, confrontation from the Godman, or in some cases elimination of the whole organism.

We must always be able to bring the recognition of our suffering back to the non-dualistic perspective so that we can recognize what is given is not given in a separate sense. There is no one paying attention to us from on high who gives us attention because we are broadcasting our need. The process is completely self-contained, inclusive, and internal. We are simply being taken care of in the process of the Law of Sacrifice. There is no consciousness and no direction involved. We must always bring the illusions that arise—the attempts of ego to convince us that in fact we are unique, separate individuals over and against other individuals—back to the non-dualistic perspective.

THE PHYSICS OF EGO: AN IRRESISTIBLE FORCE MEETS AN IMMOVABLE OBJECT

There is a tremendous amount of contrast between how individuals show up. We tend to measure ego in an individual by their capacity or tendencies, or by how they express themselves. We look at one person and say, "Man, do they have an ego!" We look at someone else and say, "Wow, is that person malleable! They don't have any ego at all. Other people just push them all over the place." Yet, when it comes right down to it, ego always works in the same way. The principle of ego is identical no matter what expression is presented in the world. Ego is ego and the principle is survival, winning to avoid losing.

Some people win by being charismatic; others win by being bumps on logs. Some win by being intelligent, sensitive, balanced, and sophisticated; others win by being outspoken, obnoxious, and objectionable. Some people win by being physically aggressive, strong, and athletic; others by being weak and passive. The principle is the same regardless of the expression or form. *Whenever two egos meet, what you have is an irresistible force meeting an immovable object.* This doesn't only apply in the negative sense in terms of arguments and disagreements. It also applies to conventional love affairs and agreements—whether they be contractual agreements or simple agreements about which movie to see, what restaurant to eat at, which spiritual meeting to go to.

Non-dualistically speaking, because separation is an illusion to begin with, what we have is ego with a big "E." Ego moves to substantiate separation so that it *appears* as if we have a lot of separate egos vying for superiority. Yet, what we have in truth, regardless of form, is an irresistible force meeting an immovable object. When two people have a relationship in any fashion or form, communicate positively or negatively, agree or disagree, what you have under all circumstances—unless they are spiritual slaves moved by Grace or turned toward a Godman—is one force trying to survive meeting an identical force trying to survive. Both are trying to win to avoid losing. The meeting of the two is always identical. There is never an imbalance. Some people win by winning; some people win by losing. Whenever there's an argument, somebody wins, somebody loses, and both people "win" in terms of ego. The force that meets is always identical.

FISSION AND FUSION

According to the laws of physics, when a nuclear bomb is exploded, a new or an altered form of energy occurs as the result of fission.[11] Because you have an irresistible force meeting an immovable object, there is never fusion, real communication, or relationship. You just have ego meeting ego and they are identical and always perfectly equal.

Regardless of what it looks like on the surface there's never an imbalance. The individuals who happen to be communicating don't join; there's not a meeting of the minds. Even though someone might say, "Let's go to a Chinese restaurant tonight," and the other might say, "Okay, that sounds like a good idea," there hasn't been fusion. There has been a suggestion by one person to eat somewhere and an agreement by the other person to go along with that. If one is sensitive enough to see it, every time there is communication between two individuals or

11 Fission is the splitting of an atom into two atoms, and fusion is the process of two atoms combining together. Both release vast amounts of energy.

groups of individuals, the fission created by the irresistible force meeting the immovable object results in Ego, with a capital "E." Fission occurs through the crisis of confrontation—and even agreeing on a restaurant for dinner is a crisis of confrontation. The motivation is always the search, the need for fulfilment or agreement, the drive to win to avoid losing.

When fission occurs and Ego (with a big "E" rather than a little "e") is recognized, the whole dilemma of the separate-self needing to survive—which is a complete illusion—becomes apparent. The dilemma which creates what we call "suffering," the need to survive when in fact survival is not an issue, is a total falsehood. It's a literal and figurative impossibility not to survive. When fission occurs, the dilemma can be obviated if there is a lucid recognition that there are not two forces meeting, as it seems, but rather one force moving and creating the illusion that there are two. This applies in physics as well: there are not actually ever two forces meeting. There is simply one force being modified internally which creates the illusion that there are two forces meeting. This is the case in all of nature, in all of the processes of the universe.

EGO IS A CONSTANT: THE GAME OF SUPERIOR AND INFERIOR

It is necessary for the student to see that his or her approach to relationship with other individuals—at jobs, socially, with family, in love affairs—is motivated by the need to be superior or inferior. It is important for the beginning student to recognize that there can never be a superior and inferior, a winner and a loser, not in the sense of spiritual life or God-life. In terms of form, if you go out on a tennis court, there will always be a winner and a loser. If you play a game of chess, there's a winner and a loser, even in a stalemate. There's the one who's played a slow and compromising game, and there's the one that's played an aggressive, clean game. All approaches motivated by the need to be superior are handicapped by the God-given fact (not

"God the Father" sitting up in a big chair but "God the inclusive form of all that arises") that there are no inferiors and no superiors under any circumstances.

Some people would rather come out of the game inferior because it validates their self-image. They play guitar at a party and someone says, "Gosh, that was great! You're a really good musician." And they say, "Well, I'm not so good, but I like it." Others are very aggressive, always needing to come out on top, wanting to be superior. In our approach to every relationship or situation in our lives, we must recognize that there can't be a superior and an inferior, a winner and a loser, *because we always have exactly identical modifications of the one ego, the one force, meeting one another within the illusion.*

Ego is a constant. Every single separative human being has ego. It's impossible to have a big ego or a small ego. Those are figurative descriptions of people's tendencies and forms. Ego is a given, a constant, in every single case. When a constant meets the identical constant, only fission can occur. There can't be any kind of meeting of the minds.

EVERY ENCOUNTER IS A CONTEST

It's very important to recognize our unconscious patterns, the games we play, in our approach to *every* circumstance. You may have noticed how people at a party will automatically take on a certain body posture depending on who they are talking to—an attractive person, a plain person, an old person, a young person, a thin person, a fat person, someone who wears sunglasses, someone who wears contact lenses. We play games in relationship to every single human variable. If you pay attention to yourself, you will see how very prevalent this is. We're one way at our job, we're a different way after work when we stop for a drink with the boys. One way playing mahjong with the girls, another way at the bridge club. We're totally different human beings in each of those circumstances. If you pay even minimal attention in the world, it's obvious that people have one way of being with their parents, another with their in-laws, another with their mate, their children, their boss, or co-workers. They are the same person and yet the form is dramatically different in each circumstance. The emotional center[12] may control one reaction; someone might be just delightful in a social situation with friends but they're animals the minute they walk into the room with their parents. Another center, the thinking center, will control the relationship with peers because we know we need to be a little more perceptive and sensitive in that situation. When we don't know how to have genuine or real relationship, we change our form to suit who we are responding to.

It's very important to recognize that our games and unconscious patterns are all a result of the need to perpetuate our tendencies and personalities, which we have misidentified as our "being" or "essence."[13] We can observe ourselves closing off our body and mind with a defense mechanism of some sort—verbal, mental, physical—founded in the need to overcome the same mechanism in the other. Every single one of our games, our unconscious patterns, is a confrontation with another's games, another's unconscious patterns. We're always in a contest.

Every love affair founded in the search and not in the context of God-life is a contest. It's a contest with who's going to be one way or another, who's going to be more mellow, more sensuous, who has more stamina. Have you ever seen a couple that goes out somewhere and the man—typically it's the man—nods-out because he's tired from a hard day's work, which is all an illusion anyway, and the lady with him says, "Yeah, he's always doing that. I can go until two o'clock in the morning. He fades out at nine!"

---

12 Gurdjieff referred to centers as parts of the structure of the human machine. He described the human as a three brained being, with emotional, thinking, and moving centers that are not unified.

13 In Gurdjieffian terms, "essence" refers to our true Self, who we really are, that which we are born with. It is distinguished from "personality," that which we have learned and assume about ourselves.

We don't understand that there's an irresistible force meeting an immovable object, and that every encounter we have is a contest. We haven't seen fission. If we recognize that an irresistible force meeting the immovable object only results in fission, we're going to recognize that there is only Ego with a capital "E." We will see that in this contest, which is the search, there are no winners and no losers. We can begin to undermine the games and unconscious habit patterns so that we can meet freely without the need to compete, win, or lose. We can simply meet in relationship to whatever is arising.

EGO TRIES TO BARGAIN

Ego always tries to make a deal. I had a sign machine once, the kind that makes those magnetic signs pressed out of plastic that people stick on their truck doors. Later, I was moving and wanted to sell the machine. I found a buyer and we agreed on a price over the phone. The whole thing was set. The guy came with a truck. It took us an hour to get the machine loaded properly. Then the guy tried to pay me a hundred dollars less than the price we had agreed on, which was five hundred dollars. He said, "I'm going to give you four hundred dollars because I had to hire this truck and this guy to help me. And hey, I didn't know the machine was this heavy." I said, "Take the machine off the truck."

I had been sitting with that machine for two years. I would have given it to the guy, I wanted to get rid of it so badly. But we had a deal, and I wasn't going to take a penny less. Finally, the guy said, "Alright, alright," and gave me the five hundred dollars. The guy knew that he was on the weak side of the transaction, so he tried to make a deal. In business, if you're holding something somebody wants, you don't have to deal. When someone's got the losing hand, they'll try and bargain. That's what ego does. When ego is confronted with the communion that is prior to the knot of itself, it is faced with its own death and it tries to bargain.

The approach of the devotee to the Godman is always one of trying to get the Godman to compromise. You're either awake or not. As long as the search is moving you, ego will try to somehow get a compromise. Because ego knows that ego doesn't become extinct. You couldn't function without ego. It just flips over. It just becomes the negative of itself. You couldn't wake up or be a devotee without ego. So, ego knows what it's faced with. It knows it's faced with losing its grasp, its identification, its power. It knows that, so it tries to compromise.

One of the ways that ego tries to compromise is by creating the perfect form, like one of my students who created the form of the perfect devotee. In his head he knew exactly what needed to be done so he always did the right thing, said the right thing, acted the right way. He was beautiful. Ego will try a number of different ploys to get a compromise. It'll try nasty, it'll throw a total breakdown, it can do nice or sexy. Some ladies try to seduce the teacher or trainer in a class. When ego sees that nothing will work—not nasty or nice, not beauty, money, power, or the perfect form—it will either become aligned with the Law or try and find a compromise somewhere it knows it can win. Those are the only two alternatives ego has.

Ego may give more and more but it still keeps trying to compromise. When ego first comes to the spiritual community, it runs its number[14] right down the line. But you begin to recognize what's required of you, which is to be full of God. It's not the conditions or sadhana or meeting demands from the guru. It's not Lee that's requiring anything. The more you recognize that the world doesn't work, the more you see what's required of you. The more you see what's required of you, the more ego tries to compromise.

---

14 "Running a number" is an idiomatic expression referring to a communication or behavior with concealed motivation.

THE GURU CAN'T COMPROMISE

The Godman is in a position where he's always being asked to compromise, and he can't. The Godman is always suffering his devotees because they don't understand why he doesn't compromise. It seems fair to ask for one little thing, but the problem is that fairness is not part of the process. God asks for everything! It doesn't mean you have to give up your car, your money, or your pretty hair, but you have to align yourself with the Law. You have to give up identification with who you think you are. I grant you that it is not fair, but then God is not interested in what's fair. God is Absolute. God asks for everything, and it's either everything or don't play the game. But compromise is impossible. Not because I wouldn't like to compromise. It's just impossible.

You're asking the Absolute to do what it did in creating this whole problem in the first place. The Absolute *did* compromise itself. That's why we're all here. Why do you think there's a separate self-sense to begin with? Because God compromised. Once. That's all that was necessary. Now no compromise is possible. It's either everything or try to find compromise somewhere that compromise can be given. But compromise cannot be given here. You're faced with an absolute and ego doesn't like that. It keeps trying to make a deal and it can't.

We keep trying to make a deal because that's the nature of ego when it's faced with the Absolute. When ego is faced with the only thing that is prior to itself, which is God, God-life, the Law, it knows that no compromise is possible. Ego isn't faced with that very often. Ego's gotten into the habit of winning. But when it's faced with the impossibility of winning, it tries to negotiate a compromise. When ego's faced with the Absolute, it says, "I'll stop being angry, I'll be neat, I won't argue; anything you want. Just not *that*!" At some point, you need to recognize that there can be no compromise. There's nothing that can be done because compromise is impossible. God cannot compromise. When you're asking for a compromise you need to see what ego is doing and say to yourself, "Compromise is not possible. The guru doesn't have the power to compromise. Sacrifice, yes; compromise, impossible."

There are three things that go on amongst those in the Community: the pull to be available to one another in sadhana, the tendencies of ego and our programming (some of us are angry, some understanding, some abrupt, some very patient), and trying to get the guru to compromise. Those three things interplay with one another. We know we have to work with one another, so we think, "Maybe if we all band together we can make compromise happen."

PIERCING THE KNOT OF EGO

The thing to do is to make some willful application of sadhana and the conditions even in the midst of seeming breakdown. When you see that you're trying to compromise and that it isn't working, you do sadhana in the midst of that. If your tendencies are coming up in terms of the search, and you really see them clearly and don't indulge them, they're going to display all their wares to you. Literally, they're going to show you everything they have to offer. Ego's got all of these numbers that it's running at deeper and deeper levels. We only see the very superficial stuff, the basic psychology of the search. But if you see that and you don't indulge it, it'll keep showing you more.

If you go looking for sex and you'll settle for a five-minute tumble in the hay, that's what you'll get. But if you won't settle for that and you want to go deeper, then you'll get shown more and more. It's the same way with ego. If you're in the midst of a fast, ego says, "Why don't you have a little something to eat?" If you do, then ego won't show you anymore. But if you don't indulge it, if you don't follow your tendencies, ego will keep showing you more of its mechanisms because it wants you to buy into it.

Ultimately, if you don't indulge any of ego's numbers it will show you itself completely, right down to the base. That's how you get to pierce the knot of ego at its primal source. The less you buy into it, the more ego will show you, to try and get you to buy into it, until eventually ego shows you everything. Once it shows you everything and has nothing more to show you, ego is at your mercy. That's the point when you can just cross right over the line. As long as ego hasn't shown you everything, you're at its mercy. Knowing its mechanism in your head isn't good enough.

You have to observe, not indulge, and follow the form of the conditions as closely as you can. If you follow all of the conditions, every resistance will be triggered. Every inappropriate tendency you have will come up. Then you need to not indulge them. The process works gradually, because we're always indulging to some degree, but eventually ego shows you its whole number. Then it's at your mercy. Until then, there's just the search on subtler and subtler levels.

SACRIFICE IS INSTANTANEOUS WHEN WE SEE PRINCIPLE

There are many reasons we pursue spiritual life, like wanting a remedy or seeking to attain. All of those things involve the mind and the mental aspect of our sadhana. There are any number of reasons for what we do on a mental plane. That's where self-observation and self-remembering—which are not techniques—come in. More and more you need to see what it is you're up to on all levels of your life. If you observe what's going on and pierce the surface level, you will see the principle—not the particulars—of any incident. Maybe you can see what you're up to when you have a fight with someone, but do you see what you're up to when you're making love? No, of course not. Ah, but most people are up to something when they're making love.

What is needed is a total re-adaptation of your mental being from chronic avoidance of relationship—chronic attempts to validate, win, attain, seek a remedy—to one of constant devotion and sacrifice. That will happen gradually because so many things that arise are only seen over time. Chronic avoidance needs to be re-adapted to natural and spontaneous appreciation and to the assumption of what is your true condition.

Suppose you're out at a restaurant. When you get your side-order of broccoli it's soggy and you wanted it crisp, just steamed a touch. You call the waitress over and start complaining, and as you're complaining you see that the rest of the meal is fine. But you're yelling at the waitress like the restaurant's no good and it's all her fault. Right in the middle of this thing you're doing, you see it. Sacrificing that reaction doesn't mean saying, "Oh, never mind. I'm just in a bad mood tonight. I'm really sorry. I'll just eat the soggy broccoli." Sacrificing that is seeing your neurosis, seeing what you were expecting and what you were reacting to, and then sacrificing that reaction and responding appropriately. Maybe you say, "Look, I know it's not your fault. I really don't mean to yell at you. It's just that I'm a bit eccentric. Would it be possible to give me some crisp broccoli?"

What you're sacrificing is the chronic reaction, the contraction that you caught yourself in the midst of. You're offended because you don't like soggy broccoli. Sacrifice is not necessarily giving up the form and saying, "I don't care about the soggy broccoli," and going on to something else. It's about sacrificing the attitude, the motivation and intent. You caught yourself sustaining self-meditation. That's it. Snap. It's not a long-drawn-out philosophical thing that goes on for hours. Sacrifice is as instantaneous as the intent that's arising. Snap. It's an immediate thing, not something you work on. Gradually, more and more, you're seeing your mental space in relationship to principle instead of particulars. Eventually, your entire mental level is re-adapted to spontaneous movement by Grace.

RE-ADAPTATION OF EGO, MIND, AND BODY

But you're not done yet; you still have ego. Ego sees everything as a threat to its survival. EVERYTHING. Even orgasm! Ego is always on guard. That's got to be re-adapted. We don't do that by putting ego in the garbage disposal and seeing it get ground up. Ego doesn't go away; the knot gets untied. Since ego sees everything as a threat to its survival, the re-adaptation of ego is seeing everything as what it is.

All of the basic life-level conditions are designed to re-orient or re-adapt the body. With the mind, a new form of thinking is required. With the body, you stop taking toxins in and you exercise. With the re-adaptation of ego there is no change. There is nothing to do. You stay right in place; all you do is flip. You simply see everything from another perspective. The re-adaptation of ego is seeing everything as its existence, instead of as a threat to its survival. What do you think makes you happy? Do you think there's an old man up in the sky who makes you happy? What do you think puts a smile on your face? Ego! When you're feeling good, it's ego. When you wake up and you're happy, it is ego giving you the recognition of what language calls happiness. When ego sees that in fact it cannot be destroyed and there is no threat, ego will make you happy.

So, you don't want to kill ego or you'll never be happy. And the easiest re-adaptation is ego. The problem is that before ego can be re-adapted you have to re-adapt body and mind. Once body and mind are re-adapted…snap. Well, it's not quite a snap, but it's a hell of a lot easier to re-adapt ego than it is to re-adapt body and mind. Once your mind stops fighting, what is there to do except to live principle? Re-adapting ego is the easy one. It's the getting there that's the hard part. Once body and mind are re-adapted, it's a breeze. That's what we're working on.

Question: Is it necessary to be in the company of the guru for the initial stages of re-adaptation and how can the guru be used responsibly?

Lee: That's a very good question. It *is* necessary—not in form but in principle. Initial preparation, whether in my company or not, is just following the basic conditions. Doing that is infinitely better than nothing if one is at all interested in spiritual life—in this Community or elsewhere. But for the natural fulfillment of a perfect re-adaptation of mind, body, and ego, the company of a teacher or guide[15] is necessary so that body functions as principle rather than mind using a healthy body as its vehicle.

Once you get involved in the spiritual Community you will no doubt come to appreciate the old saying, "You never know someone until you live with them." No amount of study can prepare an individual for what arises once they start to spend time with the Community. There is a particular atmosphere, an interchange of energy, that is how the presence of Grace actively works amongst the *mandali.*[16] Anybody that comes into the field of that interchange of energy has subjective work done on their psyche. There is nothing in anyone's prior experience that can equate with the kind of work that is done when that energy is present.

TRAPS ON THE PATH

1. Expectations about Form

Spiritual students are made up of a cross section of tendencies, types, and philosophical and personality leanings. One of the traps new people can fall into is to assume that the psychological profile of those doing work in a community is indicative of some kind of spiritual end result. In reality, exactly the same psychological profiles show in any group, irrespective of whether Grace is moving in the group or not. Because we all have concepts of what it is to be spiritual, we expect people to be humble, quiet, receptive, intelligent, well-meaning, compassionate,

---

15 The guru's presence is available through the Community.

16 For a period of time, Lee referred to a group of his students as "the mandali," which was a term Meher Baba had used for those in his inner circle.

loving, gentle, peaceful, interested, charismatic, enthusiastic—and an even longer list of words! These are the qualities that spiritual people are supposed to have. People, particularly those in my company, are supposed to have not only one or two of these qualities, but all of them, all the time, under all circumstances. Isn't that what the dharma says?

If we pay even minimal attention, that's not what the dharma says at all. People listen to the talks and read the literature and interpret what they hear and read the way they want to interpret it. Nobody learns anything new from listening to a dharma talk. People generate insights about spiritual life based on things they already believe unless they begin to live with a genuine spiritual community. Then this interchange of energy that we talked about, Grace, creates a viable alternative to prior knowledge and past history. This becomes possible once we involve ourselves with such a school or community and not before. Only through inter-reaction with the spiritual community can one possibly begin to be different.

It is necessary to be different. Altering old ideas is not relevant. First of all, it's not possible. We can change the form of things but we're just putting on another suit of clothes. Nothing ever really changes until it is changed and assumed by Grace. *We* never change a thing. But it's very easy to fall into the kind of traps that the mind will gladly surround itself with in order to distract us from God and from having to be undone. New students frequently pretend to be mellow, understanding, and considerate while psychically engaging in vicious wars with other people in the group. Whenever someone's out of their sight, they'll criticize and indict them for the worst crimes against "appropriate behavior" that the mind can imagine.

One of the traps that we fall into very easily is assuming that because we have the appropriate form—we exercise, try to eat a clean diet, and meditate somewhat regularly—that we are doing appropriate sadhana. Meanwhile our mental or psychic form may be worse than it ever was before. Without sympathy to the Law at all of the levels (thinking, moving and feeling), having appropriate form is no different than the way we've always lived our lives—which has been to shift the form depending upon who is at the other end of the interaction.

2. Making Other People Our Spiritual Heroes

The average person is highly impressed with anyone they think is minimally *more* of anything than they are: attractive, athletic, intelligent, compassionate, spiritual. We tend to make other people our heroes because we're so impressionable and we don't realize that everyone is the same. If someone does one thing that's appropriate and ninety-nine things that are not, we will make that person our hero because we've seen the one thing that's admirable and disregard all the other things. So many marriages fail in America today because we fall in love with the way someone looks at a child and disregard everything else. After we've been living with the person for two months everything else about them becomes so glaring that it wipes out what we consider to be love and all we have left is animosity. Because we're so insecure and our relationship to ourselves is so weak in any kind of willful conscious sense, we tend to pick people that should be a dog's hero and make them spiritual heroes and gurus. It's very important not to fall into the trap of making senior students your spiritual heroes, because they have no more or less a capacity than you do for waking up and living God-life.

3. Thinking We Have Mastery When We're Just Rank Beginners

Another trap that we very easily fall into is thinking we've accomplished something long before we have completed the first step in what we think we've already accomplished. As new students, we may seem to have a clear grasp of teaching. The teacher will say something and we will understand it intellectually. It's meaningful to us, it strikes a chord. We say, "Ah, I know just what you're talking about." We tend to mistake the intellectual understanding of a concept with the fulfilment of that concept as appropriate activity in our lives. The two are obviously not the same thing and, even though that makes perfect sense, we continue to mistake the intellectual connection with an idea for the fulfillment of that idea in our practical lives.

We want to be very careful not to allow the mistaken belief that we've really attained something interfere with the simple process of the Work. The path is a lifetime affair. It's not a matter of, "Well okay, I'll spend ten years and wake up." You work harder after you wake up than before! Spiritual life is a matter of paying attention to God moment to moment until you die. Then it's a matter of paying attention to God in another way, without the five senses that we relate to as the body-mind. It's necessary to simply work, not to have the mistaken idea that we've attained high levels of spirituality. People who have been in the Community for a number of years are just beginning to realize how much work is necessary to really live spiritual life.

Because we are intelligent, sensitive and enthusiastic, we tend to assume that those qualities can be equated with attaining a particular level of real spiritual understanding. It's not true. We don't want to get trapped into thinking we already understand, because every minute spent under that assumption is a waste of time. If we spend two years as the guru's right-hand man or woman thinking we're hot shit, that two years is wasted time. We don't have the capacity to learn a single thing as long as we think we've already attained what it is we're supposed to be learning. We want to pay attention to that tendency.

4. Being the Special Case

Another trap that we have to be careful of is thinking that we're a special case. Every single person that approaches has an identical response to the guru, and everyone thinks that no one else had that reaction. Everybody thinks they're a special case. We look around and say, "Look at them and look at me. What's going on for me couldn't have gone on for them. Obviously, there's a difference." There is no difference. The language is different, the form is a little different, but the response is exactly the same. Everybody's reaction has been predictable because there's only one thing to realize. It happens to everyone exactly the same way. Ego is confronted by the movement of Grace in a fashion that is absolute. The response is always the same because ego's mechanisms are always the same.

Although everyone approaching real spiritual life has the internal attitude that they are someone special, different and unique, that attitude has nothing to do with the actual uniqueness of each individual—their particular tendencies, talents, abilities, physical appearance or energy level. Every individual is relatively familiar with very basic tenets of working in a community—the need for discipline over a period of years and what is required to approach the Work. At the same time, everyone thinks that they are going to be the one to fulfill sadhana more quickly than anybody else has ever done it, in defiance of the experience of everyone that has ever been on any genuine path throughout history. We all have the perspective that there is something to be attained—awakening, enlightenment, or realization—and that we're going to attain that quickly and clearly.

5. Avoiding Functional Life

Another trap that we can fall into is avoiding functional life because we become involved with blissful states of consciousness that are mindless, formless, and essentially ecstatic. Whether it is having the head-brain flooded with white light, or every cell in the body tingling with pleasure, or waves of energy flowing in, out, or through, it's very easy to get into a state of non-practical functionality due to what are called higher conscious states. We want to realize that no particular experience can be equated with God-life. It's just as necessary to wash the dishes, take care of our personal hygiene, and dress appropriately as it is to be in samadhi or *satori* [a Zen Buddhist term for awakening or seeing one's true nature] twelve hours a day. One is no more important than the other. A major trap that people tend to fall into is to lock in on the channel where ecstatic experiences are available and avoid other forms of sadhana. That's just as inappropriate as paying no attention whatsoever to the basic conditions. We want to look out for that.

6. Needing Approval of Our Work

Something else that is not only a trap in spiritual life but is a conventional trap in all forms of relationship is needing approval in order to continue doing what we are doing. The ideal student in a spiritual community will simply do their sadhana irrespective of whether the Godman ever looks at them or not. You should be able to bring strength to your sadhana without the need for any kind of attention whatsoever—either criticism or praise.

Yet, there's a tendency to assume and feel that if we aren't told how we're doing, we're not doing it right and need to do something different. I encourage this pitfall in people who are doing beautiful spiritual work by not praising them, just to see how much strength they're bringing to their work. Many people find that they're doing work that is highly accessible to Grace and yet when they don't get complimented for it, they'll try something else—which is actually getting in their own way.

We want to pay attention to the desperate need for approval and to have our activity validated. That's one of the biggest traps we can fall into and it's completely unnecessary. The best spiritual students get less validation than the spiritual students that are just plodding along still needing a mommy or a daddy at thirty years of age. It's very important to realize that we need to bring strength to sadhana, not weakness. The appropriate form of spiritual work motivated from a position of weakness and a need for praise, approval, and to be stroked is not nearly as effective a sadhana as inappropriate work approached from a position of strength, responsibility, and ownership.

THE COMMUNITY OF DEVOTEES OFFERS THE GREATEST OPPORTUNITY

The greatest opportunity is offered in the community of devotees, not directly in relationship to the icon or hero figure that is the Godman. The community or sangha offers an opportunity that's not available anywhere else in society because the movement of Grace is actively present. We get this offering through active, functional, and manifest God-life lived in the community of devotees. We work and live and pay attention to spiritual activity in the midst of the world. Still, it's very important to recognize that the opportunity offered here is not offered anywhere else in or out of the world.[17]

SYMBOLIC TALES

Editor's note: *Lee began this discourse with the story of the life of Shakyamuni Buddha told in a lively and detailed fashion. It is distilled here to an outline of events so as to focus on Lee's commentary.*

There was a man named Siddhartha who was a great prince of the Sakya family in ancient India. He was everything a prince should be: intelligent, attractive, athletic, and happy—very self-fulfilled. He grew up in the protected environment of the palace where everything

17 Though Lee often showed great respect for the historical and rare contemporary masters whom he felt had been a focal point for Grace to manifest in the world, he also said that the Work that came through each master was unique to what was needed by the universe at the time. Lee's Work as it unfolded seemed to have to do with creating "enlightened community" in the Western Baul tradition rather than identifying an individual lineage holder, and with being a vehicle for the Influence of the Divine as expressed by his master, Yogi Ramsuratkumar.

was provided: beautiful gardens, delicious food, the finest music and works of art, courtiers who were young, vibrant, and beautiful, advisors and ministers who were wise and kind, brilliant teachers with whom to discourse. When he reached a marriageable age, he was wed to a beautiful woman who was an ideal companion. They were the happiest couple in the kingdom. Their every worldly desire was satisfied within the palace and in time they became the parents of a beautiful son.

But Siddhartha began to wonder what life was like outside the palace grounds. He took a chariot ride through the city and for the first time saw poverty, illness, old age, and death. He pondered what he'd seen and decided he must live the life of a monk. Siddhartha left the palace on horseback one night and rode into the forest to join the monks there who were practicing austerities. Determined to conquer old age, sickness, and death, he continued his sadhana until he realized that they were all illusory the way mankind understood them. He realized that death was not the end, that he was not the body, and he became the Buddha.

After Buddha became enlightened, he sat under the bodhi tree and didn't move. Brahma, one of the gods, came down and told Buddha to go out and teach. Buddha did not want to teach because he was sure that no one would listen to him or understand the Law [of Sacrifice]. Brahma said to him, "You've fulfilled the Law, you've manifested the Law, and you must present it." Then Buddha said, "Okay, I'll go out and preach the Law and transform as many men as there are grains of sand on the banks of the Ganges." So, he went out begging, started preaching, and doing miracles.

Symbolic tales are wrapped around the lives of Buddha, Krishna, and Jesus, and it's very important for us to recognize that it's totally irrelevant whether the tales are literally true. What's important is that each lived and fulfilled something in their lives that we can learn from. The early life of the Buddha, from his childhood to his enlightenment, is the perfect symbolical representation of what is necessary for us to understand in order to appreciate and fulfill our sadhana.

THE ONLY THING THAT SUFFICES

Because we're all intelligent, healthy, and attractive, we may have heard the same thing that Siddhartha heard from friends or family: "You've got a good job, you're smart, you've got friends. Isn't that enough?" And it's *not* enough. Siddhartha had everything that anyone could possibly imagine as fulfillment of the worldly search: fame, friendship, power, and every material thing he could want. And no specific was enough. The only thing that was enough was the culmination of his own personal sadhana, which was aligning himself with the Law and living the Law.

Sometimes we look at what we consider to be good enough, whatever it is, and we say, "Gee, if only such and such would happen, that would really be perfect." No matter what specific you contemplate, you'll find that when you get what you think is enough, it's not enough. Once we get into spiritual life, we tend to transpose the mundane search onto the spiritual search. We read *The Gospel of Sri Ramakrishna*[18] and we say, "If only I could be like Sarada Devi or Vivekananda. They were so pure and devotional." We set up a specific in the spiritual search the same way we do in the mundane search. But no specific will ever be enough; only moment-to-moment living in line with the Law is enough. Once you've seen that the body is not going to survive, you must conquer mortality [the assumption that one is exclusively a distinct person who is born and who dies], the transitory nature of the being.

Editor's note: *As commonly occurred, Lee's discourse takes an extended turn onto subjects not directly related to the topic, which have been omitted, before returning to the point. Lee reviews some of the early history of the Community including exuberant gatherings for* satsang,[19] *trips to diners, celebrations,*

---

[18] Ramakrishna (1836-1886) was a Hindu mystic and saint who lived in Bengal, India. His devotees included Sarada Devi and Vivekananda.

[19] Until 1981, Lee referred to formal Sunday night gatherings with students as "satsang," a Sanskrit term for "being in the company of Truth."

and a pilgrimage to India when shakti *or* kundalini[20] *energy began to arise and circulate in students throughout the school. He then refers to the change in mood that takes place as students become interested in more than ecstatic experience and more committed to their spiritual work and practice.*

Sadhana can become very valuable at that point, because we get a chance to recognize that celebration doesn't only happen in a special place, time, and circumstance. What we find is that celebration is a matter of moment-to-moment presence, not just looking forward to the special moments. The possibility to celebrate is not confined to just holidays. If the only time you can really be nice to one another is on your birthday, there's something lacking, don't you think? It's not good enough. In his early life Siddhartha experienced ultimate fulfillment of every one of his senses, and it wasn't enough. The only thing that suffices is alignment with the Law under all circumstances.

TRUST AND AVAILABILITY

It's important for the beginning student to recognize a couple of principles. One is that, in terms of trust and intuition, the Godman needs to have just as much trust of the student as the student has of the Godman. If the teacher gives the person a job of washing dishes and then stands around watching over the student's shoulder saying, "You put too much soap in," or "You're going a little too fast," and is constantly hedging the job that's given, then that's about all the trust that the teacher can expect in return. If the student is required to be available to the Godman, the Godman needs to be just as available to the student.

If the Godman is directing students as if he [the teacher] is so high and mighty that there is no participation on his part, no work will get

[20] "Shakti" or "kundalini" refers to the latent psycho-spiritual force in the body that is traditionally thought to move from the base of the spine to the brain, purifying energy blockages to ego transcendence.

done. There has to be an equal availability. The teacher is available to whatever degree the student is. Ideally, the student is perfectly available. Then the Godman is in turn perfectly available and the student realizes God-nature. This is a natural process; it's just like physics. It's like two poles of a magnet. When a magnet is magnetized through the electromagnetic process, both poles are magnetized with the same degree of pull. It's not that the south pole has a lot of pull and the north pole has a little.

The process in relationship to the teacher is the same. The God-realized being has no conscious direction or conscious will. The God-realized being meets the student equally on whatever basis the student advances. If it was a matter of the Godman being able to overpower the student and submerge the student in God, Jesus would have woken up all the Pharisees. But it is not a matter of overpowering people with God-nature. The process is automatic and willful in terms of the overall movement of God. It is not willful in terms of any kind of individual process.

As the student advances and becomes available, there's an equal availability from the Godman or teacher. As the student's availability expands, it looks like the Godman is giving the student initiation and spiritual experience. The student's love for the teacher increases, but not because the teacher did anything to make that happen. The teacher is fixed, in a sense. The teacher's got a spectrum that he or she moves back and forth on, but that spectrum is totally directed by the availability of the student.

The student, on the other hand, being an individual moved by ego, retains the choice—usually unconscious, but still there—to advance however far they want to in almost all the initial aspects of sadhana. When Gift is presented, there's a tendency for students to cross their arms and take a step backward instead of opening their arms and walking up to embrace it. That's a willful process; there's choice involved in that. As long as ego moves the individual, there's choice involved in the direction the individual is moved—up to a point. There's no choice involved in perfect availability. But in the initial stages of sadhana there is choice involved that gets one to understand the process deeply enough to be open to perfect availability.

The initial process of sadhana involves a tremendous degree of trust. But there has to be an equal degree of trust on the Godman's part. To whatever extent the student trusts the God-realized being, the God-realized being will equally trust the student. A lot of people have been given jobs to do. Edit this book, hang these posters, transcribe this talk, sell these books. Everybody that's been given a job to do has been given the job based on a level of responsibility that they have advanced to with the teacher. Having the job of editing one of our books for publication might seem to be more responsible than driving the kids to the airport, yet the level of responsibility is not so much in form. The kinds of jobs that are most responsible are working with one another and taking care of the satsang hall. Taking care of the sacred spaces is much more important than any material thing that gets done. Because the vibes that go into our sacred spaces, into sanctuary, are much more important than the vibes that go into a book. Eight million people can read a book and still be asleep. But the communion between devotees and spiritual master takes place in the sacred space of the satsang hall.

The process to recognize in terms of availability is that there's an equality. As you give, so you receive. As you sow, so shall you reap. That's a literal statement. As available as you are, that's what you get.

RESPONSIBILITY FOR THE GIFT

My students will frequently say, "For a week I really understood what you were doing and everything you ever said. I was so clear! I didn't have a problem with paradox. But now I'm not as clear. All of a sudden, I am having problems again. What's happening?"

What's happening has to do with *availability*. Perfect availability is a matter of Gift; it's not a matter of willpower. However, once perfect availability is present, the Godman becomes perfectly available in turn and you literally become the same one [as the guru] for however long that lasts. When you become the same one, you must ask the right questions and be willing to follow up on the answers. You must live what it is you're feeling and seeing and experiencing when you're the same one. Because mind doesn't shut off. Ego doesn't dissolve; there's still chatter.

You must live what you're feeling, not respond to what you are thinking. Even though you are the same one, you must fulfill the Law moment to moment. If you don't, if the chatter overrides the heartfelt recognition of absoluteness, the fraction of an instant that you become less than perfectly available, the Divine becomes less than perfectly available and you spiral right back into where you were before you became perfectly available.

You walk around thinking, "Man, I had it. What happened?" What happened was that when you had it you weren't able to be responsible for it. The Law is sacrifice. What a drag, you know? All of a sudden you became the same one and it was overwhelming. It's like you look at the sacrifice of the Lord and you say, "My God, how can anyone do that?" And you become a little grateful. If you aren't willing to live that identical sacrifice in relation to whatever comes up, then in time you become less available.

BECOMING MORE AVAILABLE

There are several factors involved in availability. One is a sensitivity, one is intelligence. By intelligence, I mean common sense and not IQ. We need a little bit of common sense. We become perfectly available one day—for who knows what reason—and we have a moment or a day or a week of clarity. When it wears off, we deny what we know. Of course, in the midst of that experience, the chatter's going to be denying it anyway. The heart is experiencing absolute freedom and the chatter is saying, "You're hypnotized, it's not real, it's too good, I don't understand," and blah, blah, blah. We buy into the chatter and we say, "I guess it isn't real." Common sense says it's real. So, what if it's paradoxical? Intelligence tells you that it's real. Your heart tells you it's real. But we don't listen to that.

We don't have a habit of being free. We have a habit of seeking. Since we've got twenty or thirty or forty years of that habit—however old we are—and we've only had a few moments of freedom, we revert back to habits very easily. Then we wonder, "What am I doing this for?" Because we can see through it, but we aren't doing anything about it. Doing something about it is a matter of a willful, conscious process. Anybody could stop whenever they wanted and be more available.

How do you become more available? Many people are familiar with the feeling of a wall coming up inside you. When you are triggered, you can literally feel the shield going up. You can feel it like an elevator door shutting and closing you in. If you are aware enough to feel that going on, then you are certainly aware enough to be able to pierce and undo that. So, instead of feeling your muscles automatically go limp and realizing you are not looking someone of a different race in the eye as you shake their hand, you do something different because you can see that wall rising.

MYTHOLOGIZING THE GODMAN

One of the things that tends to come up in initial sadhana is that people buy into the myth of the Godman that is presented in his published literature. Because of this, people build up a particular image in their minds. They read the words that are used in the books—like "undermine," "crisis," "confrontation"—to describe the process of working with the Godman, and they feel tremendous fear or trepidation about getting involved with this character who has such incredible power. *Why, he can just take one look at you and undermine you. He can see everything you're thinking. You'll be transparent.*

The fact of the matter is that we are transparent because everyone is perfectly predictable. It doesn't matter what you look like, what color your skin is, what religion you've been brought up in, how much education you've had, what your tendencies are, or how strong you are. At the core of your motivation, everyone is perfectly predictable: you're seeking. What is there not to see? What is to hide? Everybody's the same.

We used to have a bookstore where I liked to sell books. I'm a retailer at heart, both in spiritual life and in business. I enjoy seeing merchandise move off the shelves. I'd go in to work at the bookstore and people would buy big stacks of books and I'd be so happy. Every once in a while, someone would stumble upon the bookstore never expecting to see [*whispers*] "the Godman." They'd walk in and there I would be behind the counter. They look at me and say, "You're Lee!" And their eyes would get wide and they could hardly speak. This has happened a number of times.

People imagine that they'll meet me and won't be able to think or talk. Funny thing—that's exactly what happens. They walk in and they can't talk. And they conclude that it must be true that the Godman knocked them out with his presence. But it wasn't my presence at all, it was simply the person's trepidation. They had built up an image, they had a certain expectation. That expectation created a response in their psycho-physical organism of legs shaking, voice cracking, and stream of consciousness stopping. People tend to take those kinds of experiences as being very significant when the real significance is simply in the process of communion itself.

Even if there wasn't a God, existence would be here. The miracle, the beauty, what we should really be grateful for, is the Graceful presence [of the realized one] amongst us. That's the miracle: God is elsewhere also. He's also on the astral plane and in the *loka* of the hungry ghosts[21]

21 Buddhist cosmology identifies six realms of rebirth and existence, which may refer to actual places or to psychological states that beings are karmically drawn to. The *loka* of the hungry ghosts is the realm in which beings continuously have unfulfilled cravings and cannot be satiated.

and in the realm of the angels and the realm of the animals. God is everywhere. But the miracle is that God is anywhere at all. The miracle is not all of the experiences, shakti, ecstasies, and raptures. Those aren't miracles; those are simply psycho-physical responses to different levels of energy and availability.

GIFT

We tend to create a degree of availability that is safe and expect the Godman to give us everything. But one doesn't get everything by being safe. We have to be not safe; we have to simply be available. Then Gift literally becomes ours. We get to unwrap it. But what usually happens is that we glance at Gift from afar and say, "Gosh, look at that." Instead of recognizing God we make an idol of Grace, because we're enraptured for one evening or one day or one week. Making any kind of experience your idol is playing it safe. Because if you have that experience you can say, "Oh, I have talked to God. God has taken me into his heart. I've rested in God's arms." If you don't have that experience, you can always fall back on, "Well, we're all sinners. We don't deserve it anyway."

But availability is an affair that works from both sides; it's mutual. If you're playing it safe and just a little bit available that's what the Divine offers you. It's not a matter of choice. Perfect availability is a response to perfect availability. Partial availability is a response to partial availability. Because the poles need to remain equal; there can't be an imbalance.

To whatever degree we are available, we get the gift of communion in turn. That doesn't necessarily mean physical attention, more responsibility, or a higher position. What we get is Grace. Life becomes simply pleasurable, ordinary. We don't go drifting into the heavens of the sixth chakra, have visionary experiences, and read the akashic records. We make ourselves available and life becomes simply, ordinarily pleasurable. That's the Gift. No more than that. At times there's rapture, at times there are ecstatic experiences, and at times we just go to the movies or hang out. There's no felt gap or need, no unconscious seeking. We are free of tension, contraction, and constriction. No more knots in the vital [the body's important internal organs] or frogs in the throat. None of that. Life is simple, life is easy, life is pleasurable. That's Gift. But we need to be available to that because Grace itself is a perfect constant. It's never more or less available.

WHATEVER CENTER PREDOMINATES COLORS EVERYTHING WE SEE

There are seven stages of life that correspond to the seven chakras. Whatever center is predominant in your life colors everything you see, like a filter. Basically, for the first seven years of life you're supposed to mature through survival. You're learning to walk, to communicate, to feed yourself, and keep yourself warm. As a baby, you're literally dependent on mommy. It's absolute survival. If you don't get mommy's milk, you'll die. If your primary center of function is the first chakra [one of the seven psychic energy centers in the body], which is raw survival, then everything that arises for you—even God-life—is literally a primal battle. If your tendency or emphasis is the first chakra, the reason you're living God-life is to survive. All problems are colored by the drive to survive. Ideally, we're supposed to have fulfilled and completed first chakra tendencies by the time we're seven years old. That's a hell of a lot to ask for in conventional society, but that's an idea of what is possible in a spiritual community.

The second seven years of life have to do with the sexual center. You begin to recognize that boys and girls are very different, and in your early teens—eleven or twelve or so—you enter puberty. In the second seven years of life we're supposed to complete our growth in terms of sexuality. We're supposed to be straight about our sexual life by the time we're fourteen or fifteen years old. This means that in our relationships, sexuality is supposed to have its place but not override consideration or friendship. But look at the average sixteen-year-old. Most teenage boys, for instance, can't be friends with someone without sexuality being a part of it. If your tendency is second chakra, which is sexual or procreative, everything you do is colored by that aspect of life. So, if you come to the spiritual community, God-life is colored by the need to procreate. All of life is seen in sexual terms.

From early teens until age twenty-one, we're supposed to complete the third chakra tendency. Third chakra tendencies are tendencies toward power. When you get to be sixteen or seventeen, those are the tendencies that are most prevalent because you're becoming independent. You get your driver's license, a job, a little of your own money. You break away from the family a bit. You get behind the wheel of a car, especially if you've got a hot rod, and it's a whole new world. It was for me. I was the second slowest runner in my high school, but when I got behind the wheel of that new convertible—POWER! It didn't matter who was smarter, better looking, cooler, or more athletic; it was who had the coolest car.

Between our early teens and early twenties, we establish our independence. Three to four thousand years ago, when you were seventeen you were married and raising a family. You lived your life early-on, because you were probably dead at thirty. If you lived to be forty you were considered to be an old man or an old woman. In modern times, twenty-year-old parents probably aren't responsible.

If you come to the spiritual community with a predominance in the third chakra, everything you do is colored by power. You want to be important in the community and have some degree of power. People that are predominantly third-chakra oriented are the kind of people who get to be an officer in a company and then work their way up to become president. They are often extremely hard-lined with their kids. They never let them alone: "Do this because I said so." They've got to fulfill that third-chakra orientation, got to be powerful and on the top of the heap. That's the filter through which they see everything they do.

What we're ideally supposed to do for the first twenty-one years of life is mature through the first three chakras. Once you've completed survival, sex, and power, it doesn't mean that those things disappear. It means that each of those tendencies serve their real function. There's a real function for power. If you're a supervisor in a business, you've got to have the respect of the people that work for you. They've got to be able to listen to you so that you have a smooth, working organization. There's a function for power in God-life. But each of those tendencies—survival, sexuality, and power—simply take their natural place in your corresponding movement in life. You don't clutch at it anymore. There's no pressure. You don't have to get laid four times a week. Whatever is natural arises in relationship.

Most people never get past the first, second, or third chakra all their lives. We end up being thirty, forty, or fifty years old and everything we're doing is still predominantly colored by one of those tendencies: survival, sex, or power. You find a lot of people in business, forty to fifty years old, leading the life of the jungle—survival of the fittest. The salesmen go out and they joke about it over martinis. "Yeah, look at who I screwed this week"—screwed, literally and figuratively. People who are predominantly third-chakra oriented are always power-tripping in sex. They *have to*—that's their tendency.

The fourth, fifth, sixth, and seventh stages of life correspond to the fourth, fifth, sixth, and seventh chakras. Those are stages that most people never even touch let alone complete. The fourth center, or the heart chakra, is the center of compassion, understanding, and love. Usually, when you get to that center, you enjoy people, enjoy life, and enjoy things. That's a nice place to be. If you're going to get stuck in one chakra, that's a nice chakra to get stuck in because you're loose, relatively happy, and easygoing. But even that center must be completed because the higher levels of human development or human possibility involve the fifth, sixth, and seventh chakras. Typically, people stuck in the fourth chakra get walked on all over the place, but unconditional love is their image of realization. They think, "If I can love everybody regardless, I'll be awake and that will be God for me."

None of the work with the centers or chakras can be specifically equated with God-life. God-life is slavery and commitment to, or movement by, the prior source that is inclusive of God itself. Once you wake up you still do sadhana. What is your sadhana? Simply optimizing human possibility, which involves the completion of each of the chakras. The fifth chakra, the throat chakra, is very much involved with *jnana* [knowledge of the total experience of reality]. It's involved with understanding, piercing insight, lucidity, clarity of observation. People that are highly inquisitive are fifth-chakra oriented and see everything in life through that filter. They analyze everything. They can take every word and nuance of a person's body movement and analyze it, right down to the twitch in their lover's face. Wow, they love it. Fifth-chakra completion is typically a very important part of Western Buddhist studies. Just see what is going on with the clarity of insight that Chögyam Trungpa Rinpoche talks about. See your mind, see what you're doing, see what you're up to. It's a function of the fifth-chakra expression.

The sixth chakra is a matter of the super-sensual dimensions: the astral worlds, ethereal worlds, visionary worlds, the heavens, out-of-body experiences. The sixth chakra is associated with the ascended masters and teachings on other planes, the akashic records, psychometry, tarot reading, numerology, astrology, materializing and dematerializing objects, poltergeist activity, even levitation. All of that really nifty parapsychological stuff is sixth-chakra associated. There are people that get stuck in the sixth chakra. They haven't completed any of the chakras but that happens to be their tendency. They see everything in life through the sixth chakra. If you go to psychic fairs, you'll see people who are stuck in the sixth chakra. They equate sixth-chakra tendencies with realization.

To review, people that are stuck in the first chakra equate realization with surviving forever. People that are stuck in the second-chakra experience realization as whole-body cellular orgasm. People that are stuck in the third-chakra experience realization as perfect control, never losing it for a second, always being on top of it. People that are stuck in the fourth-chakra experience realization or enlightenment as unconditional love. People that are stuck in the fifth chakra imagine enlightenment as knowledge of all things, having access to complete universal knowledge. Their search is for perfect knowledge. They're always reading, reading, reading. For people who are stuck in the sixth chakra, their image of enlightenment is fulfillment by having miraculous powers like Sathya Sai Baba, who materialized objects out of air. The person stuck in the sixth chakra sees enlightenment as attainment of perfect *siddhis* [supernormal yogic powers] and the ability to do any miracle.

The seventh chakra is associated with light. The seventh chakra is the culmination of the raising of kundalini in the body. It is associated with the "blue *bindu*" that is talked about.[22] In Sufism, people who get stuck in the seventh chakra are called *masts*. They are God-intoxicated and they lose all consciousness of the world. They're blissful, ecstatic, lost in a state of reverie or communion with existence as light. For people stuck in the seventh chakra, realization is a moot point, a theoretical discussion. It has no relevance to what's going on for them.

THE PRIMACY OF GOD VERSUS THE COMPLETION OF CHAKRAS

In the work that we're doing, realization is not a matter of the completion of any one of these stages. Rather it's the recognition that enlightenment is already entirely present, and a matter of the fulfillment of each of the stages as sadhana. The primacy of God is what's moving us to begin with. It's not something we need to attain through a lifetime of effort. Our natural state is ecstasy, pleasure, God.

[22] In some traditions, visionary experiences of a blue *bindu* or blue pearl—a reference for our innermost reality—are reported.

Everything else is simply sadhana. Everything else is simply optimizing human possibility but not attaining states of consciousness that aren't already perfectly present.

People will occasionally have phenomenal fifth, sixth, and seventh chakra insights. Even the worst writer will be able to record those insights in the most exquisite language, but they can't duplicate the experience. Because of the Godman's assumption [of already present enlightenment, which elicits our own true nature at times when we are available to Grace], students randomly experience the completion of different centers. The completion of those centers isn't fulfilled and manifested; it's simply tasted here and there randomly. The process of sadhana is to fulfill each of them.

To fulfill the fifth, sixth, or seventh chakras before you fulfill the first, second, or third is not dangerous, but it could mean four or five more lifetimes of work—which is nothing compared to how long we've been working already. But if you don't have the first, second, and third chakras completed, and you start doing a lot of heavy sixth-chakra tripping, you're liable to blow your body away. So the initial sadhana, and the idea behind the basic conditions, is to begin by getting through the first, second, and third chakras because we should be complete with those by the time we're twenty-one. We're all adults, and once we've gotten through those then we can go about filling our lives with higher-conscious experiences. But we can't now because it would wreck us.

THERE IS ONLY GOD

Question: You have spoken about having the knowledge that there is a God. Could that be interpreted as our signpost or guidepost?

Lee: Most of us spend our lives either trying to prove there is a God or trying to prove there isn't—when in fact every time we wake up in the morning it should be obvious there is a God. Not knowing that keeps us from [accessing] a whole level of sadhana. Just knowing there is a God, consciously and intelligently, eliminates trying to prove there is or there isn't. That's an incredible basis on which to begin to work. You might have metaphysical questions, but if you know there is a God there's a whole level of questioning that just doesn't come up anymore. You don't have doubt about the master's integrity. If you really know there is a God, you look at the whole world differently. You don't take things personally. You understand that nothing is being done to you personally by God or the spiritual master.

Our work or sadhana is going to be shaped by how we've understood the rhetoric.[23] So we want to pay attention. It might seem silly to pay attention to mere words, since what we're trying to do is work on *living* God and experience the reality of true God-life. What part do words play in such a grand scheme? Yet, since we subconsciously function by our understanding of the language, we should really pay very close attention to the way we describe our approach to God and the spiritual community.

The whole idea of knowing that there is a God is a little bit shaky because we have to know that there is God, but not that there is "a" God. That distinction is a lot more than simply a philosophical point. Knowing there's "a" God qualifies God. It makes God a thing, something limited. "A" God very clearly indicates that there is something that is *not* God. If you give it even a cursory examination, you'll realize that's the case. If we say, "I know there is 'a' God," that indicates very clearly to the subconscious that God can be categorized or is conceptual, that we can actually get an image of God because there's "a" God over and against other alternatives. If there's "a" God, that implies there are other alternatives: no God, many Gods, two Gods… It's important to recognize that believing that there is "a" God is not a valid approach in this Work. We can know that there is God but not "a" God.

---

23 Lee uses the word to refer to the conceptual description of the teaching.

If we want a really solid foundation that's not going to create problems in sadhana later on down the road, belief in or knowledge of "a" God is untrue and can be very easily undermined. Even philosophically, there are flawless arguments for "a" God and arguments that are just as flawless for no God. So, we want to begin to look at our belief systems in terms of knowing there is God, or only God, but not in terms of knowing there is "a" God. Knowing there is God or knowing there is only God precludes any alternatives.

There can be many gods in a hierarchical model *within* that overall aspect of only God. The cosmology of many traditional cultures has God, and then they have mini-gods. There is actually a world of gods, which is just like the world of humans, where there are male gods, female gods, baby gods, and mommy and daddy gods. They go to war and fight over different aspects of the world just like we go to war and fight over different aspects of the world. So, if we come to know that there's only God, within that scheme of only God there can be different planes, different levels. In fact, there can even be levels of attainment within only God. Within the inclusive process that is only God there can be people that are beginning in spiritual life, people that are advanced in spiritual life, and people that are completing spiritual life.

Believing there is "a" God is simply another belief system. Knowing there is only God is prior to all belief systems. That's the foundation on which we want to begin spiritual life. Obviously, the ideal situation for one approaching a spiritual community is to know that there is only God. If we come with that understanding, we can say, "I know there's only God; let's go from here." But if that isn't the case at heart—and it's not for anybody really—we might as well input the appropriate information as our approach to sadhana and study so we're not deluding ourselves or studying the teaching from the wrong context.

If we approach with the appropriate context of study, even if it's just intellectual, then everything else we do can be seen in that light. In this way, as we study, we can feel, intuit, or analyze how the traditional approaches relate to our present work from the context of only God, rather than studying from the context of the philosophy that there is "a" God. If we study from the concept that there is only God, we'll have a whole different approach.

The same thing applies to the seven stages of work. If we're lucky enough to approach real sadhana already knowing what our tendency is, and if we have some idea of the big picture, then instead of looking at what arises and saying, "How am I going to eliminate my identification with this tendency?" we can look at that tendency in relationship to the fact that there's only God. Instead of trying to design some kind of remedy for our inappropriate relationship to that chakra, we can realize that what's arising is appropriate at times and inappropriate at other times but in effect is just another experience. It's not something that needs to be redone, reprogrammed, fixed up, or remedied. If we have an idea of the big picture, we can look at what arises as just another experience. Our tendency may be strong, it may be predominant in our approach to life, but it's simply another experience.

We can give it space to be there and diffuse its hold on us by realizing it's just another experience rather than trying to do something about it—which we tend to do if we see things from a small picture. We want to be able to see everything that arises in terms of the fact that there is only God, not over and against the possibility that there is "a" God.

OBVIATING THE DILEMMA

When I was a little boy, I loved strawberries, but I used to get strawberry rashes. My mother would bring home strawberries and I would eat them and break out and itch because I was allergic to them. But I loved strawberries so much that I would just as soon eat strawberries and have a strawberry rash than not eat them. So, I always gorged myself on strawberries and after a couple of years I stopped getting rashes. Now I can eat all the strawberries I want and get no strawberry rash. There is no reaction anymore because I liked strawberries enough to obviate the reaction, to go through it.

There is a great parallel to that in spiritual life. When you first taste real spiritual life, two things happen. You get higher than you have ever been before. You might not know *what* God is, but you know that there is nothing but God. The other thing that happens is that something very painful arises in your life. You see that there's only God, but you also see that you never really cared about your lover. That's very painful. Or you see that you really resent your child. For six years you gave them this and you gave them that, but you really wish you had waited before you had children. That's very painful.

When you get a taste of real spiritual life, you know that there is nothing else to do. At the same time, you start to be confronted with the obvious dilemma of your life. You begin to see that you are not a happy-go-lucky bon vivant. You start to see that you have layer upon layer of programming—of negativity, jealousy, anger, and repressed emotions. It's a great dilemma. What you can do is say, "I'm going to get through it. I'm going to throw all caution to the wind, jump in, and go through it." And after you have been through it, no more reaction to the strawberries. Or you can listen to mommy telling you, "You know how sick you get when you eat strawberries!" and never eat strawberries.

Let me draw out the analogy a little further. All you have done all your life is avoid everything. You have always taken the easy way out. You haven't eaten strawberries. Then you take a mind development course and there is a very personable teacher standing up in the front of the room saying, "You don't have to be allergic. Program it. Do your mantra!" You say, "Okay." You go into meditation, and you get deeper and deeper, "*Om, Om.*" Pretty soon you reach the level where you just flow with nature and with "what is," and your allergy disappears by itself. You are not allergic anymore. You say, "Far out!" You eat strawberries and don't get a rash. It's really great. Somebody tells you about karma, about doing good and getting good back, but you don't really understand karma. You don't stop to think that "techniquing" your strawberry allergy away is a karmic act.

There is a story about a great yogi that Sri Aurobindo[24] knew who was very accomplished. This yogi had great powers and could always control his body. One day he got bitten by a cobra. Cobras are very poisonous, but this guy was a great yogi. He went into meditation and said, "The poison will not hurt me," and nothing happened to him. This yogi was involved in politics. He was in Parliament when the British still ruled India. One day, two years after the cobra bit him, he was debating another representative in Parliament. This other representative got him angry and he lost control and died from the cobra bite. That's what happens when something is repressed rather than obviated. The idea in spiritual life is to obviate the dilemma and not pretend that there isn't any. So, the object is to eat strawberries because you don't have an allergy. It's not to eat strawberries because you used to have an allergy and you took care of it. That never works.

DEVOTION

With all forms of understanding, the first step is to know where you are before you can realize where you should be. If you think you're devoted and you're not, you'll never really be devoted. A perfect devotee doesn't walk around obsessed all the time with thoughts of the guru. It's not like that. God is spontaneously generated, appropriate activity, moment to moment. Twenty-four-hour-a-day concentration on the guru is not spontaneously generated, appropriate activity, moment to moment.

Satsang is your life as it is. Heaven is here, not there. Most of you could probably think of something you'd like to change about your life. Well, what you would like to change about your life is never going to change as long as you think satsang is other than what is. If you have

[24] Indian teacher, mystic, yogi, poet, and nationalist who lived from 1872-1950.

this idea in mind of the way it is going to be someday when you get to be a devotee, all you'll do is keep trying to give up what you think is standing in your way. You will never obviate it. Satsang is simply what's present. Your life is satsang. Not meditating on or turning to the guru when something goes wrong. That's not satsang. When turning to the guru spontaneously arises in the process of your day, fine. And when it doesn't, fine. Turning to the guru needs to arise spontaneously and be a part of the whole joyous affair of your life. Turning to the guru is not what is going to make your life joyous. Your life is already joyous.

Recognize that you have chosen the hardest path in the world: the path of absolute devotion. You have not chosen renunciation or deep and demanding meditation. You have not chosen to give up the world, to seclude yourself or to undertake austerities. You have chosen to avail yourself of the demands that will require of you the greatest strength that any human being could ever have required of them. You have chosen to be transformed. To become a devotee. That takes intelligence and humility. That takes absolute commitment. That takes infinitely more strength than the average commitment to spiritual life, for the Godman will not be satisfied with anything but the totality of relationship.

QUESTIONS

What is your method of teaching?

Lee: Well, initially there are certain standard practices: meditation, study, exercise, and a lacto-vegetarian diet, and then ideas will randomly arise to do other things with my students. For instance, I asked several people to go to New York one day and to spend the day panhandling, regardless of how inspired or discouraged they got. One of the things I'll do is provide experiences for people in the group that will provoke insight into who they really are. There's a presumption in the average human being's mind that they know who they are. It seems to be so obvious that we are our personalities and our bodies, that we never question that or stop to think that maybe there is something else. One of the things that the teaching is designed to do is to get people to see that they are not who they think they are or presume themselves to be.

How is the Work that you do with your students different than the work other teachers do with their students?

Lee: There are two types of teachers: one type of teacher has the answers and one type of teacher *is* the answer. The type of teacher who *has* the answer can't *be* the answer, and the type of teacher who *is* the answer gives answers just to pass the time. So, there might be other teachers in the world who *are* the answer, like me, and the formal objective work that's done—meetings to discuss people's spiritual and practical questions or to handle business or plan events—is aligned with right-living and right-activity. But *being* the answer is really key to my work with students. Most spiritual teachers only have the answers. That's good enough for the "new age" but not ultimately good enough.

Your Work has been said to be similar to that of teachers who have favored secrecy and confusion as a means of teaching. What purpose do you feel is served by these methods?

Lee: One of the reasons for secrecy is because what we're doing is the ultimate threat to ego, and ego is what sustains conventional society. Ego often reacts with violence in response to a perceived threat. No one is going to be convinced of the importance of or need for what we're doing, so why not just let them have their conventional attitudes and when they're ready to understand what we have to offer, they'll stumble upon us. There's no problem with people finding us when they need us.

About the value of confusion, a very common psychological principle is that when we are confused and off-balance there is a greater chance to become aware of underlying or subconscious reality. If you take my statement, "I don't give answers, I am the answer," and you try to figure that out rationally you're going to get confused. In the midst of that confusion, what can arise is more clarity than is possible when you're not confused. You may think you're being clear when you are not confused and feel in control, but real clarity isn't possible then. When people are confused and have no idea in the world what's going on, real clarity is possible. It just spontaneously arises.

Why is there a need for a living teacher if this same process has been going on throughout history and information about it is readily available through written literature on the subject?

Lee: What is readily available through reading is a description of the process, not the process itself. The problem with a tradition where the teacher is dead is that if none of the students have genuinely understood the work of the teacher—Work with a capital "W"—the tradition may continue but it will continue through the interpretation of people that didn't really understand. Most living traditions die along with the teacher. If several students genuinely understand the Work, they will carry the tradition on. But if none of the students understand, the tradition will only remain a living tradition one generation or two at most. The further removed it gets from the source, the less likely it is to remain a living tradition. The students must have the same understanding that the teacher had or the tradition dies.

What do you recommend your students hold on to when they're going through life crises?

Lee: The only thing to hold on to is the intuition that God is. Not what God is or who God is—just that God is. Nothing else. Not material things, not sanity, control, or discipline; just that God is. If you're familiar with the story of the dark night of the soul of Saint John of the Cross, the only thing that sustained him when he felt abandoned by God was the surety that God existed.

The student believes that he or she is the body, mind, and personality, and that he or she exists over and against others. The teacher—in this case me—recognizes the non-dualism of God even though there certainly are apparent modifications of energy: individuals, animals, plants, objects, and so on. Yet, in truth, there is a continuum amongst or between all things. The tension between the belief of the individual self versus the reality of non-dualism frequently produces disruption in people's lives.

To use an absurd example, if one were to build the foundation of a building on sand, regardless of how strong and well-built it was, the building would collapse. In very much the same way, if somebody comes to the Community and their foundation is sand, they can get the most beautiful traditional spiritual proof in the world, but if it's on a foundation of sand it's going to collapse. So first we need to realize that the foundation is sand so that we can clear the sand out and build the foundation on solid ground.

Every individual is disappointed at some time in their growth in relationship to their initial god, which is mommy or daddy. When that child starts to date as a young adult, they'll always look for someone to fulfill the satisfaction they didn't get from mommy or daddy. When one comes to the Community there is the fire of God, the presence of Grace. We see that relationship isn't working. We're not seeing a problem with any one relationship; we're seeing a problem with *all* relationships. That's different.

Because we think we are separate from God, we are motivated to seek union. Yet there's no such thing as union; we were never separate. There is a part of us that recognizes illusion even though we are living by it. When we connect with a living tradition or a living teacher, something within our being—call it raw instinct—responds and is drawn to it.

Teaching in 1976

PART II

WAKING UP ON THE EAST COAST

New York and New Jersey, July 1975–July 1978

INTRODUCTION

Lee Lozowick said that when he first "woke up" [or had a "shift in context" in July 1975] it was so obvious that "there is only God" that he thought all he would have to do is tell other people and they would get it. He apparently had never considered being a teacher until a friend, who later became a student, suggested the idea to him. Many people who had known him, especially through the Silva Method, were invited to the first satsang which was held on September 7, 1975. At that time, Lee assumed the traditional role of guru and began to teach—but in a style that was uniquely Western. He spoke with certainty and flair, as if moved by universal forces, and a community very naturally grew around him.

Besides the regular gatherings that Lee had with students in New Jersey several times each week, public events were held in Manhattan at a rented loft and he sometimes gave talks at the East-West Center. One poster that was put up by students in bookstores and health food stores around New York City poked fun at the serious nature of the spiritual scene as well as at the Hohm Community itself, creating quite a stir. It referred to the "flush of enlightenment" and pictured Lee sitting on a toilet bowl surrounded by worshipping students.

Public talks could be rowdy affairs, with much hilarity and a sense of freedom and enjoyment that broke social norms. After-hours gatherings at the Claremont Diner in New Jersey were often boisterous, as students were young and immature in relating with the energies that they were opening up to. Yet there was an innocence and liberated spontaneity that was evoked around Lee that contrasted with the appropriate decorum maintained by diners at the other tables. There was the joy of really knowing at times that there is only God and nothing to attain.

Though anyone might be transported by getting a contact high with Lee's free state, one could also find oneself suddenly extremely uncomfortable around him for no apparent reason. There was always some confront in his presence, usually unspoken, to the secure life that one sought to perpetuate. Dynamics of psychological self-protection and the need for social acceptance became more and more obvious within oneself—manifestations of the drive for survival of an identity that was quiescent at times but always present. Try as one might to get away from this subtle suffering, it was not possible. Lessons were constantly made in Lee's company, which seemed to intensify all the experiences of ordinary life. Lee emphasized the need to really see for ourselves that no attainment could ever suffice in a lasting way—not money, fame, relationship, success, or spiritual experience—as the precursor to recognizing that the only thing that works is "living God."

Lee provided sustenance for the inner work of students through his ongoing attention and regular nourishment of dharma. Much of the teaching that he offered would take years to digest. Students related with the outer circumstances created through the guru, which drew out aspects of self previously hidden from view. Notably, there was a water polo game in July 1976 at the first Guru Purnima [the annual traditional Hindu celebration of the guru's presence in the world, observed on the full moon in July] that became an object lesson of the need for work on self, as spiritual personas were transposed into aggressive caricatures in the heat of the game.

Students who lived in Community households or who worked together struggled with the irritant of more closely seeing the dynamics of ego, animated internally and externally in other personalities. Some worked for Dharmaraj, a business of warehousing and distributing natural health-care products in the New York–New Jersey area. There was a martial arts class that Lee participated in, called "Amdo," that involved judo exercises of learning how to throw and be thrown, a very useful principle for inner work. People packed up used merchandise for sale at flea markets on weekends and interacted with Lee about selling, which he seemed to enjoy. There was little free time, as study groups, transcribing tapes, and various projects (like a food co-op) were constantly initiated by Lee. He created circumstances in which people found themselves in and out of the fire of the spiritual process in the post-Vietnam hippie culture of East Coast urban America in the mid-1970s.

The contrast between students' subjective experience and the freedom that Lee exhibited was palpable. His demonstration of outrageous behavior during talks and at unexpected times, such as shifting into the unrestrained role of a gospel preacher who had "seen the light," only tended to magnify the dilemma of one's self-contraction when the rapture of the moment had passed. It was possible to be distracted from the dilemma of the self-meditative state for periods of time, perhaps for lifetimes, but the dilemma was still there. Most people living worldly lives seemed able to avoid such considerations, but if one felt the need to look into the crux of the problem, what was there to do? Lee seemed to offer a doorway through the maze, a living demonstration of the possibility of transcending the game of ego survival. He suggested that students begin a process of re-adaptation of body and mind to spiritual life through practice of the conditions, but students made their own decisions about engaging the disciplines.

In early 1977, Lee went to India for the first time. He had privately visited with the mystic Hilda Charlton who had spent years living in India, to ask about teachers and places to visit. While in India, Lee was most impacted by Yogi Ramsuratkumar, a Beggar-Saint who he came to realize was his master in the early 1980s, through a series of seeming coincidences on this trip and on another trip in 1979. One of the significant synchronous developments of the 1977 India trip was that some of Lee's students began to exhibit shakti-phenomena on a bus on the way to Tiruvannamalai, the abode of Yogi Ramsuratkumar, being overcome by blissful states and manifesting involuntary bodily movements or *kriyas*. Over the course of years, the movement of shakti became more internal for students, as energy was unblocked and bodily integrated in Lee's company. People gradually became more available to the free state and Influence that came through Lee, who said that he *was* the teaching rather than that he communicated the teaching.

Students began to consider how the process of work with a genuine spiritual master had no cultural limitations and was accessible in the West as well as the East. There were periods of resting in Lee's presence, but they did not last long. His comments about sexuality and relationship were especially provocative and uproarious, and his criticism of ego in the world and the spiritual scene was incisive and discriminating. His comments and "being" catalyzed underlying dynamics that needed to be clarified—for example, a sense of separative superiority in the way one got in on the fun or identified with a spiritual hero. But if one looked more deeply, Lee seemed to be providing a service never encountered before through his demonstration of compassion in a stunning counterintuitive way—unsympathetically and surgically exposing ego's dynamics. Beneath psychological defenses, a space was created for an experience of the teaching to get in beyond words.

Lee appeared interested in his students developing an understanding of the living spiritual process as opposed to the philosophies of different traditions. He commented on the sayings of Jesus in *The Gospel of Thomas* and related them to dharma in the present day. Lee brought students with him when he visited teachers (and occasionally practitioners who had studied with teachers) who he respected. Such input from sources outside of the Hohm Community seemed to provide a kind of spiritual "food" that he assimilated himself, useful material for work with students, and opportunities for students to discriminate and appreciate their own path and the different streams of genuine spiritual work regardless of tradition.

Of particular note was Lee's relationship with E.J. Gold, a unique teacher who taught in the style of the Fourth Way,[25] whom Lee had met during a trip to California in 1976 and felt to have reliable integrity. He took a group of students with him for another visit in 1978. The "Work influence" that became part of the way he taught, he said, came through Mr. Gold.

Lee's use of whatever circumstances presented themselves was a teaching in itself, a creative process that had its own momentum. Lee went with students to interview a woman who had studied with Gurdjieff and brought back impressions to share in working with the rest of the Community. He visited a respected Tibetan lama who said, "There are no Milarepas in the world today," which was a comment that he sometimes referenced in making a point about spiritual practice in the contemporary world. Years later he would discover his resonance with the Eastern Bauls of Bengal[26] who would "discriminate and integrate" in their relationship to the path. Lee was teaching students to distinguish and absorb what was of spiritual value in creating a community that could live the dharma in the West.

Early on, before the Study Course (contained in Part I) was put together, Lee decided that cassette tapes of certain talks, which he referred to as "commercial tapes," would be made available to those interested in the teaching. These could be bought by those coming around who had not yet made the decision to get more closely involved, or by those who simply had an interest in his Work.

---

25 An approach to work-on-self developed by George Gurdjieff but which probably had its origin in ancient sources.

26 The Bauls are wandering minstrel-practitioners whose tradition is characterized by several principles: realization through the body; a longing for God and what is called the "Man of the Heart"; relationship to the guru; and a willingness to draw whatever is useful from any tradition for their sadhana.

After a talk, Lee would sometimes tell one of his students to "knock out" a number of copies of the tape that had just been made, which might be spontaneously titled. It often seemed that he had never thought about the material that was evoked before the talk, but that it was instead drawn out of him in response to the need of the moment.

Transcripts of these commercial tapes are presented here chronologically, in the sequence in which the talks were given.

AN OBJECTIVE LOOK AT AND CRITICISM OF MYSTERY SCHOOLS AS A REAL PATH

(March 14, 1976)

Techniques Are Founded on Changing "What Is"

In the old days, the Mystery Schools[27] were called this because you had to do a tremendous amount of work before you'd be initiated. There were different levels of initiation, years of study to go through, and various demands were made on you. Very few people made it to the inner circle.

Typically, the founders of the schools had a lot of esoteric knowledge. They read all the ancient books and they knew all the secret techniques. Every mystery school that I've ever encountered has levels upon levels of techniques at the basis of their teaching. The techniques become more powerful, subtler, more secret, and dangerous. But even the ultimate experience is still based on technique. All the mystery schools are founded on doing something to change "what is" because "what is" is not good enough. The techniques are all remedial in nature. They all infer that if you don't apply the techniques they have, you are not going to live a full life.

Ultimately, all the mystery schools—the Rosicrucians, Theosophy—are based on one basic belief system, a very scientific, physical understanding of the structure of the material universe. The more deeply one goes into the mystery schools, the more closely all the techniques and the education parallel the methodology and the philosophy of quantum physics. It's an interesting thing because the techniques were known three thousand years ago, before quantum physics was a science. There is one single difference: intelligence. Quantum physics deals with

27 The tradition of "Mystery Schools" dates back to the Greco-Roman empire and ancient Egypt. A chief feature of these schools has been the secrecy around details of initiation and ritual practices.

raw energy, energy that does have some basic intelligence. This energy knows how to form a crystal in saturated water, how to hold the moon in orbit, how to grow a plant from a seed.

The Hope of Ascending to Transcend the Body Boils Down to Separation

Theosophy holds true to the idea of human intelligence as a guiding force in the manifest physical universe. All of the mystery schools have had, at their inception and at the base of their methodology, this idea of a hierarchical structure within levels of consciousness. In Theosophy it's called "the White Brotherhood." It's a very presumptuous philosophy of a brotherhood that exists of twelve "ascended masters," as they're called. That these masters are *ascended* masters is a very important part of the structure of the Theosophical belief system.

The average person hates their body even if they are very cool about it. We've got Primal Therapy, we've got Psychosynthesis, and all this good stuff. You can get into Sensitivity Training and in two minutes you'll recognize you're disgusted with your body. You can have the most *Playgirl-* or *Playboy* "Body of the Year" and it doesn't matter. You're still disgusted with your body. For most of you, it's very easy to recognize and understand that.

As a result of that hatred of the body, all the mystery schools are founded on the teachings of the *ascended* masters. That means they're too pure to be here with us. They're out there in the ethers, flitting around at a very high vibrational rate. They did their work on earth and paid their dues and became ascended masters. So now they float around in the realms of light with hosts of angelic beings—all white with trumpets and wings—attending to their every need. The masters help us out so we get to understand [their state].

The basis of all of that teaching has come from a very deep misunderstanding of human psychology. These beings do exist. Some of you may even have been taught in your dreams by an ascended master. I'm not saying none of this is real. I'm saying that the basis for the creation of mystery schools stems from a misunderstanding of the human condition, of that which is real for you and me. Several thousand years ago very few people understood psychology. We're really lucky to be living now, when we've got a tremendous wealth of information. We can read up on psychology and understand where all this stuff evolved from. Five thousand years ago, only the very, very few masters that lived on the earth—like the few gurus who live on the earth today—fully understood human psychology, fully understood the birth trauma and the pain of separation, physical separation from mommy and the parallel pain of psychic separation from the Divine. Very few people understood all that in practical life terms. In order to justify their knowledge that there is more than our constant suffering, the mystery school teachers of the time developed, created, brought into being and sustained a whole teaching founded on *other* worlds, other-worldly teachers, and ascended masters. They say that every once a while an ascended master takes a human body to save the world.

But I'm not interested in you being a dog or a cat next lifetime, or being an ascended master, or perfecting a body of light so you never have to come back to earth again. I'm interested in the human condition. However deeply you understand what you are doing, whatever you put your faith in, that's what you'll get back. If you, as an individual, put your faith in the end result that mystery schools promise you, that's going to be your limitation. You will be absolutely limited by your conceptual structure of what a mystery school is going to do for you. Such schools are founded on technique only. The techniques get more complicated, subtler, and more sophisticated, but they're still techniques.

If you stay in such a school, you will agree to give up the possibility of a passionate existence in order to become attained, cool, controlled, and wise. You might even get into the high inner circle of the school, get to meet or be initiated into having a personal ascended master. You all know from your dreams how real alternate realities can be. You don't know they are not real until you wake up. You *can* communicate with an ascended master. He'll be real; you'll get messages. But no matter what mystery school is studied, the ultimate teaching is always philosophically the same. The ascended masters always tell you the same thing in almost the exact same words: if everybody studied in this mystery school, everyone would live in peace and harmony with one another, in brotherhood and sisterhood.

They always hold out that hope for you because it's literally instilled in the very texture and guts of the teaching. The hope is very simple. The hope is to be ascended. It all boils down to separation. It's too tough dealing with the body. Emotions aren't easy, sickness isn't easy, sex isn't easy, childbirth isn't easy. The hope at the foundation of the mystery schools was that through enough dedicated practice one could transform this body into a body of light which would not get sick or be hurt, would not die or decay. The implication is that, before you can do that, you have to cool out your head, so you'll never have negative emotions and never be upset, sad, or passionate. If you've been involved for any degree of time with mystery school groups, their brotherhood, relationship, tenderness, and friendship is not very passionate. It's very superficial, mild, sweet, nice. It looks good but any challenge rips it to shreds.

The Need to Deal with Where We Are

It always boils down to the need to deal with where you are. We all have minds and one thing that's exciting for most people is knowledge. You might really believe that when you get to the "Thirteenth Degree" they're going to have a special little secret that's going to give you the answer. You want to recognize that the deeper you get into the mystery schools, the more it is subtly implied that you cannot do anything without them. The Brotherhood watches over them, the Brotherhood gave them the permission to do this teaching. They are protected and you need their protection.

It is typical for the average spiritual teacher, guru, or meditation teacher to really condemn the mystery schools. Yet the true gurus that exist in the world have always structured their relationship in the same way as the mystery schools. The structure of the mystery school is founded on the traditional guru-devotee relationship. Everything is. There is not a single thing in the world, particularly in the domain of spiritual teachings, whose basic structure is *not* based on the guru-devotee relationship. That's just the way it's always been. The limitation is the inference or implication of the teaching itself, which of necessity limits the students of that teaching who put their faith in it. They think, "Someday I could be a grand master." That's the limitation.

Question: Is God ever mentioned in any of the mystery schools?

Lee: God is most definitely mentioned—but not right away. They say there is an infinite continuum and God is none other than the continuum. The language is very consistent with the teaching. But the implication of the practice is that the technique is what's going to get you to see the truth. "We're just telling you the truth so when you experience it you will know that it's the truth."

Another problem with the mystery schools is that the initiations are always based on super-normal, para-normal or mystical experience. Mystical experience is really great. When you are actively dealing with your life here and now, you can have all the mystical experience you want. Mystical experience is far out. When you have mystical experience or look for it to the exclusion of your life here, that's what we call "separation" or "seeking." The mystery schools imply that you should seek for mystical experience to the exclusion of your life here. Even though there is rhetoric about God, your body, and basic life-level responsibility to your family, business, or job, the emphasis on it is very weak.

What mystery school initiation is not based on is you recognizing that you married your mother or realizing that you've never loved anyone in your whole life.[28] That's what initiation should be based on! That's what our initiation is based on [laughter] …good stuff that you can deal with! How can you deal with the ascended Brotherhood? It's like going to a priest that's never been married. If you tell the ascended master, "Master, I have a problem with my girlfriend," he says, "Just meditate, my child." The ascended master doesn't know from nothing! No matter what you tell them, all they know is, "It's all light, my child." You say, "When I visit the spiritual center everybody's always eating between meals. They've all got an oral fixation. I'm having a problem with that." The ascended master doesn't know what to tell you. They don't know from oral fixations. They don't eat!

A Full Life Is a Matter of the Texture of Experience

We can call me a "*descended* master." Compared to the mystery schools, the strength at Hohm is found in a different place. What the guru implies is that a full life is not a matter of what you do, how much you know, or how widely traveled you are; it is a matter of the texture of what you're experiencing. It's not how *much* you experience; it's *how* you experience. So… [*Lee launches into a mock scenario here*], we'll build a little cave under the ground and meditate down there and give the earth energy. It's true that there are people living under the shell of the earth. When Atlantis blew up, they went down there, and they survive to this day. That's what the Bermuda Triangle is. It opens up and these people come out in their spaceships and do things. It's very

28 Lee's confrontive observation about the inability to love was based on the understanding that there can be no real love at the deepest levels when one is in the sway of the survival imperative of ego and one's focus is self-reference. Everyone also carries a primal psychological wound from early life experience that is generally an obstacle to fully giving and receiving love.

secret. Not many people know about them. Even fewer people have seen them…

When you get into the inner circles of mystery schools that's the kind of stuff you get into.

Being Happy at the Deepest Level

Let's be serious for a bit. The basis of the mystery school teaching is that if you get yourself "clear enough," if you get out of your own way, the master will take over and run your life and always give you what you want. If you just clear yourself and give it up to the ascended master, you will always be in the right place at the right time and so on. The rhetoric is exactly the same as the whole "Spiritual Slavery" idea.[29] But when you've given up to the guru, and the guru takes care of you, all you know is devotion. You're happy all the time at base level. You're happy at the deepest level that there is to be happy at. When you give it up to an ascended master, your understanding and your being at the right place at the right time is not at base level. As soon as the raw Divine comes into your life, it undermines you completely.

You've got two things going on: you've got the Divine and you've got you. Rhetorically, yes, it's all one; the Divine is constant and you're the Divine. Well, that doesn't mean much when you're suffering. The Divine is not comforting. Only a human being is comforting. You want a person to hold you when you are suffering. You don't want some nebulous transcendent form beyond time and space. The *guru* is comforting. That's why the guru is relevant. When you start to recognize that it's all agony except God, then you can be happy all the time.

When you allow yourself to be comforted by a philosophy or ideology about how it's okay after death and you're going to come back

---

29 When Lee experienced a shift in context and began to teach, he referred to his condition as that of a "spiritual slave" who was moved by and surrendered to the universal process.

anyway and all of that stuff, you can lead a very comfortable life. You can really not be too upset if someone in your family dies. You can say, "Well, I know they are happy where they are." You can go for thirty, forty, fifty years and lead a very comfortable life with a very comforting philosophy. You'll be moderately successful, you'll be secure, and have your money and your family, and everything will be fine. Intuitively, you will be where you need to be, whenever you need to be there. You can do that; many people do—because the raw Divine is evident in so few places in the world.

The problem is that, if you happen to meet the raw Divine, and if you get undermined and don't stay with that and understand it, your whole life can fall apart. If you don't have a basis for understanding what's going on, you'll be in touch with your suffering and that's all.

FREEDOM'S JUST ANOTHER WORD—UNLESS YOU KNOW THE GURU

(April 25, 1976)

Using Our Potential

The disciple very often interprets the relationship with the guru from his or her own reference points. Any decision-making that the disciple, student, or devotee goes through always comes from the perspective of who the student thinks the guru is. One of my students said this week, "I want to get to know you better because I really don't know you." Of course not. Obviously, none of you really know me… And you shouldn't expect to know me. I'm unknowable. The point is—were you to know me, you would be a perfect devotee.

All of you have interpreted what I have said the way you would have liked to have heard it and functioned on that basis. That's why people leave the Community. For example, V. had more talent than anybody you're liable to meet. But she was too busy being a tough lady (at twenty years old), too involved in feeling sorry for herself, feeling the loner, the ugly duckling, to allow herself to be revealed as the incredibly talented person that she is. It became so easy to be tough, too easy to play the role of being stupid. She had to deal with the fact that she's really very warm and sensitive and not as tough as she always told everybody she was. And she left when she was expected to be smart—because she is very smart.

You all have a tremendous depth of experiential possibility. And regardless of who you are, no one works at full potential. The average person in the world isn't working; they're just kind of floating along watching TV. Some of you have tremendous potential that you don't want to use because you won't get as much attention that way. The fact is there's no payoff for you to realize your potential because the guru is the one that gets lauded with praise. "Look at what good devotees he has!" You don't get the praise. There's no payoff initially in being who you really are. There's no payoff in being a clear, healthy, loving, successful, and talented devotee—even from the guru!

There Is No Other Payoff Than Being Alive

Being talented, healthy, happy, and doing your sadhana—that's your thanks to the Lord for creating you in the first place. There is no other payoff. You already got the payoff. You're alive. That's it, see? You've had the payoff for a long time. You don't get two payoffs. That's just the way it is. To fulfill your sadhana, and to thank the Lord for giving you the payoff in the first place, you allow the guru to uncover who you are. If you let him or her, the guru will [compel] you to be creative, happy, strong, healthy, intelligent, successful, alive in God.

Your sadhana is like forging steel. The best swords are made from the best steel. The best steel is tempered by being heated up, taken out and beaten, cooled, then put back in the fire to be heated up, taken out and beaten, then cooled again, over and over. The best steel is tempered many times before it comes to its perfect quality. A devotee is the same. The process of being tempered by the guru is one of being constantly put into the fire, brought out in order to reflect on the tempering process, put back in again, pulled out so you can re-cognize and understand the heat, and put back into the heat again.

When the Guru Makes His Point

When you're in my company, there are typically three alternatives if you decide to leave. The first alternative is to go back to doing the same thing you did before you found the guru. You have your friends, your work, and your family. You think the way you always thought before you came to the guru: "Life is sometimes sad and sometimes happy. But that's the way life is. We're only here for a short period of time." Of course, if you've been with any guru you know at least intellectually that there's some kind of afterlife when the body drops. So, you've got that to hold onto. "Well I'm pretty straight. I don't lie and I don't cheat, so I'll do OK."

The second alternative is to pretend that the guru was just a pleasant interlude in your life and spend the rest of your life un-experiencing the guru—in other words, to run like hell as far away as you can, and to continue for the rest of your life to try as hard as you can to forget the point the guru made. But when the guru makes his point, there is no way in heaven or hell that you can forget about it.

One of the people that some of you know has a daughter in a school where they have a particular attitude about God. One day the daughter said to the teacher, "God isn't up there. God is everywhere." Next thing you know, the whole class and the teacher were arguing with this five-year-old girl.

"How can you say that? It's blasphemous."

"Nope. My mommy says that God is not up there, and my mommy knows."

The guru made his point, and there is no way that point is ever going to be forgotten. Mommy is going to be constantly reminded because her daughter isn't going to forget. You know how kids are, "But Mommy, you said God wasn't up there."

The third alternative if you leave is to try to destroy everything about yourself that remembers the point the guru made in your life—through the abuse of alcohol, food, dope, sex, and so on. You will try to literally destroy the brain through the abuse of food and/or substances. Sex doesn't destroy the brain, but it gives you so much emotional stuff to deal with that you're too busy to think about the guru.

Some of you might think there's a fourth alternative where you leave the guru and either find another guru or make it on your own. There *is* the possibility of achieving the Buddha state in your life. But it's very unlikely, because if you've left one guru, you're liable to leave others for the same reason when it gets to that same point [in your process].

Many people find it very easy to live normal ashram life with a normal "guru" because it's very secure. You know when you're going to be fed, when you're going to work, when you're going to meditate. You get your body in shape and you're healthy. But how are you going to be challenged? All your decisions are made for you: they tell you to meditate from this time to that time, then eat, then work, then meditate, then sleep. It's like being a career officer in the armed services. Many people find it very easy to do that kind of sadhana. Since I have already made my point with most of you, you have a particular dilemma. You can't go to just any ashram. You wouldn't last at any ashram. They'd either kick you out or you'd take over.

When You See That the Only Alternative Is God

The other possibility, of course, is staying with the guru. To do that, of course, you need to get through the very basic stuff, like wondering whether I'm the real thing or not. Once you got through that—"Okay, Lee's a real guru"—then you need to get through self-doubt. You need to get through feeling like you don't understand. How many of you have come to me saying, "But I don't understand"? Who the hell understands? Do you think everybody else understands? If you don't understand, it's okay. Everybody has questions. So, what if you don't understand? If you believe I am who I say I am and you're devoted, you're devoted. What else is there to understand? "But what about the teaching?" You can find the teaching in any library. The teaching is the flypaper that gets you stuck first time around. So, it can be very simple. You make your decision and that's all there is to it.

At some point all of you have realized that something about your life doesn't work. Some of you have realized that *nothing* works. It's my job to get you to know that nothing works so strongly that you stop doing what doesn't work and start doing what works. It's very simple, very basic. You may have had an insight into the fact that nothing works, that your whole life is nothing more than desire for something or other. You upgrade it when you come to spiritual life. If you don't see that nothing works to the point of distraction in God, you're never going to be distracted in God. You're going to be distracted in desire—by the next pretty woman who walks down the street, or the next stud-man that takes his shirt off at the beach. You may even be distracted in your mantra! See, if you're not really in touch with your suffering, you're not going to be distracted to the point of having the only alternative be God. You *need* the only alternative to your life to be God. You can't have other alternatives. You can't have the alternative of being *almost* happy. Not here, you can't.

Grace doesn't allow any choice. But if you don't put your life on the line, then you're not allowing Grace to do its work.

Enlightenment Is the Knowledge That All Experience Is Transitory, Including Enlightenment

Some people meet me for the first time and practically go out of their minds with joy because they've met the true guru. But what's really important is that you recognize the point that has been dramatically made in your life, and that you not run away from that point.

The Buddha said, "All life is suffering." Every Buddha before Shakyamuni Buddha and all the ones after him have said that all life is suffering. You can read Buddhist texts from now until you're eighty years old and you can very passively acknowledge that all life is suffering. "Yes, yes, oh yes." But if there is no one to point that out to you graphically and dramatically, all you're going to do is be reborn again and do the same trip.

Because none of you know who I am, I can't tell you what I'm doing. But every time I give a lecture, I explain what's going on. I can make it seem reasonable to you so that your intellect will say, "That makes sense," but explanations don't really apply. What applies is that we're in a space together where there's an implied promise: God. There is no goal. You are already realized. "Prior condition" [that which always exists prior to the mind's activity] is your heritage. You *are* prior condition. I can't get you to prior condition. You have to awaken to that fact.

By virtue of the fact that there is "nobody home," the guru can be whatever he needs to be. The guru can be friend, lover, teacher, businessman, decision-maker. The guru can be freaked out, sad, depressed, happy, high, jealous. The guru can be just about anything. Enlightenment is the knowledge that all experience is transitory, including enlightenment. And it's implied that if or when you get to be a perfect devotee, you'll be in the same place. Far out!

There's Nothing Else to Love but God

Every once in a while, you get a hit of what love is. One hit of love makes it all worthwhile. There's only God. What else do you have to do? You don't have to make it complicated. You don't have to understand what's going on. You *can't* understand what's going on. *I* don't understand what's going on. How the hell are you supposed to understand what's going on? All you have to do is live your sadhana. Every time I think you need to understand, I will pull you out of the fire so that you can re-cognize your experience and understand, and then I'll stick you back in the fire again. So, if you don't understand I'll pull you out of the fire until you do. Then put you back in, see? The process of our relationship is that I'm going to keep putting you into the fire until you are tempered to perfection.

There's nothing you can do with a perfect samurai sword but admire the perfection of its blade. That means, my friends, when I stop putting you into the fire and you are perfectly tempered, there is going to be nothing anybody can do but admire your perfection. There's going to be "nobody home" for you either. You will have a perfectly appropriate action for everything. Your children and the person you're living with will be special to you because they're your children, your mate, *and* you will love them like you love anyone else in the world. When you are perfectly tempered, there are no degrees of who you should be nice to and who you shouldn't be nice to. You're in relationship or you're out of relationship—that's the way it is.

In the ultimate sense, the perfect devotee is always happy. Until you are always happy, you are getting hits of what I'm talking about. In between the hits, I'm purposely creating the environment where you can recognize how much armor you have between you and real relationship. I'm trying to distract you with other things to show you how weak your love of God is. The more I can get you to be distracted in anything else, the more clearly evident it is that you don't love God. Simultaneously, it is my job to get you to love God more than anything else in the world, to get you to recognize and to live the condition that is Grace. Because that's all there is, you know? What else are you going to love but God anyway? All else is a delusion. All else is your separate self, thinking there's something else to love but God. There's nothing else to love but God, nothing else. When I can't get you distracted in anything else, you're going to be okay.

The Guru-Devotee Relationship Will Always Be Misunderstood

It takes everything that you have as a human being to stay with the true guru. It takes strength, insight, intelligence, devotion, love, sincerity, and work, as deeply as you can get it up from your gut. The guru-devotee relationship will always be misunderstood. It is, in fact, misunderstood by half of the people that call themselves spiritual seekers. Most people today look at someone like Sai Baba of Shirdi and think, "What a romantic personality! A crazy old man, living in a run-down hovel, throwing stones at people that approached him—how romantic, how beautiful! Wouldn't it have been nice to have lived back then?" Or people look at Ram Dass's guru, Neem Karoli Baba, and say, "If only

I'd found out where he was before he died. Wouldn't it have been fun to sit with the old man, wearing his wool blanket around himself in 120-degree weather? Oh, how romantic!"

Listen, those kinds of people don't know what spiritual life is all about. Spiritual life seems romantic if you're not with a true guru. If you're with a true guru, there's plenty of romance, plenty of juicy adventure to keep you dealing with stuff. But how many real gurus are there in America? There are a lot of people that talk tough, people that are good mechanics, people that can make white light come up your spine through manipulation of subtle energy. So what?

The point is that the real guru is here to undermine your life of suffering. The only way that can be done is to get you to realize that the only thing that works is God. How are you ever going to realize that the only thing that works is God if you don't first realize nothing else works? You think sex works? You think a good meal works? You think a six hundred dollar-a-week salary works? You spend any time around the true guru, you make the commitment, and you'll see that those things don't work—until you're functioning appropriately. When you're functioning appropriately, everything works. You can make five thousand dollars a week, enjoy it, and live appropriately.

When you honestly and openly deal with who you are, you realize that romance is not on the other side of the fence. Romance is everywhere you are. It's romantic, it's really passionate to be here together, living in relationship. That's what life is all about. Life is romantic! Life is an adventure! Life is not a drudge. Look at your insights with joy. When you really know your life doesn't work, you've made yourself open to getting it to work. When you really *get it*, you don't know whether to laugh or cry, so you do some of both.

When you really know your life doesn't work, you've made yourself open to getting it to work. The fact is that relationship is beneath the avoidance of relationship. If you try to put relationship on top of the avoidance, it doesn't work.

Once I woke up, I couldn't fantasize about God anymore. There was nothing left but sex and food. And what the hell good is food? I used to dream about the day when I'd experience white light every time I'd meditate. I used to daydream about seeing Kali[30] and opening my heart to her. Then I woke up and it was all gone. There was nothing to attain, no more Kali. There was nothing but who sits in front of me.

---

[30] Hindu Goddess of death and time, who embodies feminine energy and who removes the ego and liberates the soul from the cycle of birth and death.

THE ASSUMPTIVE DILEMMA

(July 31, 1977)

Change Is Not at Issue

Student: How can I be released from the grip of my perceptions and programming regarding my job situation?

Lee: When you ask, "What do I do about something?" the answer is: you don't do anything about it. You watch it, you self-remember, you understand, you enquire. You recognize why it is you seek change—different circumstances, friends, lover, job, teacher, community, more money, less money, more responsibility, less responsibility... You simply recognize what's going on. Change is not at issue.

If change happens to be present in your life, that's peachy keen. But you don't program, manipulate, or attempt to change anything. You recognize what is most appropriate and that is what you live. Sometimes recognizing what is most appropriate does mean change. It could mean a change of job, a change of friends, a change of household. But change is irrelevant to the whole process.

Sadhana is not about manipulating through mental processes. There will be occasions when what you think is your mind will spontaneously create positive or responsive circumstances for you. That's neat, that's okay. But willful manipulation of circumstances because you have an ability to do that when you want to is not a part of your sadhana. That's resisting your sadhana, because you'll keep yourself comfortable that way for a long time. But we're not interested in keeping ourselves comfortable *(laughter)*. Okay, some of us are. The enlightened community is not interested in keeping itself comfortable; it's interested in living God. Waking, sleeping, dreaming, daydreaming, fantasizing—simply living God. Not manipulating circumstances to be comfortable.

When things are good, you do your sadhana, meditate every day and stick to the diet. You're all *Rah! Rah*! When doubts creep in, and things aren't so good, and you're feeling the pain of contraction, you tend to slack off. You say, "I can't meditate. I'm depressed. I need to eat something that's not on the diet." A typical seeker will do that. Some of you do your sadhana no matter what, whether you doubt or don't doubt. This is really a nice place to go from, because you're not under any misconceptions.

Self-Meditation

What takes place is this: under all circumstances, toward all events, literally to the death, you will sustain self-meditation. Part of the sustenance of that self-meditation involves what you know about spiritual life, the Godman, enlightenment, realization, shakti, bliss, mindlessness, prior condition. Only when *all of this*—you, this room, this building, the earth, the solar system, the nearby galaxies—becomes distracted in God, will you realize what it is that I've been communicating to you. It is not a matter of undoing your personality or experiencing mindless union with whatever you think you've experienced mindless union with, because that is not God. It's God because everything is God and there's only God, but it's not God. Even when you experience union—blissful, joyous, and without consideration for the search—what is it that you're doing? You are experiencing an event that is going to cause you to form a more solid conviction about what you think spiritual life or God to be. Experiences of satori or samadhi serve to undo the knot of contraction. There's only one dilemma, there's only one knot. But there's an infinite number of contractions and dilemmas that mind creates to sustain the search.

Many people do not understand a word I say. Considering how clearly and concisely I speak, it should be a simple enough matter to understand what I say. What, in fact, goes on is that the seeker will make assumptions about what his or her teacher or spiritual master wants or expects of them. They will assume they know what sadhana is. Then they will act on those assumptions under all circumstances. Those assumptions are never based on listening to what I say. The times when you do real sadhana, when you are perfectly turned to God, when you are living God, are when you have listened to what I've said somewhere in the deep recesses of your being. Something just randomly triggers, and you do sadhana for a time. Because it's all in there somewhere. Just like the survival instinct can randomly trigger from a myriad of associations—color, temperature, sound—real sadhana works the same way. From the deep, dark recesses of all of what you call "you," there are random times when real sadhana triggers and you do it. What you are doing at other times is never what I have suggested. Rather, you are following through with your assumption of what you thought I said or wanted, or what you expected of me. At some point you need to really see what you have been doing. When you have really seen that, you need to start listening and paying attention to what I say, because I speak very clearly if you have the ears to hear.

Change is not at issue. There's nothing to do but assume your "already perfect enlightenment." Recognize that you've never heard what I've said. I have never said that the implication of your relationship with me is that you're going to lose all individuality, personality, personal strength, hopes, dreams, desires, things you like to do. In fact, I've said the opposite. You will be shattered, you will never be the same, you will absolutely lose who you think you are, but that has nothing to do with the form your life takes. The form your life takes is the form your life takes. You will lose all the assumptions you make, all the reactive strategies you play out in relationship to that form. The basic knot, the dilemma that is in fact the crux of the existence of that form, will be taken into consideration. Not the form. The form has nothing to do with anything. The form is just the form and would not be any different if God existed or not. If God didn't exist, everything would be exactly as it is today. You all would still be here, and I would be here, and New

York with its dirty air would still be here. Everything would be exactly the same whether God existed or not. Form is not at issue here.

The perfect argument that God exists is also the perfect argument that God does not exist. Do you understand that logically and philosophically? So really, whether God exists or doesn't exist is not at issue. What's at issue is that there is the illusion of separation. There's constant self-meditation and in rare moments of lucidity, generated by your relationship to Grace, you are shown that your life is suffering. That's the point. God has nothing to do with that. So, what do we do about that?

Life Is All the Illusion of Suffering

It's one of the laws of the mental worlds that history (like good garlic) always repeats itself. So, we can learn something from tradition. We can learn something from what Tukaram, Rinzai, and Kabir—people of that ilk—have taught. What can we learn? When I read what they've taught it seems perfectly clear to me. When I perceive the institutions that have been built up around what they have taught, based on the assumptions that their students have made about them, I can recognize that history repeats itself. What we can learn from tradition is that the relationship between the Godman or Godwoman and the devotee is the only thing that makes the world real.

We have this situation. We have the Godman, who knows exactly who he or she is, and we have this assumption that we know who the Godman is. So, what are we to do about that? As long as there is this assumption, we should be doing something about it. We should be doing appropriate sadhana. What does that mean? Initially, that means listening to what the Godman says, which is a very simple matter. Watch yourself and self-remember. When you see yourself doing what you think is sadhana, because of an assumption you have made about what you think you know, allow that to break down in humor and chuckle to yourself about the time you have spent running in place.

See, the idea is not to *run* in place, the idea is to simply *be* in place. What the seeker does is run in place, assuming that is being in place. When you run in place, what you're doing is seeking. When you're being in place, the form is the same because you're still in place. You're wearing the same clothes. The difference is you're happy and humorous instead of motivated by the need to forget that you ever saw (once, sometime, in some meditation) that all life is suffering. And maybe you haven't seen that yet, and here I am trying to get you to see that. Why the hell would you want to see your suffering? [Typically] you do one of two things: you either seek to avoid seeing that all life is suffering, or you seek to avoid remembering the terrible vision that you had that all life is suffering. You don't know the vision is incomplete. Life is not all suffering. In fact, it is all perfect—bliss, happiness, God. It's the *illusion* of your life that is suffering.

The Dilemma Is Not Within

No real community will ever be large. It will be large at times, but never for any length of time. Very few people will recognize the necessity of living God. You need to sustain this recognition long enough to realize spontaneously-generated, absolute and true life in God. You're not going to have an internal vision that is going to purify you and then you're going to see the guru within. That is not the case. As a matter of fact, the guru is not *within*. The guru is not *without* either. I know that's a problem because poor mind says, "Come on, man! It's not within, it's not without, where is it?" Well, it isn't—that's the point. It cannot be attained.

Not only is there nothing to be attained, but the realization that there is nothing to be attained cannot be attained. That's a real dilemma. The seeker says, "I know there's this dilemma of separation, but that's within, right? That's down deep in my psyche somewhere." Well no, that dilemma is not deep down within your psyche. The dilemma of self-meditation is not within. It's not some knot that you have to meditate on and go within, in the deep dark recesses of your psyche, and untie. That dilemma is present right here, right now, as all of this. That dilemma is present as everything inclusively that you have ever seen, felt, smelled, heard, and tasted—subtly or physically. That is the dilemma.

Now that presents a problem that might not have been seen before. The problem that was seen before was that there's this dilemma inside and if I meditate long enough and work hard enough, or if the guru is a skillful enough surgeon, we will get to it. The problem becomes somewhat more profound at this stage of the game because the dilemma is not seen as any kind of internal process. The dilemma is seen as all of this.

Only One Thing to Do

What are we to do about that? We certainly aren't going to undo the worlds. There's not going to be one great atomic explosion of awakening. Well, there's only one thing to do. It's painful, it's a real bitch, and if you do it with honesty and real observation, you will be very happy and full and there will be lots of higher-conscious experiences along the way to keep you involved. The experiences themselves do not connote a particular level you've attained; they're just icing on the cake. And there will be those rare few of you, I'm very sorry to say, that will simply do sadhana and not have any of those higher-level experiences along the way. You won't have obviating blisses and distractions in God. [*With an exaggerated depressive tone*] You're just going to live with me, sorry to say [*laughter*]. Some of you are just going to have to do it that way… [*With an exuberant tone*] But some of you are going to have any number of visual experiences, subtle lights and sounds; phenomenal things will happen to you along the way. It's just a matter of your tendencies and your karmas.

So, there's only one thing to do… [*Lee spontaneously animates the role of Gospel preacher*]: "See the light and be born again! Hallelujah! Only the Holy Spirit can cleanse your sins and make you clean again! Jesus is the Lord and the light and the way! I have found the one way and I'm here to testify! I wanted to be cleansed in the Holy Spirit!" (*clapping and laughter*)

Back to sadhana… Sadhana is coming to intelligently, consciously recognize under all circumstances that every single event that arises in your life is dilemma and seeking for union, when in fact the whole delusion of the dilemma exists to begin with because you ignore and deny union. In fact, there is no such thing as union. What is there to be united with? Or who? In fact, there is no dilemma and no separation. There is nothing but God, nothing but what is. Maybe there's not even God. That would be a kick in the ass, wouldn't it? You get to the pearly gates and there's Saint Peter.

You say, "I'm finally going to see God!"

Saint Peter says, "Well, there is no God."

"But these are the pearly gates and you're Saint Peter!" you protest.

"Yeah, I know. Sorry, there's no God."

"Then what is there?" you ask.

Saint Peter says, "Well, when you walk through those gates, you'll find a factory."

It's true. That's what's up there—a factory. You don't get wings and a white robe. You get khaki pants and a khaki shirt. They make no distinction between the sexes and you get to work in the factory for eternity.

You say, "But what about the other place? I want to go to the other place."

"There is no other place."

"There must be! I saw *Twilight Zone*[31] and I know the way it is. I want to go to the other place!"

Saint Peter says, "There is no other place. That's just the way it is. You have to work. There's no purgatory. It's just work. You never worked when you were on earth so now you have to work."

---

31 The original TV series, with episodes involving fantasy, suspense, and science fiction, was on the air from 1959-1964.

You say, "I *did* work when I was there!"

Saint Peter says, "No, you were just a seeker."

"How am I going to learn anything working in a factory?" you wail.

It's very simple. If you don't want to work in a factory for eternity, you're going to have to realize sooner or later that nothing ever changes. It's all perfect because this is just the way it is. You're just going to have to do what you do from now on. See, we think that we're going to be transported into realms of infinite variety in taste and delight and experience. No, we're not. Maybe one of you will make it and hit one of those realms if you careen off the wave we're traveling on.

First you have to listen to the spoken, written, and recorded message of the Godman—really study it, pay attention to it, and absorb it. Not exclusive of other recommended study materials. You have to realize, sooner or later, that what you're doing is basically the same thing you did before you came to spiritual life. It's tough to admit that basically all you're doing is seeking some other form. You need to see that and enjoy that for what it is. Because if that's what you're doing, that's what you're doing. There's no conceivable hope for change—for manipulated, sought for, willful change. When the worlds move, change is appropriate and present and available. That's the only way the word "change" is relevant. Change is not relevant in the sense of anything remedial: remedial breath technique, meditation, or sadhana. No remedial form of effort is real or valid.

See What You Are Up To

So, what do you do? Listen to the teaching. Understand what you are always up to. It's not a matter of questioning what you are up to; it's a matter of *seeing* what you are up to. Don't do anything about it, don't get upset about it or feel bad about it. Just see it. Know what is necessary: absolute and total sacrifice to the life of Truth, God, Self, whatever you want to call it.

There is only God. There is nothing outside of God. There is nothing inside of God. There is no relationship that takes place in terms of God. There is only God. If you can only know it intellectually, that's the way it is. I know that it is felt at random times. Then do your sadhana, which means that when it is not felt, simply see what is. Don't question it. See what is present. Who you think you are will try and frustrate that sadhana every instant. Who you think you are will not for one second allow you to do that sadhana easily. Sadhana is a matter of very hard work, of willful and very intense discipline. When mind tells you you're serving, you're devoted, you're doing guru *seva* [selfless service to the guru through tasks that support his or her work], you're being appropriate, it's not very easy to see that is not the case. But that is necessary sometimes.

Working that way is the initial process of sadhana. When the question is present, "I've seen it's all suffering—what can I do?" you haven't seen it enough. You need to see it at levels that come closer to the absolute, which is not a level but is inclusive. Inclusive of what? Well, "inclusive" is not a good word because inclusive implies there's something to include. In fact, there's nothing to include. There is only what we see and what we don't see, and what we imagine and what we don't imagine. We can get very esoteric and say it's nameless, mention-less, description-less.

GURDJIEFF: ALL MY SINS ARE ON THE SURFACE

(September 16, 1977)

Recognizing Level of Being

G.I. Gurdjieff, the Russian mystic and originator of the path known as "The Great Work," was quite a gourmet. He enjoyed both eating and cooking. He certainly seems to have indulged himself and the question arises as to what that meant spiritually. It is said that whenever anyone made mention of his indulgence, Gurdjieff would say, "All my sins are on the surface." In other words, what went on for Gurdjieff in terms of outward appearances didn't have anything to do with the clarity or the level of his inner work, whereas what goes on for the average person—for "man" with a small "m" as Gurdjieff would say—goes down into the deep levels and isn't a surface activity. Furthermore, he had a somewhat scornful humor about people who interpreted his level of being from the way he lived.

Gurdjieff had some of the greatest spiritual minds of the century with him, and he also had some of the greatest detractors. The brilliant people of the age were just about split when it came to Gurdjieff. The predominant criticism of Gurdjieff came from people who did not understand the nature of sin. They looked at a man who simply enjoyed his senses and they called him a sinner. People who were critical weren't able to interpret the inner space of a human being or of any teacher. Gurdjieff was just one of the more flamboyant characters around.

You might wonder how someone's level of being is recognizable—how you can tell whether their level of being is high, low, or mediocre, and how you know whether someone has worked on themselves. Certainly, from a student's perspective, it would help to know that a teacher is a genuine teacher. There are a lot of people around calling themselves teachers who aren't teachers in the Gurdjieffian sense—which is not like a French instructor or a philosophy professor.

I recently met one of Gurdjieff's students who said that something she got from him—just from being with the man—was the ability to smell level of being. It's not something you can learn in the usual way. But if you know how to do this, you can walk into someone's presence, sniff them out, and know whether they are doing work or not. Modern man is almost completely incapable of recognizing level of being, and what is sin and what is not sin.

If we are going to be a part of any kind of spiritual work, we have to at least have a general idea of what our role in the Work is. The first thing this student of Gurdjieff asked me was, "What is your aim?" What transpired after that was a result of the answer I gave. If I hadn't known what my aim[32] was, then the interview would have gone completely differently. It's very important as spiritual students that we recognize our aim. When you go to a spiritual teacher, what do you want? A little energy? Some insight? Well, you don't have to go to a spiritual teacher for that. You can walk around Times Square and get a hit of energy and a realization of what life is all about. But that is what most people go to a spiritual teacher for. The average man or woman walks around sinning, never realizing what their sins are, and pulling their hair out over things that aren't sins. So, Gurdjieff's statement can be very helpful to us if we pay attention to it. He said, "All my sins are on the surface."

A Real Teacher Provides a Closeness to What Is Going on for You

We have a basic disregard for other human beings. The way to tell that is by seeing how you function in intimate situations. How are you with a lover? That is the way to tell. Not by how you are when you go out in the street and there is a bum and you give him a quarter, or when there is somebody collecting for a halfway house and you give him a buck.

32 Gurdjieff said that it is necessary to have an aim in the Work. An aim can be a possibility that we are committed to which requires discipline and dedication.

That has nothing to do with how much you care about human beings, how considerate you are, or the regard you have for other people. Most of us have a very real disregard for other human beings which surfaces most clearly in our close relationships.

One of the benefits of working with a teacher is that he or she provides you with closeness—not only closeness to one another but closeness to what is going on for you. If you are committed to a teacher, you don't have to be near him. You can be on the other side of the world and you will be provided with closeness, which is the environment in which you see what is going on. You don't see what is going on when there is distance. When there is distance, we are solid, together, and we can take care of things. We can always come out of any situation smelling like a rose.

It is very important that we recognize what sins are. Gurdjieff was a robust man. He didn't sex to take advantage of people. He enjoyed a good glass of Armagnac because he liked alcohol. What Gurdjieff did, he did without any impure motivation. That is what "sinning on the surface" is. We don't do that. We've got a very definite motivation inside that needs certain feedback, validation, and agreement. The average man or woman has a point to prove. They have a need-system, which is why they go around sexing, eating, drinking, doping, and whatever else they do. Gurdjieff didn't. Gurdjieff had a level of work that was honest, clear, and compassionate. When he talked about self-remembering, he talked about that because he remembered himself; it wasn't a theory or concept. Whatever Gurdjieff did on the surface was done without any impurity, without the desire to hurt or use. It was done without need-systems. Now he might have given "food" to someone and used them in return, but that is not using someone the way the average man or woman uses people.

When someone comes around that can discuss spiritual life, I like to talk about it and even debate a little bit. But typically, it has been impossible for anyone to debate with me without having a point to make.

One of the nicest things about our meeting with Gurdjieff's student was that she didn't have a point to make. It was just so refreshing. We sat and we talked, and the discussion went back and forth; it wasn't a one-sided conversation. But she didn't have a point to make, she wasn't arguing with me, she wasn't trying to convince me of anything. She knew that you can't convince anybody of anything.

It was never anything that Gurdjieff said that got people. It was people's inner reaction, their inner response to what Gurdjieff said—which is another way to measure a teacher. She said that no matter how hard Gurdjieff stepped on people, no matter what he did, anybody with a sensitivity to who Gurdjieff was didn't feel resentment towards him. And he really put some people through their paces. Those people simply dealt with whatever he did in a reasonable fashion—or an unreasonable fashion. Sometimes they just freaked out—but they never felt resentment as long as they had a sensing for who Gurdjieff was.

Gurdjieff used to talk about "storming heaven." The first thing you have to do—before you can get into the Work, take on obligation,[33] consciously suffer, or any of that jazz—is know who your teacher is. Then you can work. Because if you don't know who your teacher is, you're going to feel resentment as soon as a little bit of work goes on. Then if the teacher picks up on that and pushes on it a little bit, you're going to feel angry and resentful. That can be dangerous because, if we haven't dealt with that, we can get really angry.

Sins and What We Think Are Sins

The first time we went to Mexico, I was struck with how physically affectionate the Mexicans are. It made we wish I had grown up in that kind of environment. You see two guys walking with their arms around

---

33 Obligation is distinguished from responsibility in that, rather than having a duty to fulfill a certain task, one has taken on an essential role in the Work to relieve the suffering of the creation.

one another, and everyone is always hugging and kissing. It's nice. Most of us have grown up in a very puritanical environment. Maybe we have learned to express our feelings that way, but we tend to be very anxious about it. The first time I was in Mexico I was uncomfortable. Not because I was afraid of anyone coming up and hugging me—I was a little jealous actually—but my whole tendency and upbringing was to be more formal and a little distant. All of this natural, spontaneous affection that people showed to one another—especially men—was confrontive. In India, the men walk down the streets holding hands. They gaze into one another's eyes in a way that is really nice, but scary. In America, men go out with their buddies and hit each other on the back to show their affection. Women, of course, express affection to one another by talking about whichever one of their friends isn't present…

The real sins of non-relationship are inflexibility and invulnerability. We are always protecting our physical space and our psychic need-systems. Those psychic need-systems are very real to people whose needs are not being met and who feel pain as a result. Spiritual life is basically engaged on a biological level. It's about connecting the centers. You start to become aware that you've got different centers that do different things. You've got your head center doing one thing and your heart center doing another and your vital [moving] center doing another. A lot of people would love to be in their head all the time, because your head doesn't hurt and feel sadness, remorse, or guilt. Your heart and your emotions do.

Men really like to think that they are sensitive human beings. If some of you were like me, it was a very curious affair when you started to have experience with sex. No matter how well you understood the technology of things, it was different when you had to put it somewhere and you weren't sure where. There is only one little place down there where it goes. Sometimes you figure it out just by accident, but sometimes you have a problem. You hope that your girlfriend isn't more experienced than you, so she starts laughing and has to tell you, "Down a little further, man!"

Anyway, that is beside the point. That has nothing to do with sinning—except that what we think are sins aren't sins. But Gurdjieff had real problems with some of the people who came to him because many of them thought that his behavior was sinful. They allowed Gurdjieff to act the way he did because they loved the guy and were committed to his vision, but they still thought he was sinning. And when people think other people are sinning, what arises—for starters—is jealousy, envy, and vindictiveness. It's necessary for us to look at what we think is sinning and what sinning really is.

Talking about Gurdjieff, we first have to begin to develop a little bit of will. If we don't have will, we can't even stay away from a piece of chocolate candy—let alone a German chocolate layer cake. Oh, my mistake, that's the wrong food for this crowd. We can't even stay away from carob candy bars. We don't have any will. That's concerning food. When it comes to sex, forget it. Gurdjieff used to say that sex is sex and love is love. None of us knows that. Even people that go to Plato's Retreat [one of New York City's most infamous sex clubs when it was open from 1977-1985] all the time, and screw a different partner every time, don't know that sex is sex and love is love. First you have to know what love and sex are. Then you can know that sex is sex and love is love. Sometimes they go hand in hand, sometimes they don't.

If you want to be a tantric master, like some of you probably do, you can read one book on tantric sex and it looks like a good idea. You find a few consorts and off you go. It would seem that you can just use sex to work with your level of being and get a little energy going. You don't have to fall in love and worry about all the stuff that comes with it, like getting hurt. You get hurt when you fall in love because you can't help but have your territories overlap when you are living with one another. If you could fall in love and *not* live with one another, you wouldn't have your territories overlap. Then you could come and go when the mood was right. But we don't want to do that. How can you own somebody if you don't live with them, right? You can't. So, you have got to live with them and know everything they are doing. When the phone rings and your lover answers it, what is the first thing you say when they hang up? "Who was it?" It's very important that we know who was on the phone. It could have been an old boyfriend or girlfriend, or hubby's secretary from work calling after hours. We have got to recognize what sin is before we do anything else.

Two Things Everybody Needs: Their Own Work and Help

Gurdjieff's student said a lot of relevant things, but one in particular struck me as important. She said that there are two things that everybody needs: their own work and help. Nobody knows what an aim is to begin with, but by the time someone has been in the Work for a while they are able to develop a reasonable aim. But nobody is going to achieve that aim without help. We don't always know where the help comes from. I never had a guru, but I got lots of help. Who knows where I got help from? When I went to India, I got lots of help. Maybe it was coming from some Indian guru, but I wasn't aware of it.[34] Now I am a little more sensitive so I can see where the help is coming from. So, everybody needs their own work—meaning their own spiritual work—and help.

The first time Gurdjieff came to America, he met with a large group of people who were supposedly followers of his Work. He started talking to this group and by the time he was done, ninety percent of the people in the room weren't his followers anymore. Gurdjieff was offering help, but nobody wanted to accept it. He said, "Here is help," and people ran away. We have to be aware of that response to help. The principal thing in our own work is to create a level of work *inside* that

[34] In the early 1980s, after visiting Yogi Ramsuratkumar on two trips to India, Lee recognized that Yogi Ramsuratkumar was his guru and had been helping him long before they met.

has absolute integrity. "Sinning on the surface" means that there are no egotistical need-systems motivating an activity. A lot of people today think they are doing that, but they are not. People think they can sin on the surface, but it is obvious to everybody else they can't. They are not aware of how to make their centers work in appropriate relationship with one another. Instead, our centers are always fighting each other for authority and power. To have our own work we must have internal integrity.

Internal Integrity

Gurdjieff had perfect internal integrity. Whatever happened on the surface was simply activity that happened on the surface. When we do something on the surface, like overindulge in anything—food, sex, power, money—it's coming from a very deep need. It is not a pure activity. When we sex, we don't just sex; there are all kinds of other things involved. There is the person we are with, and what we need from them, and what they need from us, and how we've got to be seen, and how it's got to turn out, and how many orgasms we have or they have, and how long we make love for. There are *so* many considerations.

When Gurdjieff sexed, he simply sexed. He wasn't trying to use someone. He wasn't trying to prove that he was a man. He didn't have any insecurities about it—he simply did what he did. When he stepped on people's corns, there was no vindictiveness. He didn't pick on people he didn't like and leave alone those that he liked. There was no distinction; he simply provided what people needed with no emotional attachment. If somebody did something to Gurdjieff, he didn't hold a grudge. He worked with people based purely on what they needed.

If you study with a teacher, you need to be able to recognize the condition of your teacher. You should find someone whose inner state has integrity; who does what they do on the surface with internal integrity. If you think the person you are studying with is going to take advantage of you in any way—financially, emotionally, physically—then you should stay on the fringes of that work until you can see the teacher in a different light, or not. There aren't a lot of teachers with that kind of internal integrity around today. You could probably count them all on two hands. So, when you see that kind of integrity in someone, then you should just dive in.

We need to recognize what sin really is, which is the lack of internal integrity. It is functioning on the surface and attributing that surface activity to humanitarian motives. If you assume you are being honest, but you are really a fraud inside, you've got to become aware of your internal state. The primary level of work is to be aware of what a sin is, know your aim, be aware of your internal state, and be able to sense the internal state of someone else. Resentment is a sure sign of the need to reevaluate. There are all kinds of signs along the way. You don't have to worry about how you are going to know whether you are in the right or the wrong place. If you feel resentment towards your teacher, check out your relationship to that person. A genuine teacher will not hurt anyone in a vindictive or vicious way, but only where shock is needed. We might be upset and reeling emotionally or mentally if a genuine teacher steps on a corn, but if we feel resentment or anger toward that person, we should reevaluate our entire relationship to the teacher. That's very important.

The two things we need are our own inner work and help. We need a teacher. This notion that "everybody is my guru"—I mean, come on, give me a break. The trees are your guru? Yes, okay, you can learn from everything, but everything is not your guru. That is new-age tripe. That is a way of avoiding real work. You just stagger around starry-eyed with your head in the clouds. People like you because you smile at everybody and you are harmless. But if you want to do real work, you need a teacher, you need help.

Chief Feature

Everybody has one major impediment to spiritual work. For some people it's vanity, for some people it's pride, but it's always something so major that it permeates and is reflected in everything they do. Sitting down to eat is a reflection of pride, or the business they transact is a reflection of vanity. "Chief feature" [a term used in the Gurdjieff Work for one's major fault or weakness that is hidden from awareness] is that one main tendency that permeates everything, and then on top of that we have lots of little habits, eccentricities, and minor tendencies. By the way, chief feature never changes. We never get rid of it, but we can have humor about it, work with it, and enjoy it.

People are run by chief feature. Theoretically, what you get to do in the Work is you get to run your chief feature. You get to control it instead of it controlling you. If you look at someone who is really vain, you see that it's automatic and consuming for them. Everybody is a little vain, but some people are really vain. Some get to be famous because of that feature. People get to be millionaires because of their feature. Chief feature can be a very strong motivating force. So, you don't have to kill it; it can be very helpful. When you learn how to harness its energy, it can be fantastic.

If I had one wish for what Hohm could contribute to the world, it would be to impress even a few people with a little bit of real sensitivity and consideration in relationship to one another. That would be my greatest wish. Most of us think we are spiritual students, but you can't imagine the violence that people have inside. If people are pushed far enough, what we're capable of is really scary. If I could just get people to appreciate the gentleness of human beings and to reject the violence, to really see it and reject it, that would be very nice.

COMMENTARY ON THE GOSPEL OF THOMAS

(Christmas, December 25, 1977)

There are some things I want to consider with you from The Gospel According to Thomas[35] in which Jesus comes across as Divine and also very human. He was certainly unique for his culture and time, not someone the world had ever seen the likes of before.

Undoubtedly, the direct translation of *The Gospel of Thomas* is accurate, but what is lost is the cultural context of the time. To more fully appreciate Jesus's words to the disciples, you need to be a little familiar with the culture that they lived in. For instance, the Essenes were one of the three main sects of Judaism at the time—along with the Pharisees and the Sadducees. Jesus is thought be have been an Essene, to have come from the Essene community, or to have taught the Essenes. Probably everybody knew about the Essenes. They were different from everybody else; they were generous, peaceful, just, vibrant, alive, juicy, happy people. They were well-established and were around for four hundred years. The disciples were probably familiar with the dharma of the Essenes. If Jesus spoke in a way consistent with Essene philosophy, the disciples could relate to it.

The quotes I'll be reading are all taken from *The Gospel According to Thomas* [translated by A. Guillaumont, H.-CH Puech, G. Quispel, W. Till, and Yassah 'Abd Al Masih; Harper & Row; 1959].

When he finds, he will be troubled…

These are the secret words which the Living Jesus spoke, and Didymos Judas Thomas wrote. … Jesus said: "Let him who seeks, not cease seeking until he

35 *The Gospel of Thomas* is a non-canonical gospel of one-hundred fourteen sayings of Jesus. It was discovered in Egypt in 1945 and is believed to date back to the second century. However, its origins may date back to the historical Jesus as an independent source of Jesus's sayings from the four accepted Gospels.

finds. And when he finds, he will be troubled, and when he has been troubled, he will marvel, and he will reign over the All."

The statement, "Let him who seeks not cease seeking until he finds," is saying you must have a desire for God that is the most intense thing in your life. It is only with that kind of desire that you can get to be desireless at some point. If you are honest about seeking, you have to become sensitive. When that sensitivity becomes acute, you develop compassion. When you find what it is you have been seeking, you are troubled. You see that none of your conceptions are valid, and all of the shoring up of your identity that you have tried is invalid. Once you have been troubled, you will marvel and will reign over the All. It's not like you are controlling the All; you *reign*. What is there to control? It is not a matter of power, not like an earthly king who reigns over subjects and has to continually do something to keep power. You reign because you are the Kingdom itself. You find the whole. What is there that is not you?

Esoteric documents show that Jesus sought like everybody else. He took off when he was very young and went trekking around the world to places like India and Tibet, studying with different teachers and gurus until he found what he was looking for. When he returned to his homeland from traveling, as a young man of twenty, he was still known as the Jesus of his youth—not as Jesus the Christ. When he told his kinsmen, "I have inherited the Kingdom from my Father," the response was, "Come on, man. What are you giving us this line for? You are not the prophet. We have rabbis who are prophets. You are just Jesus." So, he was troubled when he came home and saw that people were not listening to him, that his realization was not appreciated. He set off trekking again and began to amass a large following. And when Jesus collected his closest disciples, he marveled.

Jesus said: "… For many who are first shall become last and they shall become a single one…"

When you are first in terms of spiritual life, what do you become? You become a sacrifice; you become last. Your interests and desires are secondary to who or how you can serve. Mr. Gold told his students when we visited him, "Lee is here and if you ask him a real question, he has to answer you. He doesn't have a choice." A real question must be answered. Someone who has taken on a teaching obligation rarely gets what they want, because those to whom they must sacrifice are nearly always in need. Such a one becomes last… "They shall become a single one" is the metaphysical equivalent of non-duality.

And he said, "The Man is like a wise fisherman who cast his net into the sea, he drew it up from the sea full of small fish; among them he found a large (and) good fish, that wise fisherman, he threw all the small fish down into the sea, he chose the large fish without regret. Whoever has ears to hear, let him hear."

The wise man doesn't keep all the other fish in case he can use them someday to set up an aquarium or to sell in the market. He throws them all back—except for one. When you see what is most important—we can call it "God" or "awakening"—all the other "fish" have to be thrown back.

On the day when you were one, you became two.

Jesus said: "This heaven shall pass away and the one above it shall pass away, and the dead are not alive, and the living shall not die. In the days when you devoured the dead, you made it alive; when you come into light, what will you do? On the day when you were one, you became two. But when you have become two, what will you do?"

No matter what you seek for, it is transient. Enlightenment is the knowledge that all experience is transitory including enlightenment. This heaven will pass away. The heaven above it—that you think is heaven—will pass away. All will pass away, all is transitory. The dead are the masses that are not alive, and the living who are turned to God shall not die. When real teaching is accepted, you devour the dead and make it alive. We all have an ego and the world is not ready for the real relationship that is possible when we come into the light. So, what are you going to do when you come into the light? Who are you going to talk to? Where are you going to go?

Jesus was speaking metaphysically when he said, "On the day when you were one, you became two." He was talking about creation. Duality arose when you were first conscious of yourself as God, because how could there be relationship without two? How could there be love returning upon itself without two? So, in that moment when you became conscious that you were one, you became two. That is the story of creation in very concise terms. But now that you have become two, you are separate from God. What will you do? Here we see the limitations of the mind. Because you are separate, how will you see the paradox for what it is?

The disciples said to Jesus: "We know that thou wilt go away from us. Who is it who shall be great over us?" Jesus said to them, "Wherever you have come, you will go to James the righteous for whose sake heaven and earth came into being."

Jesus is saying if he designates somebody as a teacher, then heaven and earth will move for that person. Whoever he designates will be able to do what needs to be done.

His disciples asked Him, they said to Him: "Wouldst thou that we fast and how should we pray and should we give alms and what diet should we observe?"

. . . Jesus said to them: "If you fast, you will beget sins for yourselves, and if you pray, you will be condemned, and if you give alms, you will do evil to

your spirits. And if you go into any land and wander in the regions, if they receive you, eat what they set before you, heal the sick among them. For what goes into your mouth will not defile you, but what comes out of your mouth, that is what will defile you."

Here Jesus says, "If I have to tell you what to do, you will be doing it for the wrong reason, and you will be doing yourself a disservice. If you have to ask me, 'Should I fast?' you will beget sins for yourselves. I am present here as Grace. I am not here to tell you specifically what to do. So don't do what you think I want you to do; do what is appropriate. Don't ask me, 'Should I do this, should I do that?' You know what to do. If you have ears, hear me and wake up." He is saying that what is appropriate will naturally arise.

Jesus said, "And if you go into any land and wander in the regions, if they receive you, eat what they set before you..." When the renowned Tibetan master Naropa was searching for his guru Tilopa, Tilopa would take many forms to test Naropa. Once, Naropa was trekking along the highway and he saw a filthy, ill-shaven man sitting by the side of the road gorging on the raw meat of a deer he had just killed. "Come join me in my feast!" the man said to Naropa. Being a Buddhist, *ahimsa* [non-violence] was Naropa's creed. He could do no violence to any living being and wouldn't eat a dead animal; it would be against his dharma. Naropa was disgusted and said to the man, "Never!" As he walked off, the man turned into Tilopa. This goes on as Naropa keeps coming upon situations where he is invited to be a guest and keeps saying, "No." Each time Tilopa appears and says, "You missed it again!"

If you travel as a devotee, *be* a devotee. If people want to serve you, don't refuse the hospitality. If it would ruin somebody's party for you not to eat the fried ribs they have prepared, you should eat the fried ribs even if you are a vegetarian. Don't be a big mouth and preach the dharma. Just do service. Heal the sick and eat the food which is offered because it makes the one who is offering it happy.

Jesus said: "When you see Him who was not born of woman, prostrate yourselves upon your face and adore Him: He is your Father."

Jesus is being very realistic here. He is telling the disciples, "I am not the only one. There are others. If you travel and meet someone who is awake, bow down and be reverent before that man, for he too is the Father."

I have come to throw divisions upon the earth...

Jesus said, "Men possibly think that I have come to throw peace upon the world, and they do not know that I have come to throw divisions upon the earth: fire, sword, war."

This is one of my favorite quotes. People tend to think that the spiritual teacher is here to get everybody together. Well, you can't be gotten together until you see that you are *not* together. The real spiritual master is here to show you reality, to bring division to the world. Once division is owned, once you really own the fact that you are prejudiced, then you can go about the honest work of opening yourself to those who you are prejudiced against. But if you refuse to admit that you are prejudiced, how can you possibly get together? It's always valuable to be shown something about ourselves, to have our division revealed.

Jesus said: "I will give you what eye has not seen and what ear has not heard and what hand has not touched and (what) has not arisen in the heart of man."

Jesus is saying, "I will give you what transcends the senses. I will give you what you cannot see, hear, feel, or touch—the perfectly transcendent and intangible Truth."

The disciples said to Jesus: "Tell us how our end will be." Jesus said: "Have you then discovered the beginning, so that you inquire about the end? For where the beginning is, there shall be the end. Blessed is he who shall stand at the beginning, and he shall know the end and he shall not taste death."

Jesus told them, "Just stay with me, and you will get the truth." The disciples have an incredible opportunity to experience the truth in Jesus's company. But they want to know what their end will be. Jesus responds by saying, "I just got done telling you not to pray or fast if you have to ask me, and now you want to know what the end will be? Just do your sadhana. What difference does it make what the end is going to be? There won't be any end if you can't start at the beginning!"

Then Jesus says, "For where the beginning is, there shall be the end." It might seem ridiculous and outlandish to think that all you have to do is just study a little bit, meditate a little bit, do a little bit of exercise and that's it. It might seem like that won't get you anywhere, but that is the whole picture. The disciples are looking to attain something. They are looking for the Kingdom of Heaven and Jesus is saying, "Hey, we are not attaining anything. We are just walking along the road and maybe our feet are getting blisters. That is the end." The disciples want to know, "Will we be great and famous?" Jesus responds, "Find the beginning and that is the end."

Jesus keeps returning to this theme: you will not taste death if you live God. He is saying *there is no death.* You will not die because you *can't* die. He keeps putting this out to them. Why does he do this? Because the mind has always been the same. Ego has always been propagating the myth of survival. That is what ego is attempting to secure. All our strategies are about survival and Jesus keeps saying, "What is the big deal about survival? You can't die. There is no death. Simply see that and forget about survival."

These stones will minister to you…

Jesus said: "Blessed is he who was before he came into being. If you become disciples to Me and hear my words, these stones will minister to you…"

In other words, blessed is the man who recognizes prior condition, who sees that he was before he came into manifest being. Jesus is saying, "If you simply hear what I am saying, the world will sacrifice itself for you. The stones will minister to you; they will sacrifice." Do you think stones can sacrifice? Yes, stones can sacrifice. But you have to be in a place where the stones will sacrifice for you.

The disciples said to Jesus: "Tell us what the Kingdom of Heaven is like."

As if he hadn't been telling them all this time!

He said to them: "It is like a mustard seed, smaller than all seeds. But when it falls on the tilled earth, it produces a large branch and becomes shelter for (the) birds of heaven."

Grace grows in the one who is available. A "large branch" is produced and the one who is available serves, "becomes shelter" for those in his or her environment or circle—the "birds of heaven."

Whom are thy disciples like?

Mary said to Jesus: "Whom are thy disciples like?" He said: "They are like little children who have installed themselves in the field which is not theirs. When the owners of the field come, they will say: 'Release to us our field.' They take off their clothes before them to release it (the field) to them and to give back the field to them…"

When Mary asks, "What are disciples like?" Jesus says the disciples are like little children who install themselves in a field which is not theirs. What is the field that is not theirs? The body. And your house, car, money, books, furniture—all your stuff. When the owner of the field comes along and says, "Give me the field, give me what is mine (ego)," the real disciples take their clothes off to release the field and give it back to him. Don't burn the field down. Just give the field back. It's very simple.

... Therefore I say: "If the lord of the house knows the thief is coming, he will stay awake before he comes and will him not let him dig through into his house of his kingdom to carry away his goods..."

The lord of the house is you. The thief is distraction. If you know that distraction is coming, you will be aware of it when it comes. The distraction will still be there and the thief will still enter the house, but you will be there to scare him off. You will not let the thief steal the goods of the house. This is what self-remembering is all about. If you are aware of the mechanism of mind, simply see distraction when it arises and don't let it steal faith. See distraction for what it is; it will run away.

"... You then must watch for the world, gird up your loins with great strength, lest the brigands find (a) way to come to you, because they will find the advantage which you expect..."

The part of you that is trying to outwit ego through mind is not smarter than ego. That is what Jesus is saying. So, beware of the world, "gird up your loins with great strength" because ego is going to do everything to get you—everything. You can't even imagine what your ego is going to do to try to distract you. When ego comes to get you, it will find the advantage. So what? Don't buy into it. When the distraction arises, let it pass. Nothing is permanent, not even the distractions. They will come up and they will dissolve. Just retain your faith.

When you make the inner as the outer...

Jesus said to them: "When you make the two one, and when you make the inner as the outer and the outer as the inner and the above as the below and when you make the male and the female into a single one so that the male will not be male and the female (not) be female, when you make eyes in the place of an eye, and a hand in the place of a hand and a foot in the place of a foot, (and) an image in the place of an image, then shall you enter [the Kingdom.]"

Now that is really profound. That is not alluded to in the New Testament. It's incredible that Jesus said that. When you see through duality, when you stop seeing things individually over and against other things and "make the inner as the outer and the outer as the inner and the above as the below," then you will enter the Kingdom. Jesus was also a master of tantra. When he was wandering in India or Tibet, he probably studied tantra. Tantra is a lot more than just sexual union. Ramakrishna was a *tantrika*, but not the kind of tantrika that went around "teaching" it to all his women disciples. So Jesus is indicating that you lose your identity "when you make the male and the female into a single one so that the male will not be male and the female not be female." That is perfect sexual tantra.

In a typical sexual relationship, the man always remembers that he is the one doing the humping, no matter how hot it gets. Women generally lose themselves more than men. The man almost always keeps some reserve so that he knows that he is the one that is filling up the hole. In perfect tantra, the man sometimes thinks *he* is the one getting filled up. Sometimes you don't even know who is filling who; you forget if you are the man or the woman. It can be very threatening to forget yourself that way because our roles are so delineated for us from the minute that we get a little pink or blue beanie when we are babies.

Jesus is saying that you can go the non-dualistic route of Vedanta[36] or you can go the route of *neti-neti*[37]—negating all that is. You can also make the male and the female into a single one so that the male will not be male, and the female will not be female. Then you enter the Kingdom.

"If those three ways are not up your alley," he says, "how about another one?" "When you make eyes in the place of an eye and a hand in the place of a hand and a foot in the place of a foot, and an image in the place of an image..." he is saying, "How about just taking what you've got?" You don't know you've got an eye. It is all ego. When you make a real eye in place of what you think is your eye, that is pretty good. You might think you've got hands, but you don't *know* you've got hands. So when you make a hand in place of a hand, then you shall enter the Kingdom. Jesus is giving his disciples four choices in terms of paths—four ways to go. They all get you there, but you've really got to do your sadhana.

Jesus said: "I shall choose you, one out of a thousand and two out of ten thousand and they shall stand as a single one."

He is saying that his Work is so radical that very few people will be drawn to it, but that those who are drawn will be made into one—one mind, the enlightened community so to speak.

His disciples said: "Show us the place where Thou art, for it is necessary for us to seek it." He said to them, "Whoever has ears let him hear. Within a man

---

36 Hindu philosophy about the oneness of existence which reflects the ideas contained in the *Upanishads*.

37 Sanskrit expression meaning "not this, not this" to negate identification with all worldly experience until all that remains is the Self.

of light there is light and he lights the whole world. When he does not shine, there is darkness."

The disciples said, "Show us where you are at. We are seeking it, we've got to have it, we are really hungry, we are getting upset, man." Jesus is saying, "I am available. It is your job, if you want it, to be available too." It's not like Jesus can turn the light on. He is a man of light. He can't turn the light on because the disciples want to see it. There is light. If they want to see it they must make themselves available. Jesus is turning it back to the disciples. They keep asking him to prove it to them, to show it to them. And he is saying, "The light is on. Can you see it?"

When thou castest the beam out of thine eye…

Jesus said: "The mote that is in thy brother's eye thou seest, but the beam that is in thine eye, thou seest not. When thou castest the beam out of thine eye, then thy wilt see clearly to cast the mote out of thy brother's eye."

We can see the faults of others very well, but we don't see the truth that is within. We see the mote in our brother's eye because we need to compare ourselves so as to make ourselves higher, in order to survive. We don't see the beam in our own eye. When we are willing to sacrifice, because we have seen the truth in ourselves, then we will be able to help our brother.

Jesus said: "I took my stand in the midst of the world and in flesh I appeared to them; I found them all drunk, I found none among them athirst."

Jesus says, "I have appeared. I am not otherworldly. I am flesh and blood, just like you. I have dragged you out to the desert, made you lose interest in any number of things that used to really attract you so that you'd get thirsty. You had to see an alternative."

"And my soul is afflicted for the sons of man because they are blind in their hearts and do not see that empty they have come into the world and that empty they seek to go out of the world again."

People seek to go out of the world the same way they came in, except they want to take with them what they got in the meantime. Jesus says, "My soul is afflicted," like Ramakrishna when he got on top of the Kali temple and screamed out, "My devotees, where are you?" Everybody thought he was mad. He was afflicted by the fact that he was so aflame with love of God, but there weren't people coming to him to partake of that flame. He just couldn't believe it. He went mad screaming for his disciples, "Where are you?" The same thing happened to Jesus.

"But now they are drunk. When they have shaken off their wine then they will repent."

The wine is the distraction of the world. Jesus is saying, "Now they are drunk. Why would they want God?" They have to be sober first. Once you have seen through the world, you don't have to leave the world. You simply have to know what it is and not get trapped by it.

A marvel of marvels.

Jesus said: "If the flesh has come into existence because of [the] spirit, it is a marvel; but if [the] spirit (has come into existence) because of it, it is a marvel of marvels."

The perfect disciple is an infinitely greater marvel than the Godman. The Godman is a marvel: spirit made flesh. But flesh made spirit—that is the marvel of marvels. Jesus is saying to his disciples, "Look at the possibility you have here! Look at what has been offered you! I have been a marvel, but you can be a marvel of marvels."

Jesus said: "A city being built on a high mountain (and) fortified cannot fall nor can it (ever) be hidden." Jesus said: "What thou shalt hear in thine ear (and) in the other ear, that preach from your housetops; for no one lights a lamp and puts it under a bushel, nor does he put it in a hidden place, but he sets it on a lamp stand so that all who come in and go out may see its light."

Previously Jesus said, "Don't go around broadcasting the dharma." Now he is saying, if you've got a base that is unshakeable, it cannot fall. If your house is built on top of a mountain go out and proclaim it. Shout it from the rooftops, don't hide it.

Jesus said: "If a blind man leads a blind man, both of them fall into a pit."

Jesus doesn't explain how you can tell the rascal-guru. He just says that you both fall into the pit if you are led by a rascal-guru—which is true.

Jesus said: "It is not possible for one to enter the house of the strong (man) and take him (or it) by force unless he bind his hands; then will he ransack his house."

When Jesus says that it is not possible to enter the house of the strong man and take him by force unless his hands are bound, he is talking about the spiritual teacher. You can't come in and bowl the spiritual master over with your intellect or strength. But if you get his hands tied, then you can ransack the house. You are going to ruin it. Jesus is saying not to tie the strong man's hands or try to overpower him. Ego is always trying to tie the hands of the master. Jesus was a great psychologist. He really knew the way the mind works.

His disciples said: "When wilt Thou be revealed to us and when will we see Thee?" Jesus said: "When you take off your clothing without being ashamed, and take your clothes and put them under your feet as the little children and tread on them, then [shall you behold] the Son of the Living (One) and you shall not fear."

He says, "I would be glad to show you my real Self. Are you willing to see that your whole idea of yourself is false? Are you willing to take all your clothes off and put them under your feet like a small child?" Did you ever catch a three- or four-year-old child running a number and they knew you caught them? They get this cute little smile on their face and just shrug their shoulders. They're not like, "Oh my God, I have been caught!" It's not traumatic for them. They don't care. They were just trying to run a number and you caught them, so they didn't get away with it. It is perfectly all right with them. But if you catch an adult doing their number? Oh my God! They defend, justify, and excuse. They do all kinds of fancy steps to avoid taking responsibility for their activity.

Jesus is simply saying to the disciples, "If you want to see me, are you willing to admit that all the questions you are asking me are just an attempt to tie my hands? Don't be guilty that you have run your number for twenty-five years. So what? Some people have been running their number for seventy years! You are lucky you get to work on it while you are young. Take off your clothes without being ashamed." He is talking about owning what you are up to. "Taking off your clothes" refers to an internal process.

Jesus said: "Become passers-by."

Don't get stuck anywhere. Don't think that you've got it made. Check things out, serve where you can, move on. That applies to everything. Don't be attached to form. When I was in India I found that I loved to *pranam* to the deity statues; it was tremendously inspiring. But at the same time, one can't be attached to that, no matter how much it moves one. Don't be attached to the form; be passers-by.

Jesus said: "Whoever blasphemes against the Father, it shall be forgiven him, and whoever blasphemes against the Son, it shall be forgiven him; but whoever blasphemes against the Holy Ghost, it shall not be forgiven him, either on earth or in heaven."

God the Father, Mankind the Son, Faith the Holy Ghost. Don't ever compromise your faith—the Holy Ghost—because it shall not be forgiven on earth or in heaven. Why? All you've got is your faith. Faith is the only thing that is real.

Jesus said: "From Adam until John the Baptist there is among those who are born of women none higher than John the Baptist, so that his eyes will not be broken. But I have said that whoever among you becomes as a child shall know the Kingdom and he shall become higher than John."

John the Baptist was a prophet. He had faith; he knew Jesus was who he said he was. There was no doubt in his mind about Jesus. But John the Baptist didn´t necessarily live the sadhana that Jesus prescribed. Jesus said to his disciples, "Live the words that I say and you will be far higher than John the Baptist," even though John the Baptist was the highest man born of woman since Adam. Jesus is saying that once you have entered the Kingdom you are no longer "man born of woman," because you are not separate anymore even though you still have your body, your individuality, and your personality. Jesus is saying to his disciples, "John the Baptist was the best prophet, the most faithful separate one, but any of you can do far greater things than him by just becoming non-separate."

Jesus said: "It is impossible for man to mount two horses and to stretch two bows, and it is impossible for a servant to serve two masters, otherwise he will honor the one and offend the other."

Jesus is saying that you cannot serve two masters because you will offend one in serving the other. You can't have the world and God at the same time—not until after you wake up. If God is your context, everything will be appropriate in terms of the world.

It is a movement and a rest.

Jesus said: "If they ask you: 'What is the sign of your Father in you?', say to them: 'It is a movement and a rest.'"

If somebody says to you, "How do you know that Lee is who he says he is?" you *know* because of the movement that goes on in your life. You don't know because you have been transformed. You know because you are doing sadhana, because you've got a fire going. It is a movement and a rest.

His disciples said to Him: "Twenty-four prophets spoke in Israel and they all spoke about Thee." He said to them: "You have dismissed the Living (One) who is before you and you have spoken about the dead."

He is telling them, "What does it matter if the prophets said I was coming? They are all dead. You have dismissed me and all you are concerned about is agreement. I am living here before you—to hell with the prophets! Never mind 'agreement.' Just do your sadhana. Be alive."

Jesus said: "Whoever has known the world has found a corpse, and whoever has found a corpse, of him the world is not worthy."

Whoever has seen the world for what it is has found a corpse. It was dead two thousand years ago and it is just as dead now—no difference. When you have really seen the world for what it is, you have seen the illusion, maya. There is no life in it. Then the world is not worthy of you.

Jesus is saying, "You guys are worthy of me because you have made an effort. You've had enough strength to follow me."

Jesus said: "Look upon the Living (One) as long as you live, lest you die and seek to see Him and be unable to see."

In other words, you aren't going to do it [the Work] over there; you've got to do it here. If you don't do it here, when you get over there you're going to be seeking, but you will find you've got to take another body to do it. This is where it gets done, not over there. This Gospel doesn't cover the resurrection, but the resurrection is symbolic in the sense that Jesus had to come back because the disciples didn't see it while he was here. You aren't going to see it when you die, you've got to see it right here.

What thy right hand will do, let not thy left hand know what it does.

Jesus said: "I tell My mysteries to those [who are worthy of my] mysteries. What thy right (hand) will do, let not thy left (hand) know what it does."

He tells his mysteries to his disciples who are worthy of them, but he doesn´t explain his mysteries. He doesn't tell his right hand what his left hand is doing because that is just confusing. It becomes much more obvious by the doing than from the explaining.

Jesus said: "There was a rich man who had much money. He said: 'I will use my money that I may sow and reap and plant and fill my storehouses with fruit, so that I lack nothing.' This is what he thought in his heart. And that night he died. Whoever has ears let him hear."

Never mind what you are going to do. What you are going to do doesn't mean anything because you could die tomorrow. Just do what you do. Don't plan to go out and buy seed—buy seed.

Jesus said: "A man had guest-friends, and when he had prepared the dinner, he sent his servant to invite the guest-friends. The servant came and said to the master: 'Those who thou hast invited to the dinner have excused themselves.' The master said to the servant: 'Go out to the roads, bring those whom thou shalt find, that they may dine. Tradesmen and merchants shall not enter the places of my Father.'"

Did this Community start with people who were sophisticated seekers like the "guest-friends?" No, we started with people that were just ordinary. We came like beggars because we wanted to be fed.

Jesus said: "A good man had a vineyard. He gave it to husbandmen so that they would work it and he would receive its fruit from them. He sent his servant so that the husbandmen would give him the fruit of the vineyard. They seized the servant, they beat him; a little longer, they would have killed him. The servant came, he told it to his master. His master said: 'Perhaps he did not know them.' He sent another servant. The husbandmen beat him as well. Then the owner sent his son. He said: 'Perhaps they will respect my son.' Since those husbandmen knew that he was the heir to the vineyard, they seized him and killed him. Whoever has ears, let him hear."

The vineyard is life-as-it-is. The husbandmen are mankind, humanity. The son, of course, is the one that not only tries to explain Truth but lives it. He is done in because the husbandmen who now run the vineyard—which is the manifest world—got used to running things and didn't want to give it to the owner. They don't want to sacrifice to God. They figure, "We are running the place. Who can take it from us? We've got our own strength." When the son comes, they kill him to make sure there is no heir to run the vineyard when the father is gone. Humanity is so used to running the earth. We don't want to sacrifice to God. We just want to just keep it.

Jesus said: "Blessed are you when you are hated and persecuted; and no place will be found there where you have been persecuted."

He just told the story about the husbandmen. Now he is saying, "This is the way it is, guys. You are the servants, the disciples. The husbandmen will beat you up. Blessed are those that are hated and persecuted for they are the servants of the owner of the vineyard. They are the servants of God."

Jesus said: "Blessed are those who have been persecuted in their heart; these are they who have known the Father in truth."

If you have not really grappled with faith, how strong is it? Once you've had that conflict and have gotten through it, then you have known the Father in truth. You have seen how seductive the world can be. You have been tempted and you have seen through it. God has become your priority.

Jesus said: "I shall de[stroy this] house and no one will be able to build it [again]."

Jesus means, "I am going to undermine your separate existence, and no one will be able to reconstruct that separate existence again." Once you are undone in God, that's it. No one will be able to build up the illusion again.

Why did you come out into the desert?

Jesus said: "Why did you come out into the desert? To see a reed shaken by the wind? And to see a man clothed in soft garments? [See, your] kings and your great ones are those who are clothed in soft [garments] and they shall not be able to know the truth."

He is saying to the disciples, "Don't come out into the desert if you just want pleasure. If you walk into the desert of your own volition, you better expect to be parched. This is not a nature walk. The desert is hard, cruel, hot, dry and boring." The disciples are always expecting Jesus to be a loving man, a compassionate father, a gentle teacher, a bodhisattva hero, a saint. He is telling them, "You joined company with me to work, and we are going to work. Stop trying to fit me into your preconceived ideas. Don't make me a hero." The disciples had a lot of preconceived ideas of what it was supposed to be like to follow him. They thought they would go out in the desert and see beautiful wildflowers and green bushes and he is saying, "We are in the desert. So guess what you get? Sand, windstorms, more sand—and the occasional oasis."

Jesus said: "Adam came into existence from a great power and a great wealth, and (yet) he did not become worthy of you. For if he would had been worthy, [he would] not [have tasted] death."

Jesus is saying, "Even though the Father created Adam, Adam didn't hold to the dharma and he wasn't worthy of you." He cuts the disciples down, then builds them up, cuts them down, builds them up. That process goes on through this whole manuscript. Jesus is a sly man.[38] What he is doing is constantly showing them the paradox of the teaching through his actual work with them. He is teaching them not to get stuck on criticism or praise. He does that by constantly alternating between the two so that their heads are spinning. Jesus taught very much by example as well as by parable.

---

38 A reference in the Gurdjieff Work to someone who knows the secret of the path and how to work with the mind, emotions, and body.

Easy is my yoke…

Jesus said: "Why do you wash the outside of the cup? Do you not understand that he who made the inside is also he who has made the outside?" Jesus said: "Come to Me, for easy is My yoke and My lordship is gentle, and you shall find repose for yourselves."

[Jesus is saying,] "You are the ones that are creating all the problems for yourselves. Why are you so concerned with external stuff? You are so concerned with your ego, with praise and criticism. Don't you know that the one that has made the outside has made the inside? My teaching is peaceful. I am not a tough guy to deal with. All you have to do is see it and you can find repose with me."

Test this moment.

They said to him: "Tell us who Thou art so that we may believe in Thee." He said to them: "You test the face of the sky and of the earth, and him who is before your face you have not known, and you do not know to test this moment."

He is saying, "You see all these phenomena, all these externals. You are always testing it; you always want proof. If we are supposed to go on a picnic and it is sunny that day, you see that as a sign. You say, 'Ah yes, Grace is on our side; it's a nice day for a picnic!' You wink at me and say, 'Thanks, J.C.' But you don't know to test this moment." He is telling them that they don't know how to ask a real question. All they want is proof, proof, proof. He is saying to them, "Test this moment. Look into your heart. What do you feel, and why do you need proof?"

Jesus said: "Seek and you will find, but those things which you asked me in those days, I did not tell you then; now I desire to tell them, but you do not inquire after them."

Back when the disciples were neophytes, Jesus did not tell them things because they weren't ready. Now he wants to tell them, but they do not ask. Now they've got the dharma down so they ask questions like, "Is circumcision proper?" or, "Should we fast and pray and give alms?" When at last they are in a place where they can ask real questions and actually do something with the answer, they don't ask.

Jesus said: "Whosoever does not hate his father and his mother in My way will not be able to be a [disciple] to me. And whoever does [not] love [his father] and his mother in My way will not be able to be a [disciple] to me, for my mother, [My] true [Mother] gave me the Life."

He is saying, "You cannot be my disciple if you don't hate your mother and father, seeing that they are separate and that they are trying to win and distract you. And you cannot be my disciple if you do not love your mother and father, seeing that they gave you life and are sincere and doing the best they can."

Jesus said, "Whoever drinks from My mouth shall become as I am and I myself will become he, and the hidden things shall be revealed to him."

In other words, he is saying, "Whoever drinks of the knowledge that I speak will become as I am. If you can really hear what I'm saying and drink of it—not just hear it—you will become as I am."

It's very helpful to see the way some of the real heavies of the spiritual traditions were—like Jesus, Krishna, and Tilopa. We might wonder how it was when Jesus was alive. Well, it was different than it is now, but also the same.

GROUP SADHANA, SERVICE, AND LEVEL-TWO WORK

(February 26, 1978)

Three Levels of Focus: Self, Group, and Teacher or the Work

There are basically three levels of possible focus in spiritual life. The first level is when the priority is on self. You know there is nothing to attain, but still you are *trying*. Whether you are trying to attain something or are just trying to understand what is going on, self is still the priority. The second level of spiritual life is a shift away from self, where the priority is the group or the community. The third level of spiritual life is where the priority is the teacher. At the third level, the teacher or the Work itself can be the priority. There is no difference between the teacher and the Work at that level. But there is a difference between the group and the Work. These levels basically go in order.

A lot of people think their attention is on the teacher. But if you examine their sadhana at all, you will see that their attention is really still on themselves. It's not even on the group yet, and the teacher comes way later on. The followers of *shaktipat* yogis are a good example of this. They are always running around thinking about "Babaji" [a generic Hindu name for a teacher], but what they don't understand is that running around thinking about Babaji is actually attention on themselves rather than attention on Babaji. If they really had attention on Babaji, what they would be doing is assuming the work that Babaji (whichever one it is) is trying to make available in the world. But they don't do that. If Babaji gives them a job to do, they fall over backwards getting it done, but they don't ever think to really make the work available. It would *seem* that there is attention on the teacher, but there is not.

Three Kinds of Relationship to the Guru

Additionally, there are three kinds of relationship one can have to the guru. One relationship is waiting until you are asked to do something, and then fussing and making excuses for not doing what you are asked to do. The second is where you do what you are asked (sometimes grudgingly and sometimes willingly), but no more. The third level is when you intuit what the guru wants, and you do it without being asked. These three relationships don't correspond to the three levels I just talked about: focus on self, focus on group, and focus on the teacher. Any one of those three levels of focus can be present within each of the three kinds of relationship to the guru.

For example, a person can have an upbringing that is very service-oriented. They are still meditating on self and are completely narcissistic, but their upbringing or habit-pattern is one of being service-oriented. Maybe they came from a big family and they were the oldest kid. It was just natural for them to take care of all the other kids and make meals and clean up after them—so they are used to that. This kind of person might come into a [community] household and keep it neat and clean and be very appropriate in relationship to other people, because that is their habit and not necessarily for any other reason.

So in those three kinds of relationship to the teacher that we talked about—not doing what you are asked, doing what you are asked and no more, and intuiting what is expected of you and doing it without being asked—even the highest of those could be present in the lowest of the three levels of sadhana [where the priority is on self]. Conversely, you could be sincerely and genuinely centered on group sadhana and be working for the group and still not do what you are asked. Any of the three relationships to the guru can be present within the three levels of focus in spiritual life.

Level-Two Group Sadhana

When people initially become involved in spiritual life, focus on a group level is almost impossible. Occasionally, someone will come to spiritual life from a genuine group situation elsewhere, and find it a little easier to embrace group sadhana. But even if someone has lived with other people in a communal situation, there is no community like *this* around, and so they are going to have problems blending into group sadhana in my company. Group sadhana is designed to make the teaching available, not to develop a balanced living situation or a perfectly run household. In most new age communities, the basic idea is not to make the teaching available but to have an ideal living situation—going back to nature, using alternative energy sources and so on.

When people first start sadhana, they have either seen the futility of the search and the possibility for relief in group work, or they haven't seen the futility of the search but they see the possibility for more satisfaction in a community situation. And some people are simply curious. They see that something good is going on, and even though they are relatively satisfied, they decide that they can use more experience and they might as well get involved.

In all three of these scenarios, there is still self-meditation or self-focus. In one case the person wants relief from the illusion, from a self that is nonexistent. In the second case the person wants more satisfaction, which is reinforcing self-meditation rather than piercing it. In the third case the person simply wants to jump on the boat, ride along, and then jump off as soon as something better comes along.

In terms of the work we are doing together, it has taken a number of years for a small group to get far enough along in first-level sadhana [self-focus] to begin to consider second-level sadhana [group-focus]. We are still seeking, and ego still wants to be stroked, but at the same time there is enough intelligent understanding of the dharma and involvement with the guru and the sangha to be sincerely desirous of group sadhana. What happens at this point, in terms of group sadhana, is that we think we are devoted to the teacher. That is what everybody thinks at the beginning. Occasionally, we intuit that we are not really devoted to the guru. At other times, particularly in the midst of ecstatic experience, we are absolutely convinced that we are doing sadhana for the teacher. As we get into second-level sadhana, the conviction that we are doing sadhana for the teacher is even more strongly present. But it is still not the case. We may be doing sadhana for the group at this point, but we think it's for the teacher.

But what is the group? Initially, the group is what we perceive as safe space for our self-focus. We are willing to put our self-meditation on the side for a little while to support the group in exchange for the feeling of safety and belonging. That is what is really going on in the beginning levels when the group is the primary emphasis. As the work progresses, that perspective gets burned away. We come to realize that self-meditation isn't going to make it. Every time we think we understand, the teacher changes the game. We get to the point where we're going to have to do something different.

So we get into group sadhana. Basically, group sadhana involves putting aside our personal desires for the needs and process of the group. We all have personal desires: a perfect man or a perfect woman, a Porsche, the little house with the white picket fence, a child, a certain job, fame—whatever it is. When the group becomes our priority, we decide to put aside our specific dreams because the teaching says it is all the search anyway. If you aren't happy now, you won't be happy just because you realize a particular dream of yours. So we have integrated that idea, thought about it a lot, been upset about it a number of times and figured, "Okay, now I'm going to put my personal desires on the shelf and do a little group sadhana." The thought might still stick around in the back of our minds that maybe there's some way we can do group sadhana and still fulfill our dreams, but you know the group is about making the teaching available and you know that's what you have to do. You direct your whole sadhana into group work. Things may happen in terms of the first, second, and third chakras that stroke your ego, but basically your main emphasis is on the group.

So, we decide we are a disciple doing group sadhana. We really think that our attention is on the teacher. Not true. We are doing group sadhana at the second level, but we are not doing Work sadhana or teacher sadhana. We still see the group as an extension of ourselves. We see the group as our safe space. We don't see the group impersonally. It's just the opposite: whatever we do for the group, we never forget to count ourselves in it. In initial Level-Two group sadhana, we never see the group without *us*. We support the group, we have put some of our personal dreams and wishes on the shelf, but we never vision the group without us. Why else would we do group sadhana? What would the group be without us? We don't see the group as an entity unto itself. We see the group as an extension of a number of individuals who happen to be together.

Level-Three Focus Is Sacrifice and Ecstatic Union

Level-Three sadhana is when our priority is the teacher or the Work. It doesn't matter which it is, because at that level we cannot see one without the other. We cannot see the Work without the teacher because there is literally no teacher without the Work. There could be an awakened individual, and so what? If there is no group, no community of practitioners, the awakened individual wouldn't make a bit of difference. So in Level-Three sadhana we have made up our minds, consciously, intelligently, and directly, that this is our life and there is nothing else to do.

We must die to the illusion before we can do Level-Three sadhana. Like Mohammad said, "Die before you die." That's what is talked about in terms of awakening. What is awakening? What do we awaken into? *Our Self with a capital S?* No, nothing so romantic. We awaken into Level-Three sadhana, the recognition that there is only the Law—

sacrifice. Gurdjieff called it "reciprocal maintenance." Awakening is the recognition that there is only the Law of Sacrifice and that we can either fulfill the law unconsciously—which is really a bitch because then we suffer like hell—or we can fulfill the Law consciously. That is what is talked about in the traditions as ecstatic union with God. That is Level-Three sadhana.

Ego's Subtle Interplay in Group Sadhana

It would seem that because we are doing group sadhana we don't have to pay attention to life-level responsibilities anymore and that we can deal with higher things now. We can really think about how to cook meals in a devoted space, breathing in God and giving *shakti* to the food. We don't want to have to think about the pile of dog shit on the floor, the clutter and dust on all the surfaces, the wilted flowers on the altar, or the water left running in the bathroom. We don't want to have to pay attention to those things. We want to think about more elevated considerations. But Level-Two sadhana can't be approached unless the support of the group includes an appropriate environment to make the teaching available in. How can the group make the teaching available in an environment that is uncared-for and scattered?

The big things tend to get done, which is great. This space we're meeting in was turned from a filthy, seedy place into a beautiful hall. But what about the little things? Everybody is willing to jump in and show how talented they are—so the big things tend to get done. The day-to-day little things, like leaving on the power to the stereo or leaving the water dripping in the sink might seem insignificant, but things like that really help us gauge where we're at in our sadhana. It is important to recognize that we are not going to get to do Level-Three sadhana if we don't get our basic stuff together. We need to remember the simple things like turning the water off and conserving electricity. It needs to become obvious that the individual's work is the work of the group.

People come into the Community needing education. In order to provide that, our priority needs to be the group; otherwise people will just be getting our self-meditation. If what they see is a cohesive group, that energy will drive a wedge into their armor and help them be honestly available. If what they see in the Community of practitioners is self-meditation, they are not going to be open and available. Why should they be? All they are seeing is the same thing that is going on for them. What is there to be available to? So the group has got to be in a place where new people see Level-Two sadhana being lived. Whether that perception is conscious or subconscious doesn't matter. It doesn't matter what outward form we manifest. If there is genuine Level-Two sadhana going on for the core group of students, people will make themselves available.

If we are all still doing Level-One sadhana with the priority on self, everybody in the sangha will be very helpful and caring. There will be no bitching or moaning, no jealousies, everybody will be really happy and full, but new people will not make themselves available. You would think they would look at all these friendly, happy, healthy people and say, "God, I want to be a part of that," but subconsciously people are sympathetic to whether Level-Two or Level-One sadhana is going on. What matters is that they make themselves available so that they can start their education.

We want to really pay attention to all the ways in which we are still seeing the group as an extension of self. When we begin to be aware of that, then of course we can start to dissolve it. That is not going to happen overnight; it is a process usually involving the same kind of fire we went through to get to the path. That is unfortunate, but that is the way it has historically been because of the way the mind works. It is frustrating, but nonetheless very simple to understand. You will find that once you are genuinely serving the group, your personal stuff is totally irrelevant.

Some of you own more worldly goods than others, so you have a lot more stuff to worry about. That is why Jesus said it is hard for someone who is rich to enter the Kingdom of Heaven. He said, "It is easier for a camel to go through the eye of a needle than for a rich man to enter the Kingdom of Heaven." Why? Because the more stuff we have, the more stuff we have to be concerned about. R. [a student who broke his back] is literally forced to confront his attachment to all his stuff now because all he can do is stay in bed. He can't play his guitar; he can't jump on his pogo stick. What good is all his stuff? Not much. It is helpful to see that. We all need to do that without breaking our backs. We want to be able to recognize that our stuff can certainly be helpful, and make life more comfortable, without being worried about it. Just use it when it is there and don't use it if it is not there.

George Gurdjieff went from being very wealthy to being stone broke, then became very wealthy again, and then once more stone broke—back and forth. He came from Russia with a lot of money, and two hundred students joined him in Paris and he supported them all until he was broke. They literally ate him out of house and home. So he went out and started a business and became wealthy again. Then he bought the Prieuré mansion in France. He paid for everything, and many students came and soon he was broke again. He was forced to sell the Prieuré. He was up and down in terms of his fortune in life. When he was up, he spent it, and when he was down, he couldn't have the kind of banquets that he liked, but he always had enough to eat. That was the way he worked and that was the way he demanded the individuals of his group work as well. Some were famous writers, artists, and thinkers like A.R. Orage, Jane Heap, and Margaret Anderson. These people were cultured. They were not the types to go out and work in the dirt.[39] But they did.

If you are doing genuine Level-Two sadhana, there is a subtle interplay that takes place in the responsibilities you take on and in your

---

[39] Hard physical labor was part of the work at the Prieuré that those who wanted to study with Gurdjieff participated in.

relationships to other people in the group as an extension of yourself. There is still ego's subtle interplay. Basically, you are still making the shift from self-meditation into group sadhana. Even though we may talk about levels of sadhana, it is not so linear. When a certain purity of form takes place in your subconscious, your spontaneous and natural reactions will be group-oriented instead of self-meditative, automatic habit patterns. Theoretically, if the teacher was genuinely your priority, Levels One and Two would just automatically fall into place in time. All the qualities relevant to those first two stages would just click in.

Crystallizations Have to Come Second to Make the Work One's Priority

The question is, "What is it to make the Work or the teacher your priority?" Is it *attention* on the teacher or the Work?

Attention on the teacher or the Work is really helpful in terms of cultivating *bhakti* [devotional love in Sanskrit]. Love is a nice quality to have throughout all the levels. But does that mean that your priority is automatically the Work or the teacher? Not necessarily. Even devotion that is absorptive doesn't necessarily mean that your priority is the Work. You can be absorbed in bhakti twenty-four hours a day, and that just means that you are absorbed in bhakti twenty-four hours a day.

Teachers always like bhaktis and, at the same time, a genuine teacher will encourage a bhakti-inclined student not to get stuck there. Sometimes our crystallizations[40] get in the way. People don't come and get a cosmic vision from looking into the master's eyes and suddenly everything else is secondary. No way! Someone who makes the teacher or the Work their priority has to make all of their crystallizations secondary. People go to these fabulous ashrams and the biggest

40 Physical, mental, or emotional habits that have solidified and are impervious to change. "Crystallization" is a term used in the Gurdjieff Work.

crystallizations they have are never tested. They are really polite and nice. They don't have to deal with parents, kids, sex, or their jealousy. It's great. They can think that they woke up and have gotten to the height of devotion when really nothing is going on.

People on these kinds of ashrams talk about the heat of sadhana they have going on. What heat is going on? Some other woman wore their favorite blouse, somebody else got to cook, the squash was overdone? The crystallizations that get challenged are the ones they were willing to give up in the first place, which is why they went to that kind of ashram. The work there is very predictable. If you are really sharp, you can more or less gauge what you will be expected to do. In this kind of Work, once in a while there are surprises, which makes it nice. So, skipping levels is theoretically possible, but not practically realistic.

In the garden in Johnsonburg, New Jersey, 1979

PART III

TILLING THE SOIL

Johnsonburg, July 1978-July 1980

INTRODUCTION

In 1978, Lee moved from eastern New Jersey into a large house in the small town of Johnsonburg in the northwestern part of the state. Some students lived with him and others moved into a nearby house in Hainesburg, ten minutes away. Others chose not to move and were seen less frequently. The idea that spiritual life was a twenty-four-hour-a-day affair, that life could be approached from a true spiritual perspective, was becoming more of a reality. Though spiritual life was about work and service, it was not drudgery. It was challenging and unsettling, but also deeply satisfying and engaging to begin to expand one's capacity for inner and outer work. The company of others who were doing this at the same time was both irritating and uplifting.

Lee gave the two houses in New Jersey names from Frank Herbert's science fiction *Dune* trilogy. He lived with his family and a few students in Arrakis, identified in Herbert's work as the source of the most valuable substance in the universe. Other students lived in Salusa Secundus, where prisoners lived, conditions were harsh, and warriors were trained. Dinners and meetings were held several times each week, with satsang on Sundays. No time was ever wasted around Lee. Dishes would be done right after dinner and the talk would begin.

Around this time, Lee began to teach the game of bridge as a spiritual exercise that could be used for paying attention and self-observation. Any free time and many nights were spent playing bridge. Being in the company of the guru and sangha gradually created a more objective perspective on life, distilled from the conventional frame of reference and worldview of one's previous education. A different kind of struggle was required given the recognition that fulfillment could not occur as the result of reaching any transitory goal. "Living God" was easier said than done, and the ground needed to be tilled for the seeds of true spiritual practice that Lee planted to grow. He was the reminder that the price to really know who one is beyond identification, to know love, was everything that one had learned to believe about oneself. Yet, the form of one's life might not change.

There was the uncomfortable sense that the universe moved Lee in unknown ways and that anything could happen. One's trust in him, and in the process, grew over time as students experienced the fire of sadhana that opened up new possibilities in their lives by being given what they needed to go deeper into transformational work. It was a movement and a rest. At the time, it seemed that Lee was a sacrifice for the Community, regularly speaking well into the night at meetings after dinner and being available to his students with the constancy and presence of the universe that one woke up to every day. He instinctively gave exercises to people that magnified or were aversive to their mechanical tendencies, providing opportunities for self-study and to enquire about who one is prior to the crystallized ideas that one had assumed about oneself. He had students work on specific koans that could bypass the thinking mind and elicit one's true nature, as practitioners might in the Zen tradition, and skillfully named personality features in a Gurdjieffian way that brought awareness to areas of blindness. Students worked with the consideration that "Change is not at issue" and that the transformation of ego's dynamics occurred in the cauldron of seeing oneself clearly. In time it became evident that Lee actually sacrificed to whatever was needed by the universe—which at the moment was the community of students who might provide a foundation for a tradition in which real spiritual work would be lived in the West.

With the birth of a few children in the Community, Lee began to speak about the importance of conscious attention and sacrifice in child-raising. The effect that adults' conditioned, reactive, habit patterns and an unconscious approach had on children was considered in-depth. The aim was to give children a chance to maintain a more innocent approach to life, with less introjection of the competitive survival orientation of mainstream culture that their parents had been raised in.

Physical work in the garden, which began with tilling the soil, was an element of the change in lifestyle that included growing some of the food that was eaten. When driving up to the Johnsonburg house, Lee could sometimes be seen weeding or picking swiss chard and wearing a broad straw hat in the garden.

But it was clear that spiritual work was the focus in Johnsonburg and that community living was just an element of that. Though the diet was vegetarian, there were exceptions to the salads that Lee made, such as the occasion when he had someone buy horsemeat for dinner, which seemed to communicate the need to digest and metabolize both the contaminated and pure aspects of life and to dispel any righteous attitudes about diet. Attempts to fall into habit patterns were often offset by the guru's unexpected behavior. Lee could provide critical feedback and sometimes shock with personal input at just the time when one had become available to make use of it. This seemed to come from providence. There could be recoil on the recipient's part, but also the sense of Lee's regard through interactions that seemed to be objective communications of the work that was needed to bring one to the next step.

Before meeting Lee, most of his group of young Western students had little prior training or knowledge of the spiritual path. Lee spent extended time with them discussing basic principles of the dharma and creating circumstances for practice of the conditions and work on self. He often read and commented on teachings and lessons from the great traditions and from historical or contemporary teachers for students to consider. Lee also introduced material from other arenas of life that was useful for students to integrate in their spiritual process. Students matured in the recognition that there were many teachers who had charisma, intellectual understanding of the dharma, and skill in interpersonal communication; that there were those who were "rascal-gurus" or charlatans who either made power their god or who were unconscious of areas of blindness; and that there were some who communicated a genuine understanding of the Work. Still, there were few who actually lived as the Law of Sacrifice. Lee provided a much-needed education to inform students' growing relationship to sadhana. He seemed interested in planting seeds in fertile soil where there was some possibility of a harvest in the future.

Lee took three students with him when he made his second trip to India in 1979. Once again, circumstances occurred with Yogi Ramsuratkumar that seemed beyond the realm of coincidence. For example, on one occasion, Lee found the Beggar-Saint in Tiruvannamalai (which was not always an easy task for those who sought him) sitting with a young man who was reading a small yellow pamphlet titled "For the Love of God." Only a few hundred copies of this essay that Lee had written had been published, and it seemed implausible that Lee would show up at the exact time the young man was talking to Yogi Ramsuratkumar about how the pamphlet had changed his life. The communication of the Indian master—his presence, love, freedom, and humor—impacted Lee greatly, though it would be years before Lee began to speak about their timeless relationship.

Lee had students read certain books during the time in Johnsonburg, including *The Godman*, about the life of the Indian master Meher Baba. It was a challenging read, science fiction of a different sort in that it seemed incomprehensible that students had committed so deeply to Meher Baba that at a certain juncture they embarked on "The New Life" with him. During this period of time, they were required to leave everything behind, to follow Meher Baba implicitly and never exhibit reactivity in their wanderings with him, which might go on forever. Just to read the book and to consider its implications while being with Lee was stressful. But Lee's trustworthiness and obvious commitment to the spiritual unfoldment of his students inspired the beginnings of faith. Lee spoke about the communication that a spiritual master had to make to students to follow the master and leave the past behind in order for a master's Work to continue into future generations.

Certain remarkable events also occurred around Lee. There was a satsang on a Sunday evening when he seemed to assume the mood and posture of different historical spiritual masters, to actually become them for a period of time. Watching this *lila* [divine play or activity], one could "see" the master he was calling forth as a kind of overlay on himself. It seemed that one who had been surrendered was one with everything—past, present, and future—and that there was much more to reality than the limited linear perspective about life that we gradually learn to believe in as we grow up. Even though Lee's students knew that anything could happen, and that the future was unknown, no one could have imagined how his Work would unfold over time.

ENQUIRY: REFLECTIONS ON HUMOR AND LIFE

(November 26, 1978)

Enquiry Directs You Toward Revelation

Enquiry is a form of spiritual practice. In its true sense, it can be utilized in the same way as the basic life-level conditions of meditation, study, healthy diet, daily exercise, and right sexuality. If we are in the appropriate frame of mind, we can literally translate the most common everyday occurrences—a word from a friend or something we see on the highway—into revelation. When appropriately used, enquiry can simply be another grounding, practical, life-level condition, not a technique that is used to get us anywhere.

The most famous form of enquiry is Ramana Maharshi's, "Who am I?" Ramana Maharshi recommended enquiry to turn the questioner in upon himself, but not as a technique to get an answer. Even though enquiry is traditionally stated in the form of a question, the question is not stated in order to get an answer. It is stated in order to create the most appropriate channel for one to experience revelation. If anyone asks the question, he will immediately have the right answer intellectually. But it is not a matter of right answers. Enquiry is a matter of a spontaneous reflection—on what the question directs you towards. It is not a matter of technique or seeking. The question *will* direct you somewhere if you keep allowing it to arise. If you continue to turn what arises, through the process of enquiry, in that same direction, then ideally you come up with revelation. There won't be a verbal answer to the question "Who am I?" There will be revelation. Who you are will become present.

We all have karma at deep primal levels that goes back hundreds of thousands of years. Then there is what we have accumulated since birth, the stuff that's not so much genetically moving us but that is just the crap in our current memory banks. If we recognize something deeper through enquiry, that recognition is going to be filtered through all the immediate stuff that is on the surface. Then we might have a satori or flash of absolute knowledge, and yet not be able to practically apply it even one percent. Initially, we need something directed to that particular programming, which is why we talk about basic sadhana first. Let's get our bodies straight, our diet straight, our sexuality straight, and then we can start to deal with emotions and the play of subtle energies. Why even seriously consider the subtle energies if we haven't dealt with the very basics? Why bother dealing with anger and jealousy if we haven't dealt with our sexuality? Sexuality is what permeates anger and jealousy anyway. If we start to work on jealousy but we have not dealt with sexuality, nothing is going to ever be resolved—though we may have temporary insight.

Revelation Can Be Found in the Most Mundane Circumstances

There is an interesting form of enquiry that can be practiced which is ideally suited to our culture and the technology of our minds. We've got a modern technological structure to our mentation that wasn't around one hundred years ago. Along with the world having undergone an industrial revolution, our minds have undergone an industrial revolution. So we need a form of enquiry that is specifically and directly suited to our culture, mental technology, and upbringing. The form of enquiry that I want to share with you arose in a way that really highlights how each of us can find revelation in the most mundane circumstances. Our tendency is to want to find revelation in cosmic experience that happens randomly. Yet true revelation is found in the process of ordinary, mundane life. This form of enquiry came in the remembrance of a humorous experience that happened a year ago.

I was thinking about a friend who didn't have a job or any visible source of income but managed to live pretty well. He was the kind of character that could get along just about anywhere with relative ease. I had the highest esteem for this guy. One day he and I had a discussion about how he used to be a super-motivated man. But the day that [the guru's point was] made with him, he completely lost all his motivation about everything—the motivation to earn money, get a new car, or find a nice place to live. He didn't care where he lived, he didn't care what he ate, he didn't care who he slept with or if he slept with anybody at all. After a year and a half in the Community, it became apparent to him that he should get off that position and begin to be motivated in some sense.

He went about doing what he was best suited for, which was selling real estate. As soon as he started working again, he immediately lined up a major sale. It was under contract and he figured that he was going to get a five thousand dollar commission.

"When I get this commission," he said to me, "I'll just donate the whole thing to the Community. I don't need the money."

I said, "Great. Fine." I didn't plan how to spend the money; I figured we could do that with relative ease after we got it.

Well, the deal got held up by red tape and legal problems so that, as time went on, it became a fantasy that he would donate the commission to the Community when the deal closed. He didn't yet have the check in his hand.

At one point, all of the legal problems were resolved, and it seemed to be a matter of weeks before the closing, at which time he would get his commission check. When it became apparent that the fantasy was about to become a reality, a few of us—he and myself and one or two others—were sitting around talking. We got to talking about real estate and about his work. Thinking about how in two weeks he was going to have five thousand dollars for fifteen minutes of work, he suddenly sat bolt upright and said, "Who am I kidding? I'm not going to give the money to the Community!" We all laughed. I just chuckled because I didn't expect it anyway. He left the Community—just like that—because he realized that his entire involvement had been a fantasy. When it was about to become real, he thought, "Who am I kidding?"

Well, it struck me just like it must have struck Ramana Maharshi: who was this man kidding? All he had to do was realize who he was kidding and what a revelation that would have been!

In that moment I realized that this was an opportunity that could not be passed up for the mandali to perfect their student-sadhana and become disciples, at last, by utilizing this process of enquiry: "Who am I kidding?" I am very serious. This is just as good as "Who Am I?" It's better, in fact, because our whole life is not only a joke, but so are we. Trying to kid somebody is the basis of everything we do from the moment we are directed and motivated in the body. Who are we trying to kid?

Each one of us knows how everybody else is avoiding sadhana, but we don't know what *we* are doing. On a very superficial intellectual level, if we start to consider who we are kidding, we'll know that we are not kidding anybody else. Everybody else sees us just as clearly as we see them, believe it or not. We walk around doing our number while everybody else is thinking, "Why can't he see what he's doing? My God, it's so obvious!" Meanwhile, when we are looking at someone else with a knowing glance and thinking, "Why can't she see what she is doing?" we are implying that we know what we're doing. In truth, we are doing exactly the same thing as the other person. We are just not seeing it.

Enquiry is a form of practice that one can use—not to get anything, not to use as a mantra, but as a beautiful form of reflection. We are simply contemplating what is arising. The beautiful thing about "Who am I kidding?" is that "I" am the one who is doing the kidding as well as the one that is being kidded. So when we say, "Who am I kidding?" we are reflecting upon both who I am to ask, "Who am I kidding?" *and* we are reflecting upon the source of who it is that's being kidded. The "who" refers to the all-pervading Divine and "am I kidding" refers to what is being kidded.

Why is anything being kidded? Because we have identified with our body. We absolutely think we are our body. When somebody criticizes us, what are they criticizing? Not some illusion, they are criticizing us. We take everything personally. Don't think that your practice is being undermined because I have explained "Who am I kidding?" It will reveal who it is that creates the illusion to begin with. Do you think your body creates the illusion? Do you think your mind creates the illusion? Neither your body nor your mind has the independence, the intelligence, the strength, or the will to create the illusion. Who creates the illusion? "I" creates the illusion.

Identification, Taking Things Personally, Societal Structures as Forms of Ego

We can trace every single structure of society, without exception, back to the form of ego. That is why you have a corporation over and against a sole proprietorship. If you own a sole proprietorship and somebody screws you out of a thousand dollars, it's your business and your loss. It comes out of your income tax at the end of the year. But in the legal sense, the idea of a corporation is that a corporation is a separate legal entity that things can be done to in place of things being done to the individual. The idea of a corporation didn't arise from some smart lawyer wanting to save on income tax. The idea of the corporation arose as a strategy of ego to substantiate survival. If all of this stuff in the world of business is being done to us personally, what a threat to survival! But if it is being done to the corporation, a completely impersonal legal entity, then we can survive even if the corporation gets slaughtered. If the corporation loses money, the individual businessman who owns all the stock is still drawing the same salary regardless of how much the corporation loses.

It is the same thing with this whole idea of taking things personally. If we identify with the first three chakras, we literally think we are the body. We think that whatever goes on in the world is being done to *us*. We take everything personally—right in the first three chakras. When we go over to someone's house and the sink is dirty, we think a direct insult is being done to us personally because we identify with the body. We think that everything that goes on in the whole world is personally being done to us. Our "vital" gets wrapped up in a knot because there was a plane crash in the Pyrenees. We hear about political prisoners being tortured in Argentina or Brazil and we think it's being done to us.

But we aren't about to get off our asses to make a commitment to a more humane world. No. We have the electric dishwasher, clothes-dryer, hairdryer, can-opener. We use enough power in one day to supply the whole city of Yellow Falls, Wyoming for two weeks. We hear about what they are doing to people in Chile and we are so upset that we can't make love that night. But we are not about to open a can of food manually, let alone do anything that contributes to a more humane world. We are not about to keep the thermostat at sixty-eight degrees as recommended. Screw saving energy! We can't make that kind of a commitment. Yet we get constipated, literally, because there is eleven-percent unemployment. We think it is being done to us. We take it personally in the first three chakras because we think we are the body.

Or we identify with the psychic self, which is even worse. We sit in our comfortable house sipping our mineral water, contemplating the incredible dinner we are about to eat of carrots and celery and brown rice with a little bit of soy sauce (not too much) and onions fried in ghee. We are centered in the psychic realm contemplating devotion to the Lord. We literally think we are our minds. We don't get things so much in our bodies. Why should we? We know the mind controls it all. What we believe is the motivator of our health. We believe good thoughts and we are healthy. So those of us that think we are our minds don't get sick much. We don't feel it in our body, but we feel it in our minds.

What happens when those of us that think we are our minds take things personally? We get angry, guilty, jealous, distracted, and depressed. All of our responses take place on a "higher" level than the body. We think we are our minds and we take everything personally, under all circumstances, unless we know who we are kidding. If we ask, "Who am I kidding?"—and that is the exact statement, it shouldn't be interpolated—there is nothing to take personally when we find out who we are kidding. Otherwise, if we identify ourselves as the mind, we take personally whatever arises in the world.

We don't understand that we are corporations, in a sense. This body and mind is literally a cosmic corporation. It is an entity unto itself, no matter whether the entity wins or loses, survives or goes bankrupt, or gets taken over by a conglomerate—which is what the Community is. It doesn't matter, because the body and mind are simply an entity. The one that needs to know "Who am I kidding?" is the one who makes up the entity, who moves the entity, who the entity couldn't exist without. But that one never gets hurt. That one occasionally gets fired but moves on to another job, which is reincarnation. That one always has a job. As long as the corporation survives, that one always gets a paycheck every week, and medical benefits, and a retirement plan.

That is what we are: a corporation. What a perfect analogy. The corporation is a legal entity, and the stockholders of the corporation don't have to worry about personal survival. Who moves and sustains the corporation? Although it is a legal entity on paper and it moves and works in the world like an entity, the corporation is none other than the warm bodies that make it up: the comptroller, the board of directors, the president, the vice-president. And what would the president and the vice-president be without secretaries? Nothing. Most of these corporate guys are creatively brilliant. They come up with ideas that would knock your socks off, but they couldn't type a letter if their lives depended on it. The corporation could not exist without its working members.

The Divine Is Inclusive of the Illusion

The Divine is all-inclusive. The Divine isn't some pure and ecstatic perfect Self seen over and against the illusion. The Divine is the illusion also. But the identification with the illusion is what needs to be undermined. When we identify with our mind and someone attacks the "corporation," we take it as personal attack on the mind. The response is in the mind. We get angry. Why? Well, not for any valid reason, but the mind gets angry. Spiritual seekers that identify with the mind always identify with ecstasies and blisses and transcendental experiences. The average spiritual seeker will tell you that their greatest meditation was the time when they forgot who they were. They closed their eyes and an hour later they opened them and said, "Wow!" They were gone somewhere. But that is just unconsciousness, confusion. They forgot the body and thought it was ecstatic communion with God.

Whatever we identify with is what we think God is. If we identify with the body, we think God is the body. When the body is about to die, we think that God is going to die. Sometimes we pray, but we don't really believe in it. Nobody ever finds solace in "last rights" when they are in control of their wits. People find solace in last rights when they've lost control of their wits. We find solace when the rational mind has died and the consciousness is freed up from identification. No one finds solace from that kind of ritual if they identify with the body and they know the body is going to die. Because the body is God to them. If they are in control of their wits, God is dying. Here is this priest telling them about the afterlife. Forget it; God is dying. God is not going to help them. But once they've lost control of their wits, then they can find some solace in the fact that they are not dying after all. They just drop the shell, the suit of clothing.

The average spiritual seeker thinks that the mind is God. That's who we think we are when we identify with the mind. When we have a cosmic experience, we think we have seen God face to face instead of realizing we just had another experience. We had an orgasm of the mid-brain instead of an orgasm of the genitals, but we haven't been any closer to seeing God. Those of us who have had experiences of this kind of attainment can feel disdain for people at a bar cheering on a football team and think, "If they only knew they are suffering!" We imagine that we know the ecstasy of meditation, but all we have seen is a few of our nerve endings fire off. We look at people that are not involved in the pursuit of esoteric knowledge like they are no more than pigs or cows. We are really bent out of shape when our children don't let us read from the Buddhist texts, but they are just kids and they want to play. We can't handle it when somebody makes noise when we're trying to meditate. We think that our meditation is God and we take it personally when something interferes with that.

Then there are those who identify with the super-mental realms. The super-mental realms are the realms that are not located within the radius of this here flesh and blood. Even those that identify with the mind recognize a focal radius related to the body. But in the super-mental realms, we can get out of that whole relationship and identify with what most religions call the soul or with what some people call the astral or ethereal body. People that identify with that realm tend to hold all basic human relationships with disdain. They go to sleep at night and travel the astral realms. They know that when they die something is still going to survive. People like that tend to totally disregard the form of the body and the form of the mind and tend to fixate exclusively on an orientation not delineated by any kind of environment or physical location. This kind of person always has their head in the clouds; you can't bring them down to earth. Sometimes they don't even eat. You have to lead them down the street because they are always meditating. They are just way off the deep end.

There is the possibility that we identify with one of those three realms (physical, mental, super-mental) as an exclusive fixation. The process that goes on when we fixate is that we think that level is God.

The Perfect Time to Enquire

To get back to enquiry… You can reflect upon your situation—whatever you identify with—by exactly recognizing what has arisen and simply thinking to yourself, "Who am I kidding?" Now the beauty of this is that every single last thing that arises is illusory, so everything needs to be enquired of. Every single experience and event that arises in our lives, significant or mundane, must be enquired of—pain, hunger, guilt, jealousy, anger, ecstasy. There will be the tendency to say, "Who am I kidding?" when we get angry, but what about when we feel good, loose, and free? That is as good a time as any to say, "Who am I kidding?" That is an even better time! Because when you get angry at the guy on the highway, you know that's who you are. When you are floating around in the bliss of communion, that's when you should really say, "Who am I kidding?" Because the next day you will be just as fickle as ever, bitching and moaning and going back on all the agreements you made when you were feeling good.

Those agreements we make to one another in a spiritual community are exactly the same as a legal contract. For most people, it's against their moral integrity to go back on a legal contract. But we make commitments to one another in the heat of feeling good, and those commitments are dashed the minute we don't feel good. We forget about them and pretend we didn't make them. We swear on a stack of Bibles we never made that commitment. We wipe it out of our minds, we erase it. Yet it is much more dangerous to invalidate that kind of a commitment than a legal commitment. The most you can get from a legal commitment is sued. If you break a commitment made in the company of the spiritual master, you incur karma that you don't want to incur. It keeps you far more distant from God to incur that kind of liability than to be sued if you don't pay your credit card. Yet we do it all the time. We need to enquire under all circumstances, even those circumstances when we are free of debilitating emotions and we are really feeling good. When we look at one another and love one another genuinely for that moment, we need to enquire, "Who am I kidding?"

If you seriously reflect upon "Who am I kidding?" you are likely to realize who you are kidding. Who "I" is that is doing the kidding, who and what it is that's kidding, what the kidding is, and who is asking "Who am I kidding?" Realize that and you will be awakened, enlightened, and all that business. That's the fulfillment of your sadhana. Don't use enquiry for one specific type of experience. Use it at all times. Use it over pleasurable experiences, unpleasurable experiences, cosmic experiences, suffering, and when you are in the midst of the most lucid recognition that all life is suffering. "Yes, I see it, I know who I am, yes." That's the perfect time to say, "Who am I kidding?"

FAITH

(January 1979)

Remembering Revelation When It Fades

Anytime you get a work exercise[41] there are two things that can come out of it. One is a specific revelation that each exercise can generate. For instance, within a day or two of starting an acting exercise, R. had the exact insight the exercise was supposed to generate, and he wasn't even into it that much. But a much more important aspect is whether you are able to reflect upon that revelation in a way that is meaningful in terms of surrender. R's description of what happened for him was exactly what's supposed to happen, but then what do you do with it?

So, it's a two-part deal. You can talk about the revelation, but what does it mean if you aren't integrating it? Sadhana is not just doing an exercise and getting a revelation. It's taking the fruit of your work and using that fruit. It's not just that you have a revelation and that's that. Sometimes the utilization of it is a matter of remembering what it is you knew when you had the revelation and functioning according to that memory strictly on faith. Because quite frequently, when you are remembering what it is you knew, you don't know it anymore. Within a day, the revelation may seem to have happened lifetimes ago.

Things that arise that you know are beyond verbal communication frequently have to be worked on strictly by faith because that revelation doesn't continue day in and day out, twenty-four hours a day. You can have a genuine revelation where the light dawns and you say, "Oh, so that's why!" It explains everything, and the next day you can understand in your own way what it meant to you. When the field of the revelation

---

41 When moved by the transformational process, Lee gave exercises to students for their own benefit and sometimes also as vehicles for communicating his Work in the world.

isn't there anymore, you have to take it on faith. And taking revelation on faith can create a conflict, because it requires that you invalidate a lot of your previous experience. When the revelation is actively present, it's relatively easy to invalidate your previous experience. But as soon as it starts to fade into the past, ego will always try to invalidate the knowledge that you have as a result of the revelation. So, with every insight, you have to be sure to assimilate what you've learned.

The revelation R. described was beyond his usual sleeping existence, but there has to be a parallel drawn between that insight and your day-in and day-out mundane existence. Something has to be made of the revelation. If nothing is made of the revelation, regardless of how intense or real it is, it's just like any other insight. If nothing is made of it, it gets relegated to the dusty corners of your mind and is usually forgotten given enough time. If you pay attention to the things that are significant in your life, you'll get a very clear idea of what it is that's going to confront the fulfillment of the revelation. Because once you truly understand, it's always a fight. It doesn't matter how smart or philosophical we are. We've got twenty-five, thirty, forty years of one way of thinking, seeing things, perceiving, understanding.

You have a revelation and you are living Truth for a day, a week, or a month and all of a sudden that Truth is not felt anymore. It's not in your cells—it's a memory. It requires a tremendous amount of faith to continue to function in the same way when the feedback isn't the same. When the revelation is overflowing, you walk through the world and nobody can touch you. You're living in a way that is extraordinarily different. Then, when the revelation starts to fade and you attempt to live in the same extraordinary way, suddenly people get to you; you're worried you're going to lose your job, you're concerned about what people think of you. It requires a tremendous amount of faith to maintain the extraordinariness of your life when the heat of the revelation starts to cool down. But that is what's required; that's what has to be done.

The Revelation of What God Is Requires a Leap

You all know the intensity of having a revelation, not just an insight. A revelation is when you make a connection—like when you figured out how to multiply, add, and subtract. To get from all of those numbers on paper to doing mathematics required an incredible leap in consciousness. And it's infinitely harder to learn how to add than it is to learn how to do differential calculus. Once you learn how to add, you've got it. From addition, you can go on to all the heavy stuff like subtraction, multiplication, division, and work with decimals. The revelation of what God is requires a much greater leap in consciousness than the leap required to learn addition, subtraction, and multiplication. The revelation we are talking about is as different from everything we know, think, see, and believe as addition is from strict visual perception.

But once that leap is made, once we learn the principle, we can apply the logic of God-life to our ordinary lives in the same way we apply the logic of addition to higher mathematics. To live in an extraordinary fashion when the revelation is not peaking requires discipline, strength, and commitment. It's truly a matter of functioning on faith. We have to believe that we know what we are doing because those around us will do everything they can to bring us back into the fold. On a strictly psychological level it's them and us. The psyche of the "thems" will try and bring you back into the fold to validate their own existence.

The Insecurity of Ego Takes Even One Exception as a Threat

There's a story about a very powerful king. In his kingdom there were a few people who were mad. The mad people looked about the same as everyone else, especially if they were dressed and washed. Sometimes you couldn't even tell the difference. The king was a little worried because he didn't like mad people. So he asked his court magician, who happened to be the renowned sorcerer Merlin, what to do about these mad people.

"I want to be able to recognize them," the king explained.

Merlin said, "If you put a red mark on their foreheads, they will be clearly recognizable. But there's only one problem."

"What's that?" the king asked.

Merlin said, "Well, sometimes normal people see this red mark and they think it's attractive, so they put a red mark on their forehead too. But once someone puts the red mark on their forehead, they become a little mad themselves."

The king said, "I don't care! Let's mark the foreheads of the mad people and take our chances."

So the king sent his couriers to find all the mad people in the land and put red marks on their foreheads. Just as Merlin had warned, people who were not mad started to think the red marks were very attractive. One by one, these people began to put a red mark on their forehead. Before the king knew it, everybody in the kingdom had a red mark on their head. The poor king was the only sane man left. He spent all his time locked up in his palace—very wealthy, lots of things to do, plenty of diversions—but without another sane human being around to keep him company. The more the ranks of the mad increased, the madder they became. By the time everyone in the kingdom had a red mark on their forehead, they were raving lunatics, just completely insane.

The king called Merlin again and asked, "What can I do? How can I change this?"

Merlin said, "Unfortunately, you were so intent upon this project that I didn't have a chance to tell you that once people get red marks on their foreheads, they can't reverse the process. They are all just hopelessly mad."

The king cried, "What will I do? I've got nobody to play chess with, nobody to go hunting with. Without someone to share my diversions with, they are all empty."

Merlin said, "Well, you are going to have to figure it out."

The king thought and thought and decided that the only thing to do was to put a red mark on his forehead too. He put a red mark on his forehead and lived happily ever after—crazy as a loon but happy as can be.

The analogy to spiritual life is that the psyche of the common man and woman—which is asleep and only pretends to be awake—finds even one exception to the rule to be a threat. Even one exception out of billions of people on the earth is considered invalidation to the sleeping world. The only chance that God has of waking people up is because ego is so insecure. Can you imagine that something so strong, powerful, creative, and dynamic as ego can be so insecure that no matter how many people function in a completely egotistical way, one exception is too big a threat to take?

Faith Is Necessary to Maintain an Extraordinary Relationship to Life

What we find is that, if we have faith and are truly functioning in an extraordinary way, we get bombarded in a way that feels very threatening. If you are in the heat of revelation, you don't notice the bombardment because there's only the Self anyway. Who is there to bombard who? If it's truly revelation, there is no one to undermine you, no crisis to confront; the bombardment is not recognized. But as the heat of the revelation starts to cool, you start to recognize that faith is necessary to maintain this extraordinary relationship with life. You see that this extraordinary passion, this extraordinary romance is being attacked from all sides. Not just from without, but even more strongly from within. Doubts, fears, and confusion arise. It requires more and more faith to maintain that extraordinariness. To maintain that extraordinariness long enough is actually a kind of madness.

Many people who are God-realized are clinically mad. Sooner or later that's attractive enough that other people want to put that red X on their forehead. The funny thing about putting the red X on your forehead is the longer you wear it, the madder you become. If you pretend you're realized long enough, one day you are going to be. You'll be just as "mad" as anybody that didn't have to pretend to begin with. The story of the king and the mad people had a happy ending: eventually everybody had a red X on their forehead. It doesn't apply to the world-at-large, so *this* story [life on earth] doesn't have such a happy ending. But it certainly applies to those on the spiritual path, to those who are attempting to access an alternative dimension from the conventional world. It applies very realistically.

You can maintain extraordinary revelation through faith with a little discipline thrown in. A couple of cups of faith, a pinch of discipline, and a tablespoon each of compassion, understanding, consideration, and empathy. That's all you need. One big stew! But faith is necessary. It's not that we don't have faith. It's just that we are so absorbed in this survival business that we never seriously consider our faith. If you think even superficially that the Godman is who you're giving him credit for being, where's your faith? Never mind awakening, never mind being a devotee, forget about creating sanctuary and all that stuff. There's nothing to attain. Just figure out who God is…by hook or by crook; that's all you've got to do. Everything else will take care of itself.

You should realize that there is an Influence going on in your life. Divine Influence. Divine Influence will make you an offer you can't refuse! If you don't think there is Divine Influence moving in your life, then you shouldn't be here. But you should be convinced of that by now, and you should have just a little bit of faith. Come on! I've got faith. I didn't have faith when we started. When we started, I just had raw arrogance, but that was honed down fast. Now I have faith. Is this going to work out? Yes! I'm sure it is!

Every time the Buddha was asked, "Will I wake up this lifetime?" he said, "Yes!" Buddha had a card up his sleeve because we are already awake. He never lied. If somebody was on their deathbed and they said, "But I didn't wake up!" he would answer, "But you are already awake! You just have a little more work to do." Hundreds of thousands of bodhisattvas lined up and he told them all that they would wake up this lifetime. "Just say one line of the Diamond Sutra and you'll all wake up," he said. And they all said one line and there it was.

You really ought to have some faith. It doesn't mean to just sit back and everything is going to be taken care of. You have to put gas in your car. It's not like, "Oh I have faith!" and you just get in your car and drive and never need gas. You've got to be reasonable. But you're not reasonable; you're unreasonable. Have a little faith! There *is* something going on. You all know that, so why don't you give it a little credit? If you gave God even a fraction of credit that you give your own minds, imagine what would happen. But we give our minds so much credit!

I saw a movie yesterday and in it there was an old lady and her daughter setting a table. The daughter says, "Ma! Why do you always put the spoon up here?" And the daughter takes the spoon from the top of the plate and puts it on the side of the plate. The mother picks the spoon up and puts it back and says, "I've been setting tables for fifty years. Don't tell me the spoon's in the wrong place!" But who says the spoon has to be at the top of the plate? Emily Post? Gloria Vanderbilt? Is it a cosmic truth? Imagine discussing something serious when we can't even handle the spoon being in the "wrong" place. That's the kind of faith that we have in our minds.

We read something in the *New York Times* and right away we're an expert. Somebody starts talking about politics and of course we have an opinion. We are all experts on law, medicine, sports. We watch a football game, and we shout at the TV, "Block that kick!" My God, we have such faith in our minds! We know *nothing*, and we think we are experts at everything. The accountant comes in and we tell him what to do. We meet with our lawyer and tell the lawyer what to do. We have a visit with the doctor and tell the doctor what to do. If we had even ten percent of that much faith in God, think what would happen! We wouldn't be devotees or awake or provide sanctuary, but we'd at least begin to understand what God is. We need to just discover who we are.

It's not a matter of becoming stronger or clearer. It's discovering who we are.

You are holding the guru responsible for your ecstasies, your depressions, and everything else because the guru is supposed to be the mover—the creator, the sustainer, and the destroyer. When you're creating, you say, "Oh Krishna!" When things are going pretty well and you're working hard and learning about yourself, then the guru is being the sustainer. Then, when the bottom falls out, the guru is being the destroyer and you say, "Oh man, Lee undermined me again." That's the mind's recognition of these experiences. But where's your faith?

Allowing Life to Unfold Naturally

The thing to do about a crisis of faith is just be reasonable for a minute when you find yourself filled with considerations about something. See which of them are truly necessary and which are just the stuff the mind kicks out. If you're waiting for somebody who is late, you think, "I wonder if they've been in an accident. I'd better call the hospital!" Instead of just finding a good book to read or listening to some music while you're waiting, all these awful thoughts run through your mind. We're always imagining possibilities which don't do us any good. This applies to so many areas of our lives. It doesn't mean we should never buy an insurance policy. Make your preparations and then go on about doing what you're doing. But we expend so much energy worrying about this and that.

If you really consider the principle we're talking about, then you should be more willing to allow the things that arise for you to be more natural. But we don't allow things to arise for us naturally. We have to be sure of everything. We are so intent upon controlling things. Even though we don't think of this as manipulation, basically that's what it is. We're so intent upon intelligently manipulating the environment that we don't allow things to unfold for us the way they could. And that *can* happen. Things can unfold in a way that is much more natural and Divinely Influenced than they do. We tend to interfere with the Influence. There is a tremendous Influence going on, a tremendous force that's present that can activate us if we don't think that everything we do is done under our own power. That's the consideration. We think everything we do is done under our own power.

Of course, we never think of everything. We are always leaving something out, forgetting an appointment, or something like that. That doesn't mean we should just think that God will take care of it and go off on our merry way without having a date book to write down our appointments. But when you have an appointment at a particular place, having faith in Divine Influence means not fretting over the weather and those kinds of things. Just make the appointment and get in the car or hop on a bus or whatever is going to take you to the appointment.

It's really important that we are objective about our situation so that our approach to spiritual life is not simply a rejection of our upbringing. We have to be careful that our spiritual life is not simply disillusionment with the church or the synagogue or a rejection of our parents' values. Spiritual life has really got to be deeper than that if it's going to prove to be true.

THE COSMOLOGY OF DEATH: ITS RELEVANCY TO LIVING

(April 15, 1979)

We Panic Whenever We Experience a Hint of Death

We human beings have a stigma about death. Actually, it's more than a stigma; we are *terrified* of dying. Many of us have philosophical backgrounds that have convinced us that we somehow survive after death—whether it be in the bardo states or in some other world. Yet, as we get into our thirties, forties, and fifties—I think it runs in ten-year cycles—we start to see that the "Divine Path of Growing Old"[42] is true. We might live to be a hundred and twenty, but we still age. When we're young we don't get to confront death that often. Maybe we're driving along the highway in the winter and we hit an ice patch, and the car spins around and we get a few seconds to confront the imminence of death. Or we get the intuition that there is something right over our left shoulder, by our ear, and we start to feel a little uneasy. We turn quickly to see what it is, but it's immediately out of sight. We have a momentary flash of panic, but we recover and reason with ourselves, "What a silly thing! There's nothing there; it was just my imagination." As we go through life, every once in a while, we are confronted with the absolute dread, the terror, of death.

Of course, what we are really afraid of is not surviving. Death as we know it indicates non-survival to us—even if we have a philosophy of karma, or the collective unconscious, and we think we are a drop of the ocean and that, when we die, we fall back into the ocean…and all of

---

42 Reference to Lee's essay that appeared in the book, *Laughter of the Stones*, in which he wryly observes that, as we approach our death, completion of the Divine Path is assured and we are inevitably led to that which is alluded to in the greatest spiritual traditions: Life As It Is.

that jazz. That kind of philosophy doesn't hold up to what we are always being presented with in our lives. You see your family dropping like flies from the most horrendous forms of cancer. Friends from high school have been killed in car accidents, or mugged and stabbed to death in the city. Some have even died in war. As we are confronted with death all around us we say, "Boy, I hope I live to a nice ripe old age and just go in my sleep. I don't want to be sick. One day my time will be done, and I'll lie down and just not wake up in the morning. That would be really nice."

If you are in spiritual life like we all are (we are in spiritual life, aren't we?) you might have the fantasy of a somewhat more spectacular death, like leaving in a flash of transcendental white light one day while you are in the midst of a group of admiring fellow students. Or making your poor old guru proud of you by translating into the all-pervading divine light in the middle of satsang. Boom, you are gone. What a blissful way to go. Or we imagine ourselves becoming great yogis. We go into meditation and our body just stays warm. No rigor mortis sets in, but we are dead. We have no heartbeat or brainwaves. That would be a nice way to go, leaving our body warm and fresh and our cheeks rosy. In that way we would survive but not survive. Even though we have consoling fantasies, we are terrified of dying—plain and simple. We panic whenever we experience even a hint of confrontation with death.

We have the good fortune not to live in an environment in which we are always being threatened with the possibility of death through natural catastrophe. If we were to live in certain areas of the world where there are hurricanes, tidal waves, tornadoes, earthquakes, and flash floods, we could get up in the morning to find a fifty-foot-high wall of water coming at us down the valley. We don't live in a physical environment where things like that happen, yet we are still regularly confronted with the fear of death. Sometimes we hear about a catastrophe—an earthquake in Guatemala, a tornado in Texas—and we get a sympathetic shiver. There is a kind of telepathic race consciousness that some of us are more sensitive to. We can imagine ourselves being there and we think, "Oh man, that must have been awful!"

We Paradoxically Court Death Every Day

The interesting thing about all this is that every single day of our lives we go about courting death—willfully, consciously, and with a purpose that is almost vengeful. We not only court death very clearly and directly, but we literally invite it with open arms—all the while terrified every moment of death. Some of us court death in an obvious fashion. We race cars, play football, and go hunting without wearing our red caps and jackets—which is one of the surest ways to court death or at least be horribly maimed, crippled or worse. Others go fishing and simply take the chance of being at the mercy of somebody that doesn't know how to fly-cast well. Then there are those who engage in more risky forms of activity like mountain-climbing, ski-jumping, tobogganing, or hang-gliding—all of which are very fine ways of courting death. We are begging for punishment of a physical form. We are literally encouraging the extinction of our existence, "dying to get into the graveyard" as they say.

People out in the world are killing themselves, just as sure as we are sitting here, through all the addictive habits that they have. Not only through addictive physical habits (smoking, alcohol, use of drugs), but addictive emotional habits like anger, jealousy, vindictiveness, and vanity. For the average slob, all of these things cut their lives in half just as sure as the Pope is Catholic. Most of us, of course, court death in less dramatic forms. Because we are spiritual students, our form of courting death is very sophisticated. We eat the right foods and we exercise and it's very important that our bodies are healthy. We get high colonics, and God knows what other kinds of torture, all in the name of being healthy and extending our longevity. Yet even *we* court death in subtle ways.

Spiritual students tend to court death through emotional channels like competitiveness or by lying to themselves: "I can't help myself. I tried, but I can't help myself!" We court death through the tension created by swearing allegiance to the Godman and then not listening to what he says… The crime of this whole thing is that you all probably work harder than ninety percent of the world, but you don't *work*. So even though in a relative sense you are really working hard, I don't buy it—and I think you don't buy it either. The tension between not working and the face you are presenting [your stated commitment] is sure death.

You might ask, "Why is it that we literally court death?" (I knew somebody would ask why!) Death is the thing that we are most terrified of, and it is the thing that we go about actively preparing ourselves for probably from the time we are four or five years old. I remember my mother telling me that when I was two years old, I was skipping along having a wonderful time with my parents and just ran out in the street for no reason. I wasn't looking on the other side of the street to see what was there. Out of nowhere I just ran out in the road. There was a big Cadillac burning down the street and the driver screeched his brakes on and stopped with the front of the car just touching me. It was that close. When he got out of the car, the poor driver was shaking. My mother picked me up, took me home and said, "Don't you ever do that again!" She was really freaked out.

Children are not that sophisticated. When they want to go, they just go. They jump off the house, run in front of a car, or jump in the water. There is no neurosis surrounding it, no fear involved. Who knows why they want to go? There are all kinds of reasons. Children who are one, two, and three years old are still connected to intuition. Where are they going anyway? Children don't think in terms of extinction. But we do. Adults think that when we die, we're going to be extinct. We don't think in terms of the race. Every self-meditative individual thinks they *are* the race. On a subconscious level, ego makes us think that we are so important that our death should be avoided at all costs. People court death but paradoxically (or is it "occidentally" because we're in the West?) have a phenomenal will to live.

Basically, we are convinced that death is extinction. Even if philosophically we are convinced that we survive somewhere, or become angels, or lead a good life and go to heaven, when it comes down to the actual fact of dying, we think in terms of extinction. On one level we are terrified of death and on another level we encourage it. And we frequently *do* encourage it. For instance, people are always not paying attention when they drive. I used to go out disco-dancing even when there was three feet of snow on the ground. Hot nights were Tuesdays, Thursdays, and Sundays. When it was Tuesday, Thursday, or Sunday it didn't matter what was going on outside—electrical storms, hurricanes. Actually, I was intuitively trying to find the bardo, but the closest thing I could find were the bars. They had bands that sounded like the music you get in the bardo anyway.

Why is it that we encourage death all the time, even while we are terrified of it? It is sort of basic stuff, but sometimes we need to hear basic stuff over and over until we realize how basic it is. Ego knows that there is no such thing as non-survival, but the point at which it knows that is the exact tangent between the primacy of God (or the natural divine expression of the Will of God) and separation. There is only one tangent point between the primacy of God and separation, and ego is on both sides of the line. Ego is within either circle. At that one perfect tangent point, ego knows that non-survival is ridiculous, that there is no such thing as non-survival, that non-survival is in fact survival. But outside of that tangent point it's all about survival.

The Pull to Survive Keeps Us Separate from God

Ego is literally functioning as if it could become extinct at any moment. Since the evolutionary pull—it is not really a push it is a pull—of every species and every form and spectrum of existence is to survive, ego is in the same circumstance. Its pull is to survive. But that very pull to survive is the thing that keeps the human being separate from God. That very tendency that says you could die at any moment and be extinct, that you must survive at all costs, is itself the thing that keeps us from realizing that survival is not at issue. What happens is that a part of our essence knows that the only way that we are ever going to be minimally at ease, the only way that we are going to be able to play a little bit, instead of being heavy about everything (including our moments of happiness), is to realize that survival is not at issue. We are so heavy about even our moments of happiness. "I thought if I could be happy, things would be fine. Here I am, happy, but I am so heavy about it." If happiness is like carrying the weight of the world on your shoulders, imagine what it feels like if you are not happy!

We have to know that there is only God. The part of us that knows that survival is not at issue is constantly encouraging us to die. It figures that if you die and you are still alive, then you'll get it. We haven't yet. We have died lots of times and found ourselves still alive. We have been born again and died again over and over and we still haven't gotten it. Intuitively, we know that if we could just figure out that survival is not at issue, we could be a little easy with ourselves. You know, we are not easy. It's a shame we are not easy. We should be. If we die and realize we haven't died—wherever we are—we could be a little easy. Ego on the other hand, thinking that death is extinction, does everything in its power to avoid dying. So we have the tendency of ego trying to avoid death, and the tendency of the intuitive side of us trying to create death to convince us that it's okay.

Certainly this intuitive side isn't trying to create awakening. How could it possibly do that if there isn't such thing? We are already perfectly identified with whatever is arising. If what's arising is that we are asleep, that is what we are perfectly identified with. That in itself is enlightenment. We are not being pulled to wake up, because we can't wake up. The intuitive tendency that is trying to get us to die knows that to wake up is absurd, that there is no such thing as waking up. Enlightenment is whatever happens to be arising. If that is unconsciousness, we are enlightened in our unconsciousness. A change of state from being asleep to being awake is absurd.

The Intuitive Pull to Die Within the Dream

The intuition that is pulling us to die is perfectly non-dualistic. What it is doing is pulling us to create circumstances within the dream to get us to turn towards God; it is not trying to get us to break out of the dream because the dream itself is enlightenment. Perfect identification with whatever is arising in the dream itself is enlightenment. So, we can't wake up out of the dream in that sense. The intuition is not trying to have us see God. What an absurd thing. How can we see God? God is perfectly obvious to this intuition. It is just what is going on in any given moment.

There is an intuitive pull to die within the dream so that we see that survival is not an issue, to simply get us to be a little easy, a little light; to get us to be a little happy, a little pleasurable. It is not to wake us up. When we talked about enlightenment the first three years of the Community—God, what a mistake. Being somewhat naive and new at this business, I didn't know. Now we all want to wake up, and that is not the game. The intuitive pull is just to lighten up a little bit, just to be a little happy, a little at ease. Just to rest a little bit. We don't rest. We are constantly tense. It doesn't matter what our bodies do, we are tense. We are tense all the time because we are guarding our treasures: the family jewels, our precious little personalities, our precious college degrees, those of us that have them. We are constantly protecting our tenure in one way or another and we are tense.

This intuitive pull is simply to get us to be a little bit at ease in the dream—just to get us to rest, to relax for a few moments. It is not to get us to wake up, become enlightened, fall into God or satori or samadhi.

It's none of that. Whatever you are doing right now is your satori. If you don't dig it, then you think satori is something else. But satori is whatever you are doing right now. If it is inherently miserable, that is your satori. If you are in rapture, that's your satori. Satori is satori. It's whatever is going on. The pull within the dream is to get us to be a little bit at ease within the dream, so we can play. We can't play. We are too busy being jealous, protective, staking out our territory, breaking things and hoping nobody will find out. We can't play. We can't enjoy one another. I am able to enjoy you maybe that much [*Lee indicates a tiny amount*] because there is so much tension. And I enjoy you more than anybody else possibly could. I am working at five-percent capacity, which is agonizing, annoying, and really frustrating.

You don't have to die to see this pull to die. What I am supposed to do is get you to see it without you having to die. Talk about movement within the dream! I am supposed to get you to see that you can be a little bit light, a little easeful. You can love a little bit, you can rest a little, you don't have to die. It's okay. You can play, in the dream. There is no "you" to be enlightened; enlightenment is whatever is arising. This is samadhi. This—right here and right now—*is* samadhi. Basically, we need to recognize the crisis within us. We need to recognize that dichotomy [the pull to die and to survive], to see that contradiction, so that we can recognize that both of those powerful evolutionary tendencies are illusory; neither one is necessary. They both exert an incredible amount of force on our being, but they are both unnecessary. They are not *irrelevant*, they are simply unnecessary. They are very relevant—we are suffering, we are in pain so they are relevant—just completely unnecessary. If we can see that they are unnecessary, we can gradually begin to have a little bit of ease.

I was so naïve when the Community started. I just figured I would tell you the truth and it would be so tacitly obvious that we would be "the Joyous Community"—a hundred fools awakened to God having a good old time. I was *so* naive. Since then I have read the traditional spiritual literature (Christian, Hindu, Jewish, Buddhist, Zoroastrian, Muslim) and all of the traditional literature has said that what I used to call "waking up" is just the beginning. When you realize that there is only God, that's when you start. I thought that was the end. I thought I was done. Talk about naive!

When We Are Easeful, We Can Get Off the Wheel

We need to be able to look with clarity at our state of existence so that we can see these two conflicting tendencies in the play of the worlds. So that we can see that we are machines. We run here, we try to die; we run there, we try to survive. We run here and have some good sex and we say, "Oh, I am alive again!" We go out the next day and have three martinis for lunch and we say, "*Ha ha*, I am killing myself!" We go home that night and watch our six-foot TV and think, "*Ha ha*, I'm surviving!" Then we go to sleep and take our sleeping pills—"*Ha ha*, I'm dying!"

We've got to be able to see those tendencies, to see that every day when we walk into the house after busting our ass at work trying to win, the first thing we do is engage our family in a form of war that is deadly and life-negative. We spend all day trying to win and we come home and try to die. Every person you know does it.

If you come home alone and don't have a family to confront, you'll do it another way like going out to the singles bar to try and die. If we simply see the pull of those tendencies, we can be a little easy. That's the ballgame. The ballgame is being a little bit at ease; the ballgame is not waking up. The ballgame is just a little bit of rest. When we are easy then we can get off the wheel, right? When we are not easy, we are bound. When we are easy, we look at the wheel and say, "Oh, a wheel, I think I'll get off!" When we are not easy, that's impossible.

MOSES AND THE PROMISED LAND: A PARABLE REVEALED

(May 10, 1979)

The Opening of the Red Sea and Moses as a Bodhisattva

The parable of the Red Sea is about the surrender of life into the Promised Land. What happened when the Red Sea opened was that Moses and the gang crossed over. The sea closed up when the Pharaoh and his troops went in, and Moses and the gang stopped being pursued. The pursuers, of course, are all the tendencies and distractions that keep us from living God-life. But the Promised Land isn't right there once Moses gets through the Red Sea. He's still got a bit of a hike ahead of him. He's not being pursued anymore, but he's still got to get to the Promised Land.

Where do you think the Promised Land is? What do you suppose the parable of the opening of the Red Sea—so that Moses and the gang could go through to the Promised Land—has to do with? Nothing can stop water. We make buildings to resist earthquakes, but when a tidal wave hits, they are flattened anyway. Water in dreams is the movement and texture of our lives. That's standard dream symbology. We're born from the water of the womb. The parable of the opening of the Red Sea indicates the surrender of the irresistible power that is water—our lives, ego. When we surrender that, the Red Sea opens, and the Promised Land is there.

In the parable, Moses was the Godman and the people that were with him were his devotees. Reaching the Promised Land was not getting to a physical location. It was Moses translating his followers into his condition. You know what happened when they saw the land of milk and honey? Moses didn't go in; he stayed behind. Moses was a perfect *bodhisattva*.[43] He refused to enter *nirvana* until every sentient being had achieved enlightenment.

---

43 In the Buddhist tradition, the bodhisattva is one who refrains from entering nirvana in order to free all sentient beings from suffering.

Everyone Has to Enter the Promised Land Under Their Own Steam

Moses brought his people to the Promised Land, but they had to enter under their own steam. He said, "There it is. I'm not going." That's what the Godman does. He takes you to the Red Sea, stops the pursuers, obviates your tendencies through Grace and your sacrifice and devotion, and takes you right up to the Promised Land. It's up to you from there. The people who were with Moses were pissed off. They said, "Come on man! Our feet are covered with blisters. We're starving and there's no food. You're telling us about the land of milk and honey. Where is it?" Moses said simply, "I know it's there. God is telling me." They get to a mountain and Moses says, "I've got to go up this mountain, guys."

Moses goes up on the mountain and while he is up there, the people make a golden calf. They couldn't wait for the Promised Land. Moses came down from the mountain with a new teaching on tablets and he throws down the golden calf. The people say, "Give us a break, will you, Moe? We can't wait for a Promised Land. We've been waiting for too long." He finally convinces them and gets them to the Promised Land. He stays back and off they go.

First you wake up. First you melt into the heart. Then you've got to find the Promised Land, which is sacrifice. Moses sacrificed; he didn't go. The people went up to the top of a hill and there was the land of milk and honey. "You were right, you old so and so!" they shouted. Off they went, running down the hill, 'cause that land of milk and honey sure looked good. They were hot and thirsty after coming off the desert.

The Land of Milk and Honey

What does "the land of milk and honey" symbolize? Honey symbolizes *amrit*, nectar, which is produced in states of meditation when your [pituitary] gland secretes a particular fluid that's never secreted under any other circumstances. It's divine nectar that is secreted because of a high spiritual state. Milk is sexual fluid. Sexual fluid, when wasted and not used in a manner consistent with true tantra, simply expends your life [force]. Sexual fluid that is preserved and used in appropriate fashion is sustaining. There's amrit in the upper part of the body and sexual fluid in the lower part of the body. The two points form a circle of descending and ascending energy in the body. That's the land of milk and honey. But even though people love it, the higher principles of spirituality shouldn't really be talked about in the beginning. First, people have to become responsible. You've got to know how to wash the dishes before you worry about the land of milk and honey.

Bodily Surrender

The only thing that is inherently pleasurable—without tension, stress, motivation, or the need to sustain it—is the Law of Sacrifice. Whatever arises, including heartache and sorrow, is inherently pleasurable when it's because of the Law. Everything else dies. Everything else is sustained by tension—even the pleasure. You might think you are happy, but there's nothing but tension underneath it. Trying to be better and better, "every day in every way"[44] is not the Law. It might temporarily alleviate some minor problems, but you all know it's not the Law because many of you have tried it.

I admit that I can be a bit of a cut-up at times. But that's all a distraction. I just want to see whether you really get it when I'm being humorous, whether you're using what's going on beneath the surface. When you see what's going on beneath the surface, then we can just laugh and enjoy one another all the time. But we can become so serious when we get into God-life. We tend to restrict the movement of shakti instead of just laughing and not worrying about who's around. We tend

[44] This is a reference to a positive aphorism used in the Silva Method, which Lee formerly taught, for re-programming one's way of thinking.

to shut it off because we're a little embarrassed about it. Why not just enjoy yourself, let go and give in to it?

One time, a group of us got a whole Chinese restaurant laughing. None of us knew what we were laughing at, but we got into it and pretty soon everybody in the place was laughing. Cooks came in from the kitchen. They didn't know what was going on, but they started laughing along with everybody. When you SURRENDER to laughter—your gut, lungs, throat, arms and head—everybody starts laughing. They don't even know what's so funny, but people are rolling on the ground.

The same thing applies when you are moved by bhakti. When you realize how much you are in love with God or the guru, you're so thankful that you want to cry. But you worry that, if you were to surrender to it completely in the grocery store with a cart full of food, you would lose control. You wouldn't. The same thing would happen that happened in the restaurant with everybody laughing. If you were to surrender to being moved by bhakti, everybody around you would light up. *The whole supermarket* would light up. But we don't surrender because we worry about our reputation or peeing in our pants. We worry about all kinds of things.

Reputation

Editor's Note: *Lee speaks to his students about relationship with the human form of the guru and about the transformative possibility of trusting a true guru to create circumstances in which to work with the illusion of reputation and with whatever is needed in our process over time. As was often the case, Lee introduces his point in a lively and unexpected way.*

You have to be willing to put your reputation in my hands—not in Lee's hands. Lee's not responsible at all. He just wants to be left alone to read spiritual books and to meditate. Lee wants to go to the movies, gorge himself on delicious gourmet food, and ride his motorcycle. He doesn't want to be responsible for anybody else.

Actually, Lee is as responsible as hell for a man. Most men make Lee look like "Mr. Responsible." If women would only get that men are irresponsible before they coupled up, it would solve ninety percent of the problems in the world. The way life is these days, women are men. They find a man and say, "Be a man." But you can't be a man and tell your man to be a man. Your man wants to be woman anyway. Do you know how many men would give their right arm if their wives would get on top once and let them lie there and be passive instead of having to hump away like a goddamn bull? I'm not kidding. Ninety percent of America's problems are because women are men and men are women. You think God-life is impossible. God-life is a breeze compared to asking some of these guys to be men.

I can't help being responsible. It's not a matter of legal, moral, ethical or physical responsibility, or of being a hero. It is an absolute divine responsibility, and I have no choice about that. I'm asking you to put all the responsibility in my hands because partial responsibility does one thing and total responsibility relieves me of any of it. When you fulfill God-life and surrender, then you take on a portion of my responsibility for everybody. That sounds awful for the seeker. I mean, you don't want to do that. You're struggling just to have a little peace of mind. I embarrass the hell out of myself because I don't care what people think of me. It's one of the best ways I have of working with you, but I can't use that because you haven't entrusted your reputations to me. I've got real talents in certain areas and I can't use them. You're the ones that are going to make the teaching available. If you don't allow me to be responsible for your reputation, we'll end up with nothing happening—except some fabulous books. When you entrust your reputation to me, I will be so outrageous you will not be able to do anything but laugh. You will not be crippled with embarrassment and shame. You'll say, "God, why didn't I do this before?"

There are two stages: first you entrust your reputations to me, then you entrust the Community's reputation to me. And in your hearts, make your time with me sanctuary. Sanctuary for you is having your relationship to me be as reverent as you understand it should be. You have to create that. I can't do anything about it. Not only can I not do anything about it, but once in awhile in a really profoundly devotional moment I'll blow the whole thing just to give you the idea that you need to be stronger about it. I'll take a mood that is just overwhelming me with its love and crush it by making everybody laugh about farts and screwing. I can't let myself say, "God, you know, it's *working*." Because if I let myself say that, I'm dead in the water. Because it is working, and it isn't. I will do you a disservice if I leave you half-cooked, half-tempered.

Becoming a Tempered Sword

You know the analogy of the tempering of a sword. There are swords made in China that are two thousand years old and still so sharp and perfect that they could cut down a tree with one swing. Imagine if a warrior went into battle with a sword that had been taken out of the blacksmith's forge half-tempered. He would come up against an enemy and have his sword crack in half against the enemy's sword. You are the sword in this analogy. God is wielding you. If you are half-tempered when you go into battle and crack in half when God's life depends upon you, God will not be pleased.

I'm the sword master. I'm the one that knows when that sword is done. If I take you out before you're done, I'm committing spiritual suicide. So, I can't take you out before you are done. I'd like to, I really would. I'm always being moved by those moments when the Community is so devoted. You are always moving me to say the sword is done. But I know the sword isn't done. If I take the sword out before it's tempered, God is going to get into a fight and not have a proper sword. We have to keep working until the work is done.

ONE MOMENT IS THE GUARANTEE OF IMMORTALITY

(May 31, 1979)

The Innumerable Benefits of Honoring the Three Treasures

There is a story of a drunk who staggered into the Buddha's monastery, fell down in front of him and said, "I want to be a monk." Buddha had the man's hair shaved off, gave him an orange robe, and set him up with the other monks. After a couple of hours, the man got sober, looked at his robe and felt his head and said, "My God, what have I done?" He tore off the robe and ran away.

Buddha's disciples were confused, as disciples tend to be when the master does something that should be clearly obvious. They said, "The guy was drunk and didn't know what he was doing. You are the Tathagata, the all-knower. You knew that when he got sober he was going to regret his decision. It seems like you were prostituting the work and the priesthood."

Buddha said, "There are three treasures: the Buddha, the dharma and the sangha—the teacher, the teaching, and the order of monks. These three jewels are the most important aspects of spiritual life. The drunk knew to come to me and to fall at my feet—as drunk as he was—and ask permission to become a monk. In that sense, he honored the Buddha—one of the three jewels. He was drunk, but in his drunkenness, he realized that becoming a monk was a departure from the way he had always lived and that there were rules and regulations that being a monk entailed. While he was drunk, he honored the rules and so honored the dharma. He became a monk for a couple of hours. It was not very long, but in his drunkenness he agreed to have his head shaved and to don the saffron robe of a Buddhist practitioner. So, he honored the sangha, the community of devotees. Even though he sobered up and didn't like what he had done and ran away, the fact that he honored the Buddha, the dharma, and the sangha for two hours will bring him innumerable benefits in lifetimes to come."

To further illustrate the fact that the drunken man earned a future lifetime of blessings by honoring the three jewels—even if only for a matter of hours—Buddha told the story of one of the first nuns in his community. She was a very wealthy woman who left her family and her riches to become a nun. The monks used to teach the men, and the nuns would teach the women. This nun would go around to all the families of high society and talk to the women about becoming nuns. And the women would say, "Oh, but we are young and beautiful. We are not going to become nuns. We are hot and lusty. We are married, or we want to be married. We couldn't possibly follow the precepts." The nun would reply, "Oh, just put on a nun's robe and give it a try. Sit at the feet of the Buddha." They wondered why she was so insistent. "You know that we are going to break the rules," they said, "so why are you still asking us to become nuns, even if it is only for a day or a week?"

She said, "In one of my past lives I was a prostitute. I earned my living using sex and crude language to entertain men. Once, in the midst of a drunken party, one of the men brought in the stolen robe of a nun. While we were all laughing and drinking, the man said, 'Hey, let me see what you look like with this on.' I put on the robe of a nun and we laughed and ridiculed the religion of the nun from whom this robe was stolen. But because I put on the robe of a nun of the Buddha, the living God—even for a few minutes in jest, even to ridicule what it meant—I was born in my next lifetime as a devotee. It doesn't matter if you are young and lusty and don't think you will keep the precepts. Put on the robe. Come and learn about the Law."

We tend to question either the strictness or the laxity of the guru's ideas and requests in relationship to people that approach the Community. We are impatient and imagine we are going to be damned if we don't surrender to God this lifetime. We don't want to wait another two hundred lifetimes. But perhaps the only reason we are here is because three thousand years ago we met someone who was in the company of a genuine teacher. Maybe we went to a meeting with him just for fun and sat and listened. Maybe that is why we are here.

We need to be understanding about the fact that, even if we see the need to do spiritual work and not continue to suffer lifetime after lifetime, other people don't. In one sense, who isn't drunk that approaches the Community? Who approaches the Community with clarity, understanding, and strength? Nobody does; everybody is drunk. But the fact that we approach honors the Buddha. The fact we read a book or two and are willing to consider the ideas is honoring the dharma. The fact that we are willing, even for one night, to indulge the company of devotees is honoring the sangha. If someone approaches and is blessed with even an hour's worth of our hospitality, who knows what it could mean next lifetime or a hundred lifetimes from now?

Relationship to the Master Is Not a Temporal Affair

Of course, the question then arises about how much to give and how open to become to others who approach. We can understand that this lifetime is simply a blink of an eye, that the relationship and communion with the spiritual master is not a temporal affair in truth. Dualistically speaking, sensually speaking, of course it is a temporal affair. But the real happiness of our situation and the real bliss of God is in the recognition that it is not a temporal event. Yes, we share friendship and laughter together, but the texture underlying all that arises between us—pleasant and unpleasant—is not a temporal affair.

If we realize that, it gives us an entirely different approach to people that come to the Community. It's not that we give everybody free rein to come and go as they please and do whatever they want. That is not the point. The point is in recognizing what the approach is founded on, in what it can mean, and in giving people a chance. It is said that just a piece of the robe of a monk worn on your body—even as a patch on another piece of clothing—brings the blessing of the Buddha which can open the door to the heavens for a person.

Buddhist cosmology is very clear in terms of the atemporal nature of the real connection between the Buddha, the dharma, and the sangha. The Buddha is the dharma and the Buddha is the sangha. But because we are bodhisattvas and not Buddhas, we approach as if the Buddha is the Buddha, the dharma is the dharma that we have to study and learn, and the sangha is the company of friends surrounding the Buddha. But in fact, Buddha-mind, as they call it in Zen, is the sangha. Buddha-mind is not what the sangha is trying to attain through living with the Buddha. The work itself is Buddha-mind. The sangha itself is Buddha-mind. Sadhana—not the attainment or the perfection or the completion of sadhana—is enlightenment. The fact that you are working spiritually in the company of the Godman is Buddha-mind—not the fact that you believe you are suffering and think that working with the Godman will alleviate, eliminate, or remedy that suffering. That is an illusion. It is an unfortunate illusion that we fall prey to all the time, but it is still an illusion.

The fact of doing sadhana *is* Buddha-mind. Of course, *not* doing sadhana is Buddha-mind also. We can live as successful Buddhas or as failed Buddhas. We are Buddhas either way. Failed Buddhas are the ones that don't realize that sadhana is the only appropriate thing to do. Successful Buddhas are the Buddhas that are doing sadhana. A little bit of sadhana and we can be successful Buddhas a little bit; a lot of sadhana and we can be very successful Buddhas. We can be like Shakyamuni Buddha that everybody has heard of, or we can be like all the other Buddhas that nobody has ever heard of.

So, when people approach, we need to pay attention to the honor with which they approach. We also need to pay attention to whether they are following or breaking the precepts of our company. If they are going to live in the sangha and honor the sangha, they need to honor the precepts, the Law. We grant them hospitality and honor when they approach with respect. If the precepts are broken the minute they "sober up," don't invalidate the prior hospitality. Don't say, "Man, I never should have trusted them!" Because why shouldn't you have? When you trusted them, you should have trusted them.

We will not let people take advantage when their approach is dishonorable. But when their approach is honorable, we'll give them another chance—even two or three chances. But, when people come for their second or third chance, the precepts get harder. "When you first wanted to be a monk, it was simply a matter of shaving your head and wearing a robe. But now that the order has been around for a number of years there are more requirements besides shaving your head and wearing a robe." People are always given the benefit of the doubt.

The important thing is to realize the atemporal nature of the affair. We may have a certain heartfelt response to being in the company of the guru, to doing sadhana in the company of devotees, but we need to realize that a heartfelt response might not be present in others. We need to realize more and more what a tremendous blessing it is just for people to be in the Community for even a week for two. When someone decides to leave, ruthless compassion is letting them leave. We know they are going to suffer. We also know that next lifetime they are going to be incredibly benefited just by having been here a week.

Possibility Does Not Equate with Capacity

Conventional compassion is not allowing people their drunkenness. It is treating adults as children, not allowing people to have the strength to make their own decisions. Conventional compassion is being so involved in wanting people to get what it is we are doing that we don't allow them the space to make their own decisions. We can be like a lot of cults that do that if we want to behaviorally modify people, if we want to become just another conventional training ground for people who want to better themselves. But in a genuine tradition that offers Truth, people are allowed to come and go as they please.

Who is it that has allowed ego to propagate the illusion? God, of course. You think ego is doing all of this outside of God's power and Influence? Ego isn't creating the fact that all life is suffering independent of the Influence of God. God's Influence is inclusive. God is compassionate and is allowing his creation to do as it will. That we have become this way to begin with is simply through God's strength of character. If God didn't have as much strength of character, he wouldn't let us make mistakes—even deadly mistakes. Look at your own personal situations. You are not here because other people have convinced you to stay or because of what they have gotten from me. You are here because you have the strength and the insight to be here.

Maybe other people make your life here a little easier or a little harder at times, but basically you are standing on your own personal strength. You are standing on your own feet, with your own intelligence and your own clarity of knowledge. That is why you are here. We need to allow other people to do that. The people who have the capacity for superficial work will do superficial work and burn out after a while. But if that is their capacity, we need to make that available to them. That is why we don't need to do public work in a sense. We don't need to advertise satsang. Anybody can find us. We are not a secret school; we are not hidden. If anybody is the least bit drawn to spiritual work, they will find us. We simply need to make available the space for people to express their capacity.

Obviously, everyone has the same possibility, but there is a difference between having the same possibility and the same capacity. Anyone can walk in here and have Gift showered upon them and wake up tomorrow. Of course, that can happen; a fluke is always possible. But the possibility of real sadhana or discipleship does not equate with the capacity to accomplish that. It is not that someone with a highly refined and sophisticated education has a greater capacity to live spiritual life.

The two do not necessarily equate. Why can't people that are so brilliant see the obvious? There are a million levels, a million "I's"[45] functioning in this mind-body.

Who are we to say what somebody's capacity is? We have no idea what somebody's capacity in the Work is. We couldn't map one single psyche if we had a lifetime to work on it. The most we can do is map the gross areas of consciousness. But to be able to map someone's capacity for spiritual work is impossible. The fact that some of us are still here after four years is really improbable. Yet, here we are. We can't map someone's capacity. We can simply make available this environment in which people's capacities will be taken to the limit.

The presence of the Godman offers the possibility that everyone can realize that there is only God. We are all of one substance. Infinity is one thing that the Godman's presence offers—the possibility for all of us to realize our inherent Buddha nature, that we are already enlightened to begin with, that there is nothing to be attained. The second thing the presence of the Godman offers is taking your capacity to the limit. Karmically speaking, you can't do better than that. Whatever anyone's spiritual capacity is, it will be fulfilled here.

We need to begin to see the bigger picture, the principle. Form has to do with form, principle has to do with principle. If we see the principle of capacity, we will be a little gentler with people and recognize when someone has reached their capacity. How do we know when someone's capacity has been reached? We don't know. God knows. God will take care of it if we get out of the way. There is no such thing as an accident. Even when birth control is used, a child can be conceived against all odds. If God wants somebody here, that somebody is going to get here—like it or not. We need to recognize the principle that we

---

45 Observing the multiple "I's" or aspects of ourselves that manifest in different situations and in mechanical ways, and the lack of a "Real I" that is stable and unified, is part of Gurdjieff's teaching.

don't know when somebody has fulfilled their capacity. We have no idea in the world...but we think we do.

We tend to give people way more than they need. Give them whatever they need in the moment, but don't offer somebody the world if all they want is two-and-a-half acres in Nebraska. We are always giving people more than what is necessary in the moment. Simply give them their appropriate due. When you give somebody a break once, they always want it again. When I was in the stamp business, once a customer got me to go down on my price, they would bargain every time—I mean *every* time. Of course, I would simply raise my prices, give them their "bargain," and get the price I wanted anyway. People will take and take. It's not because they are vindictive; it's just ego's nature. So give people an appropriate response—openly, clearly and hospitably—but no more. Don't trust them; nobody is trustworthy when they are being moved by ego and not by God.

CHILDREN

(October 1979)

Change Due to Spiritual Influence

Most of my students have seen a form of change in their spiritual sadhana that is very different than the conventional form of change. That change is so different from the conventional change you can hold onto, which you still tend to look for as assurance that your spiritual work is going as it should. Yet most of you don't need conventional kinds of changes because you've seen enough really dramatic movement in your life. It's not the kind of thing where you were totally shy and suddenly you're bubbly and you can relate to everybody, but a certain real, absolutely tangible inner change has occurred. That's infinitely more important than any of the conventional changes we look for.

Being a better mommy, a better daddy, or a better friend are the kinds of changes that come naturally over time as a result of this Influence. And regardless of spiritual life or Divine Influence, you just see things differently as you get older and have more experience—unless you're a complete stone and that's not the case for any of you. That's the Divine Path of Growing Old. It's not some great Grace from God. You just happen to be a little more mellow. You've watched children grow up, you've seen more of the world, you've had thirty years of conscious living. Things look different.

Children Expose Unexamined Expectations

Children are great at exposing our unexamined expectations. It's clear that most women have very definite ideas about how they're going to bring up their little darlings. Most men do not and would not know what a kid wanted or needed anyway. Men want little boys who will grow up to be football or basketball stars, if they're tall enough. But they don't want their sons to ever really be independent; they don't want their sons to be true.

Have you ever seen how all kids do the same things? When they get embarrassed in a store, every two-year-old will run behind mommy's or daddy's legs. They hide their head, and then look out and hide their head again. But children don't have to do that. Most children have that shyness or fear of strangers because that's the vibe they grow up around. All kids aren't like that. Some kids are really outgoing and expressive; they're not scared or embarrassed. Parents who have children like that go through all kinds of numbers because we want our children to love and rely on us exclusively. If you're a daddy and your child falls down and skins their knee, when you run over and pick them up to comfort them they don't want anything to do with you. They want mommy. They struggle out of your arms and run into the house screaming, "Mommy, Mommy! I hurt my knee!" Daddy is left standing there thinking, "I've spent my life with this three-year-old and they won't let me comfort them!"

Pink booties for girls and blue booties for boys have nothing to do with children. It's all a matter of territory. It's true that babies are cute, adorable, lovable, and open, and that they do and say the most priceless things that we will remember all our lives. But they grow up, and if you want them to grow up and still be warm and loving and cute then you have to begin now.

What We Teach Children

In popular cartoons, we always see the Elmer Fudd character being made a total fool of and the heroes—Bugs Bunny and Daffy Duck—pounding on some poor unfortunate fool who's always getting the shit end of the stick. Boy, do we identify with that. We love it. If you are a baby, born from a nice warm womb into a bright hospital room, who gets smacked on the ass and has silver nitrate thrown in your eyes, you feel like the world is intruding upon you and trying to kill you. Harmless little ways of releasing that energy come out of that feeling—like Daffy Duck, Porky Pig, and Bugs Bunny cartoons. And we always want to be the hero. Those things arise innocently out of an intuition of what life is doing to us.

It's amazing what we offer as examples to our kids. We teach them to be cunning—literally. When I was five or six years old, if I didn't want to go to a party, we would call up and say I was sick. I never had to take my own consequences. We have to be very careful not to teach our children to get away with things using physical charm and cunning. (Those two are deadly.) It's not the way to be with children. Once I had a job helping teach third grade in Newark at an alternative public school. There was one little kid who was totally wild. He got in a big fight one day and one of the teachers disciplined him. His mother happened to be there—she was on the board of directors of the school—and she said to her son, "Don't listen to the teacher. Come here, baby." She hugged and kissed him and that was it. There was no discipline the teacher could use on that child as long as the mother was going to undermine it. The teachers there were always frustrated because the children really responded to discipline, but when the parents invalidated it, like this mother did, it made the kids wild. They went crazy because the boundaries were unclear.

We teach kids those kinds of values. That kid probably grew up to be the toughest kid on the block. As long as he's the toughest kid on the block, there is nothing he won't do—even when he gets to be thirty years old. It won't mean a thing to him to wreck cars and do whatever else he does. So, we have to be very careful not to instill a sense of cunning in our children. It's amazing how many parents don't care if their kids copy off of other kids' papers. One father I know of actually does all his daughter's homework. She hands it in with his handwriting. When the teacher asks, "Did you write this?" the daughter says, "Yes." It's perfectly obvious she didn't do it. We teach our children to be con artists. It's amazing how widespread this is. I assume that you all have some sense of integrity and that you wouldn't do that. But you're really in a small minority. The time to start is when children are young, when they will listen to you. Bring them up right when they're little and they will be okay. They'll still fight you when they get to be teenagers, but they'll remember what they learned.

This brings back a childhood memory from when I was eleven or twelve. Growing up, in my house my parents spoke politely and clearly; they never cursed. Not "hell" or "damn" or even "darn." So I didn't curse either. I knew the words, but they weren't a part of my language. I was riding in the car one day with my mother and father. My mother was driving because my father didn't drive. (He was quite a visionary. If he got an idea, he'd have to pursue that idea to its end regardless of what else he was doing at the time, so it was best that he didn't drive.) My mother was behind the wheel of the car and I was singing and talking with her, and all of a sudden another driver cut her off. She slammed on the brakes and let loose a stream of profanity. I looked at her in shock. And she realized that she had never said a curse word in front of me for eleven years. (God, what control! We need devotees with discipline like that.) She got this look of, "You caught me," on her face. She smiled and looked away.

I think I'll remember that moment for the next thousand years. There are maybe ten things when I was growing up that struck me with the force of a lightning bolt. That was one of them. My mother was only trying to bring me up a certain way. She wasn't a hypocrite. At eleven years old I felt, as all eleven-year-olds do, that whatever was good for adults was good for me. I can trace the beginning of my being very loose with my language from that day. It's amazing how things like that stick. I can relive that moment anytime I want because it struck such a chord in me. At the time I just shrugged it off.

Children Still Have a Sense of Fantasy

Your spiritual life today is exactly like your lives as children. The only difference is that now you have the strength, will, and intelligence to be different. When I was maybe five or six years old, I had a fear that if I slept with my head out from under the covers, a tiger would eat my head. For a year I would get in the bed and pull the covers up over my head when the lights were turned out. Even at that age I knew it was absurd. I knew very clearly in my own little mind that without a doubt there was no tiger there and that no tiger was going to come and eat me. I knew for an absolute fact that I would wake up fine the next morning, with no teeth marks, if I slept with my head outside the covers. Despite the fact that I absolutely knew that, I kept pulling the covers over my head every night.

That's what we do in spiritual life. The difference, as adults, is that we don't have to pull the covers over our heads. Children still do, because children still have that sense of fantasy. They know there's no tiger there, but there might be. It's possible.

Adults don't have that sense of fantasy anymore. As adults, we're very grounded. We've had love affairs break up, businesses fail, gotten fired from jobs, and had our father die just when we needed him most. For adults, "What happens if I surrender?" is the tiger. But an adult can reason that out, be clear about it, and not cover their head. As an adult you have the will and the intelligence to be different. As you mature and realize that you're being different, you'll finally just be able to go to sleep without any tension.

Children don't get used to it. When you're five years old, you can go to sleep without covering your head for a year and still be scared every night and not get used to it. You've woken up, so far, every morning, and weren't eaten up, but you still cover your head. You still have that sense that there *could be* a tiger. You know there isn't a tiger, but covering your head relaxes you. We have to be different as adults. When you wake up in the morning and you realize it's okay, you start to be different in relation to that, instead of going for four years not covering your head but still thinking the tiger is going to get you every night. You're mature enough not to continue doing that.

Children Keep You Straight and Are Interested in Whatever Interests You

Most of the mothers in the Community wouldn't think of telling their child the story of Ramakrishna's life. They imagine that no little kid would be interested in that. But you'd be amazed at how enthusiastic four- and five-year-olds get about Hanuman, or Sita and Rama [characters in the *Ramayana*, one of the epic stories of ancient India]. Kids really love whatever stories they are told. They love stories about the saints. Children are interested in whatever turns you on. Anything you like, they like. They also love all of the fairy tales that teach them to be afraid, because those fairy tales have got hundreds of years of parenting tradition behind them and nothing is going to destroy that. Kids pick that up right out of the air.

Student: On the subject of reading to children about the lives of the saints, it doesn't seem like it would be enough to just substitute a book about Krishna for a Grimm's fairy tale because you'd still have to make Krishna more than just a story-book character.

Lee: The stories definitely need to be explained to children. The *Ramayana* requires clarification from an adult. But once the stories are explained, it becomes very clear to them. The best thing you can do is bring your child up on God, and by the time they're four they will be keeping *you* straight. It's fantastic. Besides being loving, warm, cute little things, children are the best reminding factors [a Gurdjieffian principle that refers to something that helps one to remember one's work] you can imagine. Certainly, when you tell children stories about the saints you have to put the stories in context. If you tell children a story about someone like Tukaram who just sang to God and then fell over in an ecstatic trance, it's great. When they ask questions, it may make us think about why we're not more turned to God.

Our Unconscious Assumptions about Children

I've been reflecting on how we give animals human qualities, feelings, and traits. We tell them what to do based on having given them those traits, as if they felt like we do. We do that with a lot of animals, especially ones that "talk"—like tiny birds. The way some people talk to those little lap dogs they carry around literally makes human beings out of them.

We do that with children too. We unconsciously make assumptions about children, as if they felt and thought and intellectualized as we do. If you ever watch kids, most of them love to get thrown in the air and get hung upside down; they think it's the greatest thing in the world (although I always hated being thrown around as a little kid). Daddies tend to treat their kids like footballs. They throw them around and up in the air. Mommies tend to assume that children don't like having that done to them, because they wouldn't like it at all if someone did that to them. So, we're always laying our trips on our children, which are nothing more than programming. We assume they think the way we think, and they don't. They're smarter than we think they are. The other day something happened with a child and her mother said, "Oh, she's just a baby." This mother is always saying her child is a bright, intelligent, and enthusiastic baby, but something in her doesn't give the child any credit at all.

There's tremendous resistance in adults to give children the credit they deserve because they don't talk and relate the way we do. That's really what is going on underneath. When babies cry and are upset, you can't sit them down like you would a fifteen-year-old, or even a five-year-old, and say, "Come on, what's the matter?" An older child can tell you what the matter is, but a one-year-old can't. Sometimes you feed a baby or change their diaper and it's okay, and sometimes it doesn't work. Sometimes they don't want that. Every once in a while, they're not satisfied no matter what you do. One of the important things in developing our ability to communicate to *anyone* is to allow whatever space is present to be the space that's present.

There's a subconscious approach to children that we really must deal with if we're going to have children that are sure of their humanity. Otherwise, they grow up with a tremendous feeling of not being anyone because we don't give them credit for being anyone. We don't relate heart-wise. We love our kids. They make us cry when we see them do something like take their first step. It's a gigantic move for that little lump of flesh. But we relate on a whole different level as adults.

When children are around, we want to make sure that we relate to them on the level that children relate on. We want to give them credit where credit is due. We're always making assumptions about babies based on our childhood training. We don't see that our training was nothing more than reactivity. We don't want to lay that same kind of reactivity on our child. We can't expect to do that perfectly, but we can minimize the negative effect we have. If you train children to think that shit stinks and you shouldn't pee in front of anybody, when they get to be nine, ten, or eleven, they'll have a thing about their bodies. If children are to develop an all-around healthy attitude, we need to not lay our trips on them. We've got to pay attention to the assumptions we make about children and beware of putting our reactive habit patterns on them.

You have to be very careful. If a child is sitting at the table and someone brings out pumpkin pie or some other food we don't like, and we go "Ugh," you can see how the child takes in that reaction. That's why children grow up with particular tastes. Some people won't eat anything without ketchup. It all how you are programmed. It's amazing how few adults will try a food they haven't had before. They wouldn't try eel or rattlesnake unless they were strapped in and having their skin peeled off.

There's obviously a consideration of safety. You're not going to let a child run into an open oven or stick their head in a microwave and turn it on. But often we're not just taking safety and objectivity into consideration; we're strictly reacting habitually. Give children credit where it's due and don't say they're "only children." They are, but you'd be surprised at how much they understand. We're surprised every time we get a glimpse of what they understand, but we still don't get it.

A child will try out a word and see what the reaction is. It gets cataloged. Children do a lot of experimentation. They have a tremendous volume of information in their little heads before they start speaking, but they don't start using it until they can mimic the adult gods and goddesses in their environment. If you only speak in full sentences in the presence of a child, they will start speaking in full sentences. If you're always giving them nonsense baby sounds and baby words, that's the way they learn to talk because they think they're supposed to talk that way. They don't know any better. They think they're supposed to do whatever you show them to do.

If you think children are not going to like a whole bunch of foods, that's exactly what they're going to do because they think they're supposed to do that. So, we want to give children credit where it's due and not lay our numbers on them—our sympathies, our habits, our this and our that. It's unbelievable how many parents will smoke in front of their child and say, "It's an awful habit. *My* child will never smoke." Have you ever seen a two-year-old walk around with a cigarette in their mouth pretending to smoke? At two years old they find the pack of cigarettes, pull one out, and put it in their mouth. They don't know about lighting it or smoking it, but if they see all the adults around them with cigarettes in their mouths, they think that's what they're supposed to do. Children just want to be a part of what's going on.

At The Farm [an intentional community founded by Stephen Gaskin in 1971, based on principles of nonviolence and respect for the earth] down in Tennessee, children are disciplined by being sent away from where it's happening. That's all. When the child is ready to take part in what's happening, they can come back. They get good real fast because they want to come back to where it's happening. Children want to be a part of what's going on, and they learn to be a part of it through mimicry. Because they don't know what it is to be a part of society, they learn from us. If we're being redundant and bitchy, cynical and complaining, that's exactly what our children are going to be. They're going to complain the same way we do as soon as they can talk. It's scary.

Make a Difference When They Are Young

Little kids want to take part in the environment, and we want to be sure to encourage that. If you let a child know what taking part in the environment means, they can take part at their level. There is a very real way that four-year-olds can be with adults in a social environment, but they have to learn what that is. They learn when they're little—when they're one, two, and three years old. When they're seven and eight, they don't learn anymore. When they're seven and eight they will listen to you because you're bigger and you can punish them, but they don't learn. They've already learned a long time ago.

If children are trained in a way that is appropriate, they remain a part of the family. But what happens in society is that families tend not to be families anymore. Watch what happens when you don't control your children anymore. As parents, we can train children to be picky and fussy. And they will be just like us, except we get to be the ones they are picky and fussy about. You want to pay attention to how you're being with kids. When a child is four, five, or six years old you can still make a difference. By the time they're nine or ten, the most you can do is change their act. They're already very well trained.

Children are so spontaneous with their feelings. It's very important to us that children like us, and we figure that something is really wrong if they don't. Sometimes we get so bound up with all the rules about how to be with children that we can't just hang out with a kid. Just be conscious of the principles of the relationship and do the best you can. What happens is that you find that you all have good kids. But that's not enough. The world is full of good kids, and it's still falling apart. Just having a good kid isn't enough. Something more is demanded in this age and time.

With children in India, 1979

BETTER TO BE HAPPY

(November 18, 1979)

Our Problems

We all have little dramas to varying degrees. One week it's our mother, the next week it's our child, then it's our housemate, our lover, or just indigestion. If you stop to pay attention to your life, there are troubles hourly, daily, weekly, and monthly. One day we have a bad knee, or we eat too much sugar, or there's a lot of pollution in the air, or we run into a traffic jam. Then there are weekly problems like conflicts with our housemates, whether we should we go to see this teacher or that one, and there's a really good movie playing but we're broke, and payday is not until next Friday. Then we have monthly dramas. We're watching our astrological chart and our biorhythms, our palms and tarot cards. And there are also longer-term problems like spiritual life, God-realization, "already-perfectly-present-non-dualist… *blah-blah-blah.*" There are all kinds of things that go on that disturb us. Then there are the miracles that happen, which are even more distracting. Someone gets enlightened for a week and knows the answers to all the koans, or someone gets healed overnight.

We have yearly problems too, called birthdays. We're one year older. When you're twenty-six you don't care if you're one year older; you like your birthdays. Your friends remember you, you get a few cards from people you haven't heard from in a year, you have a little party, you see your families. When you're thirty-five, unless you've totally ignored generations of programming stored in the very chemistry of your cells, you start to pay a lot of attention to your birthday. The yearly problems also include anniversaries and other people's birthdays that we have to remember, as well as Thanksgiving, Christmas, and every other God-forsaken holiday. Every single day that we have to send a card is another yearly problem. If you owe fifteen or twenty cards that's fifteen or twenty yearly problems. We're so busy dealing with all of these temporary problems that we never get to see what's really going on.

We have all of these ordinary problems, and then we have the problem called "the Work"—with a capital "W." The Godman is always talking about the Work—in a relatively mediocre fashion with the random, rare flash of eloquence. (I used up my brilliance a couple of years ago. The first two years were really exceptional; I'm sorry some of you missed it.) But somehow along the way we've lost the idea of happiness. At least I have. It doesn't seem to me that any of you are happy unless you and I have a very different idea of what happiness is. And it seems that a lot of that has to do with me. You're always blaming me for your happiness, so I guess you have to blame me for your bouts of agonizing depression and the dizzying level of mediocrity as well. If you attribute the *kriyas, mudras,*[46] and ecstasies to me, you have to attribute all of the other jazz to me as well. But it's *all* jazz, because I don't see anybody being happy. If I saw anybody being *really* happy then I would say it's not jazz.

Maybe we better look a little more deeply into the nature of our experience. We're struggling so intensely that we have to pretend that we're happy. Sometimes we forget that we're pretending to be happy for long moments that go for weeks. Every once in a while, we're sitting and meditating and a sorrow comes over us. We lament, "Oh, what am I doing? The guru gives me so much even though I never do my sadhana. Oh, it's all the search!"

Let me tell you a little bit about what our problem is. Once you have said or done something, you can never take it back. You can

---

[46] Sanskrit: *Kriyas* are spontaneous involuntary movements or postures due to the increased flow of life force through the body. *Mudras* are symbolic or ritual gestures or poses, mostly performed with hands or fingers, which facilitate the flow of inner energy.

never take back the least slip of the tongue. Children, in particular, "get" everything. Children are more like sponges than sponges. Some of them even look like sponges, like loofahs, unless mommy is particularly offended by a child looking natural and combs their hair and puts bows in it. A child hears everything a parent says. "Pew, look at this load of poop!" Do we really expect a two-month-old baby to make their shit smell like roses? Is it any wonder that as adults we think our genitals are dirty and smelly?

The problem is that we don't know any better. Our heads know better. We read all the books on bringing up children and we have lengthy philosophical discourses on whether we should circumcise a child because of the trauma that it causes, but we don't even watch what comes out of our mouths. A child hears every word. If we aren't different from the minute the child is born, that child is going to soak it all up. Do you think the child will be natural and real? When we play little baby games because that's the way you're supposed to be with a baby, that's what a baby learns. To be a baby. And once the baby learns to be a baby, a baby remains a baby forever. Most of us have learned to be babies and look at us. We're either babies or "kids," but we're very rarely like children because a child is natural, true, real. But we'll be damned if we want *anyone* to be natural, true, and real.

It's Possible to be Exalted in the Presence of God

None of this is necessary. It is possible to be really happy—not to just be in a good mood once in a while—but to be *exalted* in the presence of God when we sing "*Om Nama Shivaya* [a traditional Vedic mantra and one of the chants that was sung regularly in the Community for years]. If we don't begin to see that kind of happiness in ourselves once in a while, we should look at why. It's not good enough to be distracted in miracles. It's not good enough to think that the Work is so important that we make everybody around us miserable as long as we don't forget our commitment to the Work. If that's how it is, there's either something terribly wrong with the Work or something terribly wrong with us. Unfortunately, after lengthy and soul-searching deliberation, I think it's us.

If being in the presence of the Godman for so many years makes us unhappy, we better start seriously looking at what's going on. If only one person knows something, it's the same thing as it being unknown, wouldn't you say? Because nobody believes him anyway! After all, there are still people that don't believe we landed on the moon. [*Lee speaks with veiled sarcasm*:] Can you imagine how gullible we all are that we were watching a bunch of dots on our TVs assuming that we were seeing a spacecraft that cost billions of our tax dollars landing on the moon, which is nothing but a barren rock that's got no value anyway? By God, we're gullible.

However, there's hope. But there's a problem with that, because as long as there's hope, there's also hopelessness. We all like hope. It's inspiring. Today is November eighteenth. It was almost sixty degrees out today and I bet some of you were thinking, "Oh, it was such a nice day for Lee's birthday! It's winter; it should be fifteen degrees with snow and sleet. But it was warm and sunny. And did you see the sky last night? There were so many stars just covering the heavens. It must be a miracle!" But what good are miracles if we're not happy? This is not a lark for me. It's about time you took a real good look at what's going on. The fact that you cannot take back anything you've ever said or done should give you grave cause for concern as long as you continue to function in a conventional way. There is a possibility for you not to feel terrible, guilty, and hopeless about this.

Suffering an Illusion

Genuinely and truly, I guarantee you there is nothing real about your unhappiness. Some of you really feel it and some of you really emote it and some of you just really think it. So that's certainly real. But the genuineness of your unhappiness is not to be found anywhere. In your heart? Nah. Your heart is just a muscle. In your heart chakra? Well, it's either open or closed or somewhere in between. You aren't going to find the evidence of any unhappiness there. The spiritual heart? That you won't even find, try as you might. All you can find is the reflection of your unhappiness—your thinking, emoting and feeling. So, what are we going to do about this? What are we going to do about the fact that we are all suffering an illusion and we refuse to give up the illusion? And what am I going to do about the fact that I occasionally see you ecstatic with devotion, melting right into the floor or against the wall or whatever you happen to be leaning on for support at the time? It is true that there is occasionally a light in your eyes that is absolutely brilliant.

Despite all of that, it seems that my presence in your lives is making you both ecstatic and absolutely miserable. Or if not miserable, at least as serious as death warmed over—especially the philosophers. The way philosophers respond to my behavior is by getting serious, by trying to figure me out and find all the hidden meanings. But they say there are no hidden meanings. Oh, God, I hope that's wrong. There must be a hidden meaning somewhere!

The last thing Neem Karoli Baba[47] said to one of his students was, "What am I going to do? Nobody understands me." I'll be damned if that's going to happen to me. We have quite a dilemma here, if you ask me. *You* don't think we have a dilemma. You're just sitting around and I make you laugh. You have ecstasies once in a while and you're always having lessons made in your lives. You're always learning things. What more could you ask for? I'm always exhorting you to follow the conditions. And since you don't do them perfectly, I'm always forgiving you and that makes you feel good because I give you so much attention.

---

[47] (c. 1900-1973) Hindu guru and a devotee of Hanuman, known in the West for being the spiritual master of a number of Americans who traveled to India in the 1960s and 1970s.

I forgive the things you do because they aren't conscious. If it was anything but the machine, then I wouldn't forgive you. You wouldn't need forgiveness. Because it's the machine, you don't have to worry. It's okay, even though being unhappy is a real drag. Not for me. I've been around unhappy people all my life. You don't think the big men on campus and the fraternity jocks were my friends when I was in college, do you? I always hung out with the losers. But there's some great benefit to hanging out with the losers because they're usually so off the walls that they don't know any better than to be happy. Actually, all of us losers were probably the happiest people in the school. We just walked around with our head in the clouds, looking forward to the next date—whenever that might be—and maybe a kiss goodnight.

Even the tape recorder is whining! (laughter) Here we sit laughing and enjoying ourselves. Don't forget we're in trouble. If you consider that everything that has ever happened in your environment can never be erased, we shouldn't be trying to get better under any circumstance. It's a totally useless process. I mean, we couldn't re-do one percent of our chemistry if we worked our whole lives. We might get a little centered and healthy, our bodies might get a little cleaner, we might develop manners. Maybe it wouldn't be so bad to have that kind of community. We could use a little manners.

There certainly are a lot of heroes out there in the world—and even a few to be found here—but that doesn't mean we've re-done anything in our unconscious except maybe an infinitesimal amount. Because everything is the same as everything else…but not always! There is "a red shirt and a green shirt" [to trigger the survival reactions of the machine] everywhere you go. You could be the calmest, most centered person in the world and any day, out of nowhere, boom, the sky could fall, leaving you frazzled, crazy, and miserable. Out of nowhere it could happen at any time to any of us. It doesn't, generally, because we're very contained. We don't want to get too far out of our skins because we might get free! God help us. Can you imagine what would happen if we got free? If you worked and paid your own way through college, there is no way in hell you are ever going to get free and invalidate fifteen thousand dollars-worth of higher education. [Cost of education was much different in 1979.] What would happen if you were really alive? Everything you've invested your whole life in would be invalidated.

We're trying to understand spiritual life within the given parameters of our previous education, but it's an impossibility. Since all those nasties that mommy and daddy and our friends said to us are working and moving and doing the dance of the seven veils in us, trying to re-do all of that business is just a hopeless case. Some of us can rap the dharma out, give seminars, and attract people to the Community, but basically we're not happy. I see some very bright eyes and some incredible ecstasies, but we're not happy. Unless of course your idea of being happy is different than mine. But my idea of being happy?… Let me tell you what it's *not*. It's not being so committed to the Work, whatever the hell that is, that everybody in the environment becomes miserable as a result.

I'm beginning to think it's *my* fault. What did Krishna say in the Bhagavad Gita? "I was before the world, and the world's suffering and the world's ecstasy is all my creation." *You* are already enlightened. It doesn't mean beans to you whether you come back or don't come back; *you* don't care one jot. And that sneaky, vindictive, sophisticated, incredibly powerful survival-machine is all an illusion anyway. But try and prove that and see how far it gets you. The machine isn't interested in God *whatsoever*. I know some of you feel awful because you think it's your fault. *It's not your fault.* All the misery you go through is not your fault, but nonetheless you think, emote, and feel it. That worries me because life shouldn't be that way. Your unhappiness is not what is arising randomly in the world. What's arising randomly in the world is that it's a nice day with mild weather in the middle of November and there's a birthday party with delicious food and nice music. [This talk was given during a Community celebration known as Appearance Day, which is held on the days around Lee's birthday]. If you can't allow the people close to you to be happy most of the time, you're not living spiritual life. Nothing else matters—not work, crisis, or contraction. None of that is relevant *at all* if you're not minimally happy.

The Work Isn't Supposed to Be "work"

As far as I'm concerned, you can throw the Work out of the window if you're not happy. Not conventional-world-"happy" as in it's your birthday: "Happy Birthday to you, happy birthday to you!" But you're not supposed to plod through life, gnashing your teeth. The Work isn't supposed to be *work*! Conscious suffering isn't supposed to be *suffering*. We shouldn't even be talking about the Work if we aren't happy. It doesn't matter if somebody breaks a god-damned plate or dents the silver-plated tea service that we got for our wedding fifteen years ago. If we can't be happy in one another's company regardless of what goes on, what good is all of this suffering and working? I know I occasionally entertain some of you. Once in a while I make a good point; you find some great esoteric significance in something I've said, or you have a lesson made in your life. But all the lessons in the world don't mean anything if we can't at least be a little happy together! What's the difference if everything someone does offends me, and everything I do offends another someone—ad nauseum? Why can't we be a little pleasurable? Listen, we don't all even live together. Imagine if we all lived in one big room. What about these families all over the world with fifteen people living in one room? At some point or another your happiness has to mean more than your jealousy and envy. The Work should take a back seat if you haven't surrendered. You don't spend fifteen years in spiritual life and then get to surrender. You have to surrender *first* and begin to be a little bit happy…all the time!

It would probably create a lot of sorrow for you if you came home and found your dog lying dead on the floor, but it doesn't mean you have to be unhappy. What does that have to do with happiness? If someone puts their foot in your territory you have a border clash with them. But what does our territory have to do with happiness? You read the papers, don't you? There are border clashes all over the world. Do you think that such things make any difference to the politicians or the people who make billions of dollars of profit a year for the corporations they work for? Those people just keep truckin' down the road making a profit whether there is war or famine, whether there are border clashes or monetary crises.

In spiritual life, you're supposed to be happy even though there are border clashes and wars and monetary crises, and you get sick once in a while with a virus…or worse. Who knows what's going to happen to us in the next twenty years? We could have every unspeakable disease manifest in our midst. So what? What does that have to do with being happy? It doesn't have anything to do with being happy! But because you make it have something to do with being happy, you aren't happy. You *refuse* to be happy—anytime, even when you're singing! One of the memorable experiences of my life was seeing Janis Joplin in concert. She had a tough life, but when she was singing she was really happy. For us, even when we're doing what we're supposed to be enjoying, we still aren't happy.

You can't re-do all this "stuff," neither the bad nor the good. You can look at that picture of your baby when he or she was six months old from now until doomsday. I can *promise* you that you aren't going to re-do the happiness that child gave you when that picture was taken if you live for more years than you can count. You're not going to re-do the prom and the day you were homecoming queen. You know how many homecoming queens keep trying to be homecoming queens for the next fifty years? Of course you do; you've met some of them.

You have to be different. You're never going to re-do every word said in anger, every fight you ever had, and all that stuff—not if you had eternity to re-do it. Even in the midst of being happy, you're not going to stop having fights. You *will* lose your temper and say something you're sorry for, and you're not going to be able to take it back. Listen, if your allegiance to the Work is standing in the way of being happy, throw it out the window. Never mind about the suffering of God, obligation, and essence. Figure out why it is you're not happy and get happy.

FOLLOW ME

(December 2, 1979)

A Master Must Say "Follow Me" or the Work Will Be Lost

Sooner or later, if you are associated with the spiritual master, you are going to be told to follow—very much as Jesus told the two brothers (Simon-Peter and Andrew) who were fisherman. They were just hanging out on the beach, doing what fishermen did in those days: repairing the nets and talking about the tides and the fish. Jesus came walking down the beach and, being the Messiah, he was glowing a little bit and had a big smile on his face. These guys looked up and Jesus said, "Follow me." They didn't even consider who was going to take care of the nets, or think, "I have to go tell Mom." They simply followed in that moment. They were prepared, based on their immediate response to Jesus, to give up everything and simply follow. For a fisherman in those days to give up what they had might not seem to be much to us. We might think that if we were fishermen, we would be glad to give that up to follow the master. We tend to view things from other cultures and times strictly from the perspective of our culture and time.

Giving up what Simon-Peter and Andrew gave up to follow Jesus could be equated to us giving up all of our comfort—the roof over our heads, our sweaters, our Indian and Tibetan clothes, our three winter coats, our earth shoes, sandals, boots, moccasins, car, and all of the other conveniences that we completely take for granted in our day-to-day life. It would be comparable to us walking away from whatever we were doing with just the clothes on our backs and going wherever the guy said to go. We think of the fishermen giving up their job as comparable to us working at a terrible job we didn't like and thinking, "Oh, I wish the spiritual master would come and ask me to follow. I would love to get out of this job." In terms of following, we imagine going to some cozy ashram. It brings to mind what we tend to consider spiritual life to be and what we should begin to consider in our own cases.

You shouldn't wait for the spiritual master to say, "Follow me!" That is absurd. You shouldn't expect anything like that. You should just recognize that somewhere, at some point, that is what a real spiritual master is going to ask. Someone who is not a real spiritual master will let you live on the ashram as long as you want, doing whatever you do, and that is just fine. You might be asked to donate everything that you own. That is very common these days, but that is not the same thing as being asked to follow. Jesus didn't ask the fishermen for what they owned. Of course, they didn't own anything he wanted. What would he do with a fishing net? We just don't have an equivalent in our culture to compare to what Jesus asked them to do. None of *us* do, anyway.

In this day and age, if the spiritual master asks you to follow him, he is liable to be subjected to tremendous persecution from the family of whoever he asks to follow him. If Jesus the Messiah showed up today, walked into the Vatican and said to the cardinals, "Follow me," they probably would think it was absurd. They would say, "What are you doing in robes? Are you one of those religious fanatics?" That is what would happen to him; he would be considered a religious fanatic. We would never consider what Jesus would have to offer in this day and age in our culture. But if you are serious about the spiritual path, at some point or another you have to simply follow—whatever that means. For us, it hasn't meant any great physical hardship. Or we have never been asked.[48] For us it might mean walking around India a little bit.

When we went to India, nobody that we talked to could imagine the way we traveled through the country—on second-class buses and

---

48 In 1980, Lee announced that he would be moving to Arizona. He offered students the opportunity to leave their East Coast lives and follow him, to live on the ashram he would establish. He invited them essentially into an unknown future.

trains. But we ate like royalty. We enjoyed every last grain of rice, cardamom seed, and bowl of curry, and thought it was phenomenal. Other Westerners in their yoga-whites with their malas couldn't believe we would take a bus. You can hire a car for fifteen dollars a day with a driver and translator. "Take a bus for twenty cents? Why would you do that? We all go there to see swamis anyway." "Swamis" are cultured and clean, but the people are dirty and there's disease all over. Basically, most people go to India to see some clean swami, never even considering that all of those clean swamis grew up in the midst of [everyday Indian] culture anyway. They didn't grow up in the Taj Mahal Hotel.

If we are serious about spiritual life, at some point in our spiritual careers we will be asked to simply follow. If the spiritual master has any balls—I don't know any of them who do, although there are some that have infinitely more than me—that is what they do. They simply walk through the world, pick out the ones who are theirs and say, "Follow me." Then they go somewhere together to do spiritual work. That is what Jesus did. He gathered his disciples and taught them. Then he sent them all out to heal. He didn't spend his whole ministry with them tagging along at his heels. When they had enough training, Jesus sent them out to heal. He discoursed a little bit, taught them a few esoteric techniques, made them meditate and do a little pranayama, and then he sent them out to heal. The disciples said to him, "Oh my God, we can't do this." He said, "Heal in my name." And they went out in his name and healed. The disciples did many of the miracles that Jesus was renowned for.

If the guru came to you and said "Follow me," and you realized he meant it, what would be the considerations? Well, what is it that you would be asked to leave? What do you have anyway? We think, "But what about my children? They have to stay in school. How are they going to learn to read?" I want to tell you a secret about children. If you never said a single word to a child about how to read, and all you did was read in front of them, that child would learn to read. If you read, that child will learn to read. It is much harder to learn how to do some of the things a little child does, like walking, than it is to learn how to read.

The important thing to realize is that Jesus didn't keep saying "Follow me." He didn't keep encouraging his disciples every week. If John was a little low, or Luke had a problem, Jesus didn't go to them and say, "Hey, guys, what's the matter? Don't worry. In a couple of years, it will all be over." He didn't talk to them that way. He kept bringing them back to the main point. Every time they asked him a question he said, "I am up to my Father's business." They were always thinking he was up to miracles, hoping he was up to being the king of the Jews and establishing the new social order. In Jesus's time, there was the prophesy of the coming messiah and of his being a king. The populace that was waiting for the messiah wanted someone to throw out the Romans. That was their idea of a king. The people were looking for someone who would get rid of the Romans so the Jews could have their new spiritual culture. They never considered what it is that we have to consider about seeing through the world.

Jesus is supposed to have said, "Render to Caesar the things that are Caesar's and to God the things that are God's." That is what we have to do. We have to give to the world that which is the world's, but not give to spiritual life or to God that which is Caesar's. And that is what we are trying to do. We are trying to give to God or spiritual life that which is the world's and it doesn't work; the two are completely antagonistic to each other. The considerations of conventional life are antagonistic to considerations of spiritual life.

We must recognize at some point in our lives that, if this Work is at all true, we are going to be asked to follow. If this is not true, then we won't be. And you haven't been, really. You have basically been asked to seriously consider, with all of the skills and talents at your command, what it is that you are involved with; to advance under your own power and with your own intention as far as you can, and to assume as much responsibility and obligation as you are willing to have absolute integrity about. You haven't really been asked to follow. If you *were* asked, some of you would follow but you wouldn't be ready to. You aren't going to be asked again every week. You have to put yourself in a position where you don't have to be asked or reminded.

When you are asked to follow, one of the considerations is your capacity. If you get a little hassled, the spiritual master isn't going to come around and say, "Remember when we first met? Remember how deeply committed you were?" And you answer, "Yeah, I remember that. I was so sure then."

If a spiritual master never says, "Follow me," his Work is lost to subsequent generations. Maybe he manages to establish a lot of good karma. But if the spiritual master never says, "Follow me" to any of his students (not to the whole Community, that is absurd) then his Work is lost. It's not even conceivable that it will pass on in its entirety to future generations. At best it will be fragments of the Work that will be passed on and misunderstood. Portions of it may be transmitted for a time, but a spiritual master must say, "Follow me" at some point to one or more students or else the Work is lost.

A Teacher Works at the Level of His Students

Sometimes a spiritual master will say "Follow me" at the cost of his health, but no spiritual master will say "Follow me" in the face of impossible odds. If you are living God-life five percent, you will never be asked to follow. Occasionally, you come to me with sincere and naive requests like, "Give me work! I want to do something!" We find the idea of going on the "New Life," like Meher Baba's students, very heroic when we study about it. Some of us traveled around in India for four months and didn't get sick, but if any of us had been on our back for three weeks with dysentery, we might have considered this idea of "Follow me" with a little more trepidation. One of the considerations in terms of this whole process is that a teacher works at the level his or her students' work. If the teacher gives a certain amount and the students don't use it, it is the same as the teacher giving himself disease—of the emotions and the mind, not just disease of the body. For the teacher to say "Follow me," a student has to be willing to work at a level that is at least consistent with some degree of health. Otherwise, the teacher wipes out. That is the first consideration in a teacher saying "Follow me."

The other consideration is that, were one to say "Follow me" in this day and age, that one would get a tremendous amount of attention. It was even true in Jesus's time, but to a lesser degree. On some level, *all* attention, positive or negative, supports the work, supports the process. Even negative attention is validation, because criticism indicates importance.

Editor's Note: *Lee then told an Indian story that is summarized here so as to focus on his main point: A servant boy who said that he would follow any instruction of the spiritual master died when told to jump off a cliff. The other devotees were shocked, but the master performed a miracle and brought the boy back to life. The boy then inherited the lineage at a young age.*

There is a mythological quality to the tale that makes the point about the real spiritual master's ability to provide whatever is needed for a student with faith to come to realize God-life. At the same time, Lee spoke strongly about the need to mature beyond a childish follower mentality in relationship to a teacher, to develop discrimination about a teacher's internal state, and to be responsible for one's decisions and say no if appropriate to do so.

Lee continued to comment on the story of the servant boy:

You couldn't do that in America. Think of what would happen. Nobody would wait for the servant boy to be put back together. The master would be hauled off to jail, and that would be the end of the poor servant boy. There wouldn't be a chance to do a miracle. So, we have to consider the culture that we are in. Asking someone to follow is a matter of the teacher putting himself or herself in the position of being persecuted.

Jesus didn't enlighten the disciples…or anything like that. They had the same old questions and considerations that everybody has: "What about life after death? What is it like in the Kingdom of Heaven? What about…" And what did he give them? He kept saying, "Surrender to the Father. You can only come to the Father through me. My Father does all of this. I do nothing of myself." Jesus blessed them, gave them *shaktipat* [the transmission of spiritual energy], initiated them into the Holy Spirit, and baptized them in fire.

The teacher must realize that, in this day and age, the student is liable to come up with every conceivable doubt and excuse to find fault with the Work. And you know, when the going gets rough, the rough get going. When you are asked to surrender completely, ego will activate every weapon at its command, and ego's got some beauties. If you have ever been in a mental institution and seen people throwing fits, ego will do that. I know for a fact that every one of you is capable of that kind of behavior. The spiritual master has to be in a position to look at that and say "Get off it, will you?" The spiritual master has to see ego's desperation and know that it is not who you are. It is just an act. The spiritual master has to be in a position to pierce that dynamic.

But the true spiritual master is absolutely vulnerable to their students. The spiritual master is vulnerable at the level of his students' vulnerability. If you are working at ten percent, I am working at ten percent. When I say "working," that doesn't just include building houses and that kind of sadhana. It includes the vital, emotional, and mental centers as well. If you are not really being intelligent, if you are not being lucid and objective about things—which is using your mind—then neither is the spiritual master. If your fear is at a certain level, so too is his. If ego is going to run that kind of number, the spiritual master has to be able to sustain the Work on a functional level. The

Work gets sustained on a non-functional level whatever happens. But on a functional level, we are involved in a process in which possibilities are available to us when the spiritual master can simply say "Follow me" and we follow. In fact, because the ultimate possibility is truly available here, one of the things that we should begin to pay attention to is what our role is in creating an environment in which I can say "Follow me."

More and more people will come seeking to have the true possibility given them in this lifetime. We have to recognize that very few teachers can say "Follow me" and support that with the appropriate context. The context here is one in which I can say "Follow me" and offer what that means. That is very rare in the world. If a teacher asks someone to follow them and doesn't offer them the ultimate possibility, that teacher is really in trouble. The worst thing a teacher can do, if the teacher is true, is compromise his or her Work in this way.

But it is not up to you or me. It's up to the relationship that we share, which takes our personalities out of it. If we don't work together, that ultimate possibility is never offered. If we don't work together, I can never say "Follow me." If we work together, I can. But we have to work together, because the relationship is what provides the possibility—not you or me alone. The teacher works at the level of their students. That means I have to give to whatever degree you truly offer to take. If you take something, you can't give it back immediately. You have to be willing to take it and be responsible for it, not try it out for a weekend then chuck it. This is a very important point: we have to do it together.

Working on a Level of Ultimate Value

If you create a situation where I can say "Follow me," you give the world something ultimately valuable, not something temporarily important for our culture. Most people see ultimate value as ending hunger in the world, or something like that. That is tangible. But this Work isn't really tangible. You have to see that. Together, we can provide the circumstance in which I can say "Follow me," and have the strength to sustain that.

It may or may not be necessary to drop everything. But if I never get to say "Follow me," there are people that might be in a position to take advantage of that who never get the chance to. I realize this might be very intangible, but it is of ultimate importance. To me, it's more important than anything tangible because the level of spiritual value is absolute. It would be nice to end hunger in the world, but in a hundred years we will all be dead and so will all the people with empty bellies. All of this is going to go.

If a comet comes through the solar system and hits the earth, of what ultimate value is all of this? No ultimate value, because all of this disappears sooner or later—the moon, the earth, the solar system, the sun. If you follow astronomy and physics, you know that our sun is dying. It may take five billion years, but it will happen. Ultimately, all things here die. It's a fact. When the sun turns cold, we won't have life on this planet. All things die on this plane. Even planets and suns and solar systems die. But as intangible as it might seem to this [*referring to his body*], there is a level that ultimately survives. That level is untouched by the disintegration of the solar system or even the universe. That is the level on which we can work. We don't have to be limited by this form. We can work on that level. That is what is of ultimate value to me.

When somebody dives into this Work with absolute faith, the form of their lives might not appear to be ideal to their friends and family, but the spiritual work that can result is ultimately valuable. The kind of work that can result from psychological work, from getting centered and balanced, or from humanitarian efforts, is all temporary. It creates good karma so that we have the possibility of another chance, but it doesn't create the kind of spiritual work that's absolutely and ultimately necessary.

FOOD

(March 20, 1980)

Three Kinds of Food

In the Buddhist tradition there are six realms or qualities of being: god, jealous god, human, animal, hungry ghost, and the hell worlds, such as the demons, devils, and all that jazz. The visual picture of a hungry ghost is a being with a monstrous stomach, a gigantic appetite, and a tiny little neck and mouth. Hungry ghosts can never eat enough to satisfy their hunger. They are always looking for food, but even when they find it, they can't eat enough to satisfy themselves. It seems to me that, if you pay close attention, most of us are in this category—not because there isn't enough to eat but because we don't know how to eat.

For us to survive, it is necessary to have three different kinds of food.[49] One kind is what we eat. That can be good food like brown rice and vegetables, or food that tastes really good but does funny things to the body—like angel food cake, lemon meringue pie, or junk food like potato chips and soda. We tend to feed ourselves habitually, not intuitively. Three times a day we eat all there is on the table. We have this and we have that, and we survive pretty well.

Then there is another level of food that we get through breathing. Breath is not so much habitual but intuitive. We manage to get air, but there is a tremendous amount of food in our breath that we literally don't know how to eat. If you look around, you see a lot of people who think they are alive, but you wouldn't want to live that kind of life. We manage to make it fifty, sixty, seventy, eighty years. Everybody knows someone that smoked and drank and ate whatever they wanted and lived to be a hundred, healthy as a horse. The average person is not interested

---

49 Lee is commenting on the three kinds of food—gross food, breath, and impressions—that are discussed in the Gurdjieff Work.

in knowing *how* to eat because it is obvious that we are all alive. We intuitively breathe, we habitually eat, and that takes care of that.

Then there is a third kind of food, which feeds an even subtler system in us, which is mental food. Most people get their mental food from newspapers and TV sets. Some people get all of their food from TV sets and end up being President of the United States! We don't have to learn how to properly feed ourselves because even hungry ghosts manage to live forever. It is not a very comfortable existence, but they survive forever. They're just never satisfied. If we don't learn how to properly eat, nothing bad will happen to us. We will just remain exactly the way we are.

Learning How to "Eat" Properly

If we learn how to eat properly, we can figure out pretty easily how to utilize the first level of food. The first level is very basic. Basically, we can digest anything given enough time and a solid enough constitution. You may have read in the Guinness Book of World Records about the guy that ate a bicycle. So, ingesting food is just the first part. After that, our intestines know what to do. There are certain chemicals and hormones involved, and whatever we eat gets digested somehow. But that doesn't mean that it gets used properly. Learning how to eat first level food, which is the stuff we put in our mouths, is the beginning. The second part is learning what to do with it once it gets down there so that it doesn't sit around for a few days or even years. I know some of you in the room are in favor of high colonics and enemas. (They have special enemas for hard cases like some of us, where they strap you to the table, stick a fire hose up there and heat the water up a little bit. By the time you're through, you're enlightened!) Most of us have stuff that has just leeched on to the walls in our intestines that has been there for years. So it's important to know what to do with food once you've eaten it.

We get second-level food through breathing. First of all, we have to learn to breathe properly. You have all probably seen instruction in a yoga book to breathe deeply—not into your chest and upper lungs but deeper so the belly pops out. That is pretty standard, along with breathing through your nose, because when you breathe through your mouth you miss a very important connection. But we all manage to survive; it is obvious to us that we are living. So when somebody says that we don't eat, breathe, or think properly, we say, "What do I need to eat, breathe, and think properly for?"

"So, you can develop yourself as a human being, become more spiritual, and surrender to God."

"What for?"

"Well, so you can live."

"But I am alive!"

"No, you are not alive. You are unconscious, asleep, dead!"

But it is tacitly obvious that we are alive, and that we have been able to stay alive doing exactly what we have done so far. We eat, we sex, we are alive, healthy, fine. We are a little depressed once in a while, but we go to our consciousness-raising group or a mushroom party and, before you know it, we are gossiping about whoever didn't show up that day and we feel great. We are on top of the world.

Intuitively, we know that we have survived well. Most of us are relatively successful both in a financial sense and in a personal sense. We all have friends, we are independent, strong, self-sufficient, conscious, aware. It is easy for us to buy the rhetoric. "I know I am suffering. What do I do about it?" Someone says, "Just breathe deep." We lie down and breathe deep and we have a better night's sleep than we have had in years. It's just wonderful, we feel so good.

And there are breathing techniques for everything. If you walk in the house and your child has just cut his arm off and blood is gushing all over the floor, there is a yogic breathing technique to clear your mind and mellow you out so you can deal with it. I don't know what it is, but you do some panting and before you know it you are calm and relaxed. You take your child to the hospital and even remember to take his arm, and everything is fine.

Then we get to the third level of food, which Gurdjieff called "impression" or mental food. It is the subtlest food and also the hardest kind to learn how to eat properly. We have a certain degree of discrimination within our Community. We are vegetarians. We don't smoke or drink alcohol and things like that. Yet the whole process of utilizing mental food is not one of discriminating in relationship to what comes in, but of how what comes in is used.

It is not a matter of moving out to the country and never reading newspapers so you don't read about the catastrophes going on in the world—earthquakes, war, and people starving to death. I don't recommend that you read the papers, not because what the papers say is going to hurt your consciousness, but just because nothing ever changes. The news has been like this forever. What use is there to read the paper? What good does it do you to know it is going to snow tomorrow? What is the difference? You go to work every day regardless of the weather. But for the average person, it is very important to know whether it is going to snow tomorrow or not. They want to know whether they can take another day off, drive to Vermont to go skiing, and drink hot toddies in the ski lodge.

The reason that it is necessary to learn how to eat is because the visual image of the hungry ghost is an accurate feeling-description of who we are. We are all hungry ghosts, to varying degrees, because we are not satisfied no matter what we get. Some of us have mouths that are so small that not even a little moisture could get into them. Some of us have bigger mouths. Some of us are the kind of hungry ghosts that have gigantic mouths and throats and no stomach. A hungry ghost is only satisfied for the short period of time it takes for the food to go in the mouth and down, but becomes unsatisfied again as soon as the food hits the belly. The difference between us and a hungry ghost in the

Buddhist tradition is that if you are in the hungry ghost *loka* [Sanskrit term for world or plane of existence], you can't swallow and absorb food even if you learn how to eat it properly. The benefit of being a human being and not a hungry ghost—even though we may embody that image in our approach to life—is that we can use the food that is given if we learn how to eat properly. With third-level food, that is more important than what goes in.

Using Impressions

Our Community doesn't know how to use third-level food yet. If I took my students to a whorehouse or had them read all of Marco Vassi's novels,[50] we wouldn't know how to use the impressions. And if you don't know how to use those kinds of impressions, you're in worse shape than if you didn't encounter them. Ideally, using third-level food is not a matter of any kind of discrimination. Politics, business, the financial market, sex, or spiritual literature can all provide very adequate third-level food if we use them right. If we don't know how to make use of the food in those areas, it can cause us to be more cramped than we were to begin with.

As great as we think we are, the average individual has a lot of cramps. Not physical cramps, but our entire relational ability is cramped. It's not like some of you don't have relationships that are relatively good. Of course you do. But generally speaking, even those of us that have relationships that we think are pretty good are probably enjoying twenty to thirty percent of the possibility of that relationship. We don't know the difference because we don't know how far the spectrum reaches; we don't know what's possible.

[50] An American author, mostly known for his erotica, who was a friend of Lee's.

Suppression Cramps the Body

You can go to an ashram and wear white and chant all day long, but your mind is still going to do what it does. You can stuff it down and suppress what is really going on. But, when you are not seeing who you are and things get suppressed, you get tense in different parts of your body. That intensity becomes a cramp. And that cramp doesn't allow us free communication. It doesn't allow us free relationship. Did you ever go to a creative dance workshop and watch how some people, especially men, can't move? The instructor is teaching belly dance and doing that thing with their pelvis. And you see that the guys can't move their pelvis. Or some people are always constipated because they were potty-trained wrong. There are all kinds of cramps.

The reason we want to learn to use the three types of foods is so that we can align ourselves to a life that is un-cramped, a life that is free, gentle, and peaceful. Some of you probably think you are very peaceful, but if you spend a month with me[51] I can show you how violent you are. That is another thing that cramps do: cramps keep a lid on violence. For women it doesn't matter as much. But for a man it matters a lot. If a man looks at a guy in a bar in the wrong way, he can end up without teeth.

When all your cramps are dissolved, you don't get violent. It doesn't mean you don't defend yourself. If there was a food shortage and people were trying to get our food, nobody would get my brown rice! So, you can defend yourself, but you wouldn't feel violence towards people. You wouldn't walk in the house and ask your wife "What's for dinner?" and when she said, "We're having curry tonight," knock the food off the table and shout, "Goddamn curry, for Christ's sake!" If you are honest with yourself, you see that you have urges like that sometimes. When you are not cramped up, you don't have urges like that. You don't feel angry and violent.

---

51 Lee is speaking at a public talk.

Elimination and the Need for a Reminding Factor

When you eat food, certain qualities of that food are used by the bloodstream, the glands, the bones and so on, and the rest of it is excreted in the form of fecal matter. The same thing happens with air and mental impressions. Food comes in, you use a certain quality of it that is valuable for you at the time, and the rest is eliminated. The way second-level food gets eliminated is simply with the outbreath. It's very easy, very simple, just like eating. It is very much like gross first-level food. You eat and you shit; you don't have to do anything about it. It is not very tricky. You breathe in, you breathe out. That is the way your second-level excrement gets eliminated. If you don't know how to eat gross food, it hangs around. You get fat, cellulite, arteriosclerosis, and so on. You get all kinds of things because you retain qualities of the food that are waste matter. It is not a matter of what you eat, but of how you eat. There are people that eat the worst crap, and nothing ever happens to them because they know how to eliminate what the body can't use. It's the same thing with second-level food.

If you breathe and you don't know how to use that food properly, you retain a lot of garbage that is unnecessary. When you breathe out, you aren't excreting all of the poison. Some of it is retained in the body. It's the same thing with third-level food. If you know how to cycle third-level food, then you take what is necessary and excrete what is not necessary. How is it excreted? In an innocent way through fantasies, dreams, communication, language, inter-reactions, etc. If you know how to cycle third-level food, some of it gets excreted, and what is of value gets retained. Otherwise, you retain a lot of waste material.

There are several things to learn: first, how to eat, then what to do with the food, and lastly how to eliminate what you don't need—the refuse, the poison. The best way to learn that is by having a caustic ingredient in your life, because you will never do it on your own. I never would have done it on my own. Never! I am the guy that is supposed to be a slave of God and happy all the time, and I never would have done this on my own. I was like Gurdjieff was when he was a youth…I just had to know. But I never would have done it on my own. So, you need a little push. You need something that is caustic, something that will rub you the wrong way. If somebody does something pleasant for you, you don't consider it. You don't think about it, you don't try to understand it, you don't work with it, you don't use it. But if there is something a little caustic, something that rubs you the wrong way, you will consider and ponder it, work on it. If something rubs you the wrong way every day, you will work especially hard to figure out what the hell is going on. If something pleasant happens every day and there is nothing caustic, you will not try to do something about your state of consciousness—which is cramped. You've got to have a reason for doing something about your state of consciousness. Otherwise, you never will.

Most of you are relatively successful people. Most of you are healthy, clean, and intelligent. But you're never going to do it [real spiritual work] on your own unless you've got a reminding factor in the way that Gurdjieff talked about it. You've got to have a reminding factor.

One Thing to Offer

When I am involved with people, the right thing always happens—right in the sense of what serves those people. It is not a matter of intelligence. Half the stuff I said tonight, I never thought of before tonight. If somebody asks me a question about it two weeks from now, I would probably wonder what they were talking about. For whatever reason, the right thing is elicited when it serves. That is what I have to offer you. It's not all the dharma speak and food jazz that I have been talking about tonight. I have basically one thing to offer you, which is spiritual slavery. You do what God wants you to do. I don't mean that I can get you to do that (I am beginning to doubt that I can get *anyone* to do that), but that is the offer.

LAYLA AND MAJNUN

(April 20, 1980)

Love That Is All-Consuming Is the Same as Surrender to God

The story of Layla and Majnun is a famous Persian fable, as famous in the Near East as *Romeo and Juliet* is in the West. Personally, I like it better than *Romeo and Juliet*. It's a story about two fabled lovers that is founded in fact and contains many spiritual metaphors. The main aspects of the history of Majnun and Layla are true. The translation I am using is written in prose, but the original is magnificent poetry. The love that Layla and Majnun had for one another is analogous to the kind of love that is necessary in order to please God. God is pleased by the kind of love that is consuming, maddening, all-encompassing. Anything less is not real.

Majnun, which means "madman," was born with the name Qays in the fifth century. From the start, Layla and Majnun experienced many obstacles to their love. But Majnun's love was so absolute that he became a kind of patron saint of unrequited lovers. In his later life—he never got very old—he was a hermit in the desert and people would travel many miles to find him and to hear about his love for Layla. They say that genius and madness are just a thin line apart. Majnun's madness created in him such poetic beauty that his poems were orally transmitted throughout the entire length and breadth of Arabia. His poems were so magnificent that they became the archetype for lover's poetry in all of the Arabian lands. It was his madness, which is parallel to God's madness, that drove him to such eloquence. At first it was a little disconcerting to friends and family and conventional society, but when a love like Majnun's love is true, nothing can stop it. It always inspires.

The story didn't end happily. It had a somewhat tragic ending in conventional terms, but in terms of spirituality, this kind of love is the same thing as surrender to God. When love is this consuming, what is the difference whether God is brought into the equation or not? There is not a bit of difference. Layla and Majnun never did manage to consummate their relationship. But as we go through the story, you will see that Majnun's love was so powerful that consummation of the relationship became totally irrelevant.

What was important was love, not that he lived with the Beloved.[52] What was totally important to Majnun was the *reflection* of his Beloved. The Beloved became irrelevant to him. But the reflection of his Beloved became all-consuming and literally made him a saint. Of course, the metaphor of the story, which can be taken simply as a beautiful poetic love story, is parallel to spiritual life on every level. Although this is a true story, the poet Nizami is telling a spiritual story. Although Layla was a real woman and Majnun was a young man in love, what Nizami is talking about is God.

Well, here is a little bit about the story… One of the great chieftains in Arabia was getting very old and feeling ready to die. But he had no sons to take over his kingdom—his land, animals, crops, and treasury of jewels and gold. He prayed, and eventually his prayer was answered. He went to Mecca, to the Kaaba,[53] saw the stone and prayed. His prayer was answered, and he was given a son whose name was Qays. Qays was not only strong and healthy, but brilliant as well. The chieftain was so happy to have a son at last. He gave his son everything his wealth and influence could provide—the best tutors, the best training, the best environment—and Qays grew up to be the most brilliant student, the best archer, racer, horseman, and athlete. He was loved by all the students in his school. Everybody was his friend. He was popular and extremely handsome.

---

52 In Sufism, the Path of Love culminates in a lover's oneness with a personal Beloved as the Divine so that no distinction between them remains.

53 The most sacred Moslem pilgrimage site located in a mosque in Mecca, Saudi Arabia. A stone is inset into the Kaaba's walls that, according to Islamic tradition, was placed there by the Prophet Mohammad.

One day, who comes to the school but Layla. Layla was to femininity exactly what Qays was to masculinity. The beautiful Persian poetry describes Layla as having the eyes of a gazelle, the skin of a peach, lips the color of pomegranates, and the scent of jasmine. Layla was a flawless beauty with curly, beautiful black hair and perfect eyes and lips. She was a brilliant student, a musician par excellence, lively and friendly with everyone. Qays and Layla instinctually connected to one another and fell in love. They didn't have any intellectual grasp of what was going on, but they felt the most profound love for one another, and it turned them inside out. They didn't think of it in terms of being in love with one another; they were just consumed by love, true love, love that was totally selfless.

Spontaneous Poetry as an Expression of Instinctual Love

Layla and Qays began to communicate about this to one another strictly on an instinctual level. They would sit in class, catch one another's eyes, and be lost in the glance. Neither one of them was able to bring any kind of adult reality to what was going on. The more it continued, the more lost in one another they became. Qays would be catapulted into ecstasy when he saw Layla. Or Layla would be lost for hours in rapture at the sound of Qay's sigh. Layla and Qays were so selflessly consumed by one another's presence that after a while it began to get a little scandalous because all they wanted to do was be together. Layla belonged to a different tribe than Qays, and she was a princess in that tribe. Her family began to feel that Qays was giving Layla a bad name and that she was making a fool of herself with him, so they took her out of school. Qays was crushed. He became so totally absorbed in his love for Layla that he wasn't able to function. He stopped eating, dressing himself, washing, and literally became like a madman, walking around calling, "Layla, Layla, Layla!" He began to spontaneously make up poetry about his love for Layla. Of course, Qays's family was very upset. His father was getting older and ready to die, and his only son and heir was going nuts.

"Majnun" [crazy], as Qays began to be called at this point, started wandering around town, walking through the streets calling out Layla's name and reciting poetry. He wanted to see her, so he headed toward where her tribe lived. But they wouldn't let him anywhere near her. They said, "You're a madman. Get out!" This went on for years while Majnun got more and more mad. He couldn't walk without stumbling and falling; all he did was compose magnificent poems to Layla. About this time, he was starting to get well-known. People recognized the magnificence of his poetry. Some of them started to memorize and recite it. Occasionally he would go somewhere and people would recognize him. "Majnun!" they would say, "How is Layla?" He would be enraptured as soon as he heard her name and start reciting incredibly eloquent poetry.

Asking for Help at the Kaaba

Majnun's father was at his wits' end. He's tried everything to distract Majnun—women, money, and travel—but Majnun was still lost in Layla. So his father decided that the obvious thing to do was to marry him to Layla. Then Majnun would be normal again.

His father went with a family delegation to Layla's tribe and made a proposition of marriage, offering them all his wealth and possessions just so his son could have what he wanted, which was Layla. Layla's family said to him, "It is fine that you want to offer us all your treasure, but your son is a madman. He is an outcast, crazy, a lunatic. We can't put our good name on the line for such a one!" They refused the marriage proposal.

There was only one other thing to do. His father decided to go to Mecca. He would take Majnun to the Kaaba and pray to the Prophet for help. That is how he got Qays in the first place. Maybe it would work a second time. They set off in a caravan, and he instructed Majnun on the way, "When we get there, we will thank the Prophet for your health and for our good family." (The Kaaba is supposed to be the cornerstone to the original temple in Mecca that Abraham himself built.) Majnun was mad, but he was capable of communicating. He listened to his father and said, "Fine." His father trained him in all the rituals of Islam, so that when they got to Mecca they could pray. Finally, they were in front of the Kaaba.

[Lee reads from Nizami: *The Story of Layla and Majnun*. Translated from the Persian, and edited by Dr. R. Gelpke. Boulder, Colorado: Shambhala Publications, Inc., 1978, pp. 37-38.]

> *At last the time had come; father and son stood in the shadow and protection of the holiest of Holies. Gently the Sayyid took the youth by the hand and said to him: 'Here, my dear son, every play comes to its end. Try to find relief from your sufferings. Here, in front of this temple and its Master, you must pray to be freed from your sorrow. Listen; this should be your prayer: "Save me, my God, from this vain ecstasy. Have pity on me; grant me refuge; take my madness away and lead me back to the path of righteousness. I am Love's unhappy victim! Help me! Free me from the evil of my Love." Recite this prayer, my son.'*
>
> *When Majnun heard his father speaking he wept, then began to laugh. Suddenly, a strange thing happened. He darted forward like the head of a coiled snake, stretched out his hands towards the door of the temple, hammered against it and shouted:*
>
> *'Yes, it is I, who knocks at this door today! I have sold my life for love's sake! Yes, it is I; may I always be love's slave! They tell me: abandon love, that is the path to recovery—but I can gain strength only through love. If love dies, so shall I. My nature is love's pupil; be my fate nothing, if not love, and woe to the heart incapable of passion. I ask thee, my God, I beseech thee, in all the godliness of thy*

> *divine nature and all the perfection of thy kingdom: let my love grow stronger, let it endure, even if I perish. Let me drink from this well, let my eye never miss its light. If I am drunk with the wine of love, let me drink even more deeply… Let me love, oh my God, love for love's sake, and make my love a hundred times as great as it was and is!'*

Of course, Majnun's father was distraught. In the presence of the holiest shrine in all of the kingdom, Majnun was moved not to reject the holiness that his life was about but to embrace it even more deeply. Even though he was an outcast from his tribe, which was ashamed that he was one of them, when he came to the seat of holiness he was moved to intensify his state. Majnun had listened to his father and said, "Okay, I want my father and mother to be happy. I will ask to be helped." But when he came into the presence of God, his life was absolutely irrelevant compared to the strength and the power of love.

When they returned home, Majnun's father didn't know what to do. By this time Majnun was incapable of taking care of himself. He started wandering around the desert, just going crazier, never washing. He never cut his hair, his nails were growing, he was losing weight. All he ate were scraps he found—a piece of fruit, some roots and grasses. Meanwhile, his verses were becoming more and more well-known; he was becoming a renowned mystic poet. Whenever somebody had an ill-fated love affair, they would find Majnun, sit at his feet, and listen to his poetry.

Wandering with Animals in the Desert

Majnun was not happy to have people following him around, so he wandered deeper and deeper into the desert. One renowned prince heard about him and said, "I've got to see this guy." The prince went prepared to ridicule Majnun, to make fun of him (all the princes of those days being brilliant at repartee), but when he found Majnun he was transformed by Majnun's one-pointed absorption in and surrender to his love for Layla. The prince was overcome. Being a man of honor, a knight, and a hero, he said to Majnun, "Listen, I am wealthy. I have a big army. I have never seen a love like yours. I am going to get this woman for you. Come back with me to my tent, we will eat together. You will get healthy; we will comb your hair and make you fit for Layla." Majnun was beside himself with joy. He went to the prince's tent and they ate and washed, and the prince said to Majnun, "Tell me about Layla." In response, Majnun let loose with incredibly moving poetry.

A month goes by, two months go by, and Majnun becomes strong and healthy, vibrant and alive. But after the second month, he says to the prince, "You told me that as soon as we got back you were going to raise an army and get Layla for me. You have lied. What kind of a friend are you? You have been having me tell you my poetry, but you have forgotten about Layla." The prince realizes the truth of what Majnun has said and replies, "I am a man of my word. I told you I was going to get Layla for you, and I will!" The prince gets up his army of men and they go to Layla's camp where he sends a message: "I am a prince and I have my army here. We've won a hundred wars, and if you don't send Layla out here for Majnun, we will come in there and take her." Layla's father sends back a message saying, "We will never surrender Layla!" A pitched battle ensues.

At first, Majnun is watching the battle, dreaming about getting Layla, but soon he realizes that it is Layla's relatives that are being killed by the prince's army. He wanders the battlefield, torn with misery, rooting for the enemies. One of the prince's officers sees this and tells the prince, and the prince realizes this is not the way. He orders his army to retreat. He tells Layla's tribe that Majnun doesn't want this war, that Majnun is on their side and wants to quit. Layla's tribe agrees to quit as well. They go back to their respective camps and bury the dead.

Now Majnun goes farther out into the desert and he starts to befriend the desert animals. He comes upon an antelope caught in a hunter's trap and releases it. One day, Majnun is meditating and a fox comes up, sniffs at him and sits down next to him. Pretty soon all kinds of animals show up—lions and cobras, foxes and wolves. Whenever people come, the animals protect Majnun. He wanders the desert with a troop of animals following him. When people bring him offerings of food, he takes the food and gives it to the animals. The rich people who bring him rich, delicious food get really insulted and say, "What are you doing?!" But Majnun just eats a little grass and a couple of roots. He says, "These animals are my friends. I don't want your offerings. Layla is my only food."

One Name Is Better Than Two

One day, Majnun comes across a group of people, all of whom know him or have at least heard of him. Who among the Arabs had not? Suddenly he notices a scrap of paper at his feet, tossed by the wind, that bears the names Layla and Majnun—an anonymous tribute to their loyalty. There is nothing else, just the two names joined together. Majnun snatches up the paper, peers at it and tears it into two, scrutinizing the part with the name Layla. Then he tosses it aside, keeping the half with his own name. The people looking on are amazed. They would have expected anything but this.

Surrounding Majnun, they ask him excitedly, "What does this mean? Tell us, why have you done this? Here you were united and now you have separated yourself. Why?"

"Because," Majnun says, "one name is better than two. One is enough for both. If you knew what it means to be a lover, you would realize that one only has to scratch him and out falls his Beloved."

But the people are still not satisfied. "Very well," they said, "one name is enough for both. That is what you say. Maybe. But why then did you throw the name Layla away and keep your own name? Why not the other way around?"

"Because one can see the shell but not the kernel," Majnun says. "Do you not understand? The name is only the outer shell. And I am the shell, the veil. The face underneath is hers." At this, everyone is transported into ecstasy by the beauty of his speech.

Time passed and Majnun's father died and Majnun grieved. He threw himself down at the grave, beat his head on the gravestone and refused to move. But no matter how total his love was for his father, it could not compare to his love for Layla. Eventually, he was shooed away from his father's grave by his own clansmen, who still considered him an embarrassment even though he was renowned throughout Arabia. So he went back into the desert and continued to wander to and fro attracting disciples who followed him. Every once in a while, someone would find Majnun and ask him, "Tell me of Layla!" And he would be transported as he told them about her. He would jump and dance and leap in the air. He would become so ecstatic that he would spin around the desert like a top, making little tornadoes [in the sand].

What Remains of Majnun Is the Beloved

One day, a young man who was also forlorn in love came to Majnun and said, "I want to be your disciple."

Majnun replied, "What do you know? You are just a kid. You don't know anything about love."

The young man said, "I will sit at your feet. I want to memorize your poetry and bring it to the world. It can't be lost."

Majnun warned, "You don't know what you'd be getting involved with. You can't live like I do."

The young man replied, "I am going to be your disciple. I can do it." The young man showed Majnun the food he'd brought and said, "Listen, you've got to eat, man."

"I don't want that food," Majnun replied. The young man was well-meaning but clueless about Majnun's state. Majnun looked at him and spoke.

[Lee reads from Nizami, p. 184]

> *'Who do you think I am? A drunkard? A love-sick fool, a slave of my senses, made senseless by desire? Understand: I have risen above all that, I am the King of Love in majesty. My soul is purified from the darkness of lust, my longing purged of low desire, my mind freed from shame. I have broken up the teeming bazaar of the senses in my body. Love is the essence of my being. Love is fire and I am wood burned by the flame. Love has moved in and adorned the house, my Self has tied its bundle and left. You imagine that you see me, but I no longer exist: what remains, is the beloved…'*

The young man was taken aback, finally starting to get that he didn't understand. He said, "I really made a mistake. You are the master, I am the disciple. Whatever you say, I am going to live here with you."

Majnun shrugged his shoulders and said, "All right. But you'll see, you won't make it."

"Yes, I will," the young man replied.

The young man lived with Majnun for a long time, many months. He sat at his feet and memorized all of his poetry. "Tell me of love!" he said, and Majnun was inspired to go on and on.

By this time Majnun had truly become consumed. There was nothing but the Beloved; there was no difference between Majnun and the Beloved. He had become God, he had become Love, he manifested only that. After a couple of years, the young guy couldn't take the wilderness and the wild animals, and he left. But he left having memorized all of Majnun's poetry. He became a balladeer, singing and reciting the poetry throughout all of Arabia.

In the meantime, Layla's family decides it is time for her to marry. She is eighteen or nineteen years old, and one of the greatest princes in the land comes courting. Of course, by this time everybody has heard of the love of Layla and Majnun and of his poetry to her. This prince goes to Layla's tribe and says, "I am wealthy, I've got a great army and I think I'd make a good husband for Layla." After some deliberation, they finally agree and the marriage is arranged.

But Layla won't let this guy touch her. The prince is reasonable; he thinks that Layla is young and a little hysterical over Majnun. He thinks he can win her over with his charm if he lets it rest a while. Every day he visits her, and wines and dines her, and months go by and he still hasn't touched her. Finally, he gets impatient and tries to take her in his arms, but she repels him forcibly and in no uncertain terms. She says, "Nobody will ever touch me but Majnun. I did not choose this marriage!"

Well, the prince is not too pleased with this, but he is a nice guy and has a little sensitivity. So he thinks to himself, "Her love is so pure that just to be near someone with a love that profound is enough for me." He stops wanting her physically. He visits her once in a while to just look at her. He feels that to be near her love is enough food for him.

Last Vision of Layla

One day an old man arrives and finds Layla in the garden. He tells her that he has heard of the love of Layla and Majnun and that he has traveled far to meet her. "Oh, tell me of Majnun!" she exclaims. So he tells her all about Majnun. She is overwhelmed and she says, "I have never been able to tell anyone before how I feel. As a woman, I have not been allowed to express my love like Majnun. I have never even told my parents how I feel about him." She pours her heart out to the old man. "Majnun's love is on the surface. He is consumed and surrendered to it, but I have had to keep my love inside." When the old man tells her that he is going to find

Majnun, she says, "You must take him a message!" She writes a message to Majnun and the old man speeds out across the desert. He doesn't stop to eat or sleep until he finds Majnun. He finds him and tells him he has been to see Layla and tells him about their conversation.

"I have a note for you from Layla," he says.

Majnun takes the note and he just can't believe that it's from Layla. He smells it and tastes it and looks at it for a very long time before he can even read it. Every few minutes he asks the old man, "Tell me truly, is this from she?"

The old man assures him, "Yes, Yes! This is from Layla."

Finally, Majnun opens the note and after he reads it, he asks the old man, "Will you take a message back?"

The old man says, "Yes, of course!" The old man is so pleased to be a messenger between these great lovers.

Majnun scribbles a note and the old man takes it, meets Layla, and gives her the note. When she gets the note, she says to the old man, "I've got to see him!" She starts weeping torrents of tears. "Tell him I will meet him."

So the old man charges back on his camel and tells Majnun that Layla wants to see him. "Oh!" Majnun exclaims. He's beside himself, dancing around the desert.

"Come on," says the old man. "Let's clean you up before you go." So he cleans Majnun up a bit and takes him to Layla's garden.

Layla comes out. She is standing at the door and Majnun is waiting. She looks at him and she is shocked. The last time she saw him, he was tall and handsome and healthy and in the vibrancy of youth. Now she looks at him and he is a bag of bones and his hair is matted. He is a madman. The old man urges her, "Go to him!"

"No, I can't," she replies, "It's too late. We are both consumed by love, but we can't be together."

Just then Majnun turns around and sees her. He just lights up and he runs towards her. "No!" she shouts. He stops, looks at her and turns and runs out of the garden with that final image of Layla sealed into every cell of his body.

The old man is completely bewildered. He says to Layla, "I figured you would run away together." Layla explains that because their love is totally selfless—there is no one but Layla in Majnun's case—he has become the Beloved. Majnun is simply a reflection; there is no Majnun. How could the two of them be together? Majnun is complete unto himself. His love for Layla is more important, more profound and real than any kind of personal relationship they could have.

Majnun continues to wander the desert, totally delirious with the image of Layla as he has seen her. Layla's suffering has made her age prematurely. Her hair is now grey; she is wrinkled, her eyes dull. But to Majnun she is still the sun and the moon and the stars. He is now a total hermit in the desert with his animals following behind him, taking care of him, making sure no one hurts him. If people come to be his devotees, he runs away. He doesn't want to see anybody. All he does is live in his cave spouting poetry.

"One Tent Will Hold Them in the World Above"

After a time, Layla dies, her life made complete by seeing Majnun in the flesh one more time. Everybody mourns and they bury her. Somehow, somebody gets to Majnun and yells out at him as he is running away, "Majnun, I must tell you about Layla." He stops and lets the person come close. The person says, "Layla has died," and tells Majnun where she is buried. Majnun runs to her grave and falls on it. He already is her; he is the Beloved. His love is so profound that he has become the Beloved. There is nothing for him to do, nothing to achieve. Years ago, he had already become everything there was to become because his love literally consumed him. He falls on Layla's grave and cries out, "I want to join you so we can gaze at one another!" He stays there and finally dies. All his animals are just sitting there watching him lying on Layla's grave. People who have been coming to visit Layla's grave see all these animals and stay away.

[Lee reads from Nizami, pp. 198-199]

> *Majnun remained as lonely in death as he had been in life. Having found his rest, he was safe from wagging tongues; for a long time no one knew, no curiosity disturbed his slumber.*
>
> *Some say that he remained laying on the grave of his love, where he had died, for a month or two… that as much as a year passed.*
>
> *People thought him still alive! Whenever they came to watch from afar, they saw wild animals surrounding the grave. Protected by them, Majnun slept safely like a king in his litter. Even now, they did not leave their master, unwilling to believe that he would never awaken again. Patiently they waited and Layla's tomb seemed to have become a home for the roving beasts.*
>
> *Afraid of such guardians, people did not dare to approach. They thought and said to one another: 'The stranger is lying on the grave as usual.'*
>
> *Thus the dead man was left alone; even beasts which feed on carrion did not touch him. What little remained of him fell into dust and returned to earth; in the end nothing was left but his bones.*
>
> *Then only did the animals abandon their watch; one after the other they disappeared in the wilderness. When the magic lock had been removed from the hidden treasure, people approached to solve the riddle and found what remained of Majnun. Death had completed his work so well that no one felt fear or disgust. The white shell, its pearl vanished, was washed clean and men let jeweled tears of mourning flow into it.*
>
> *They all wept—members of Majnun's and Layla's tribes, as well as others, strangers of pure heart mourning the lovers, renting their garments in lamentation. And Majnun was buried at Layla's side.*

Two lovers lie awaiting this tomb
Their resurrection from the grave's dark womb.
Faithful in separation, true in love,
One tent will hold them in the world above.

After it became known that Majnun was dead, he became even more of a legend than when he was alive, his poetry recited and loved throughout Arabia.

In the darshan hall, Arizona ashram, early 1980s

PART IV

INTO THE DESERT

Arizona, July 1980–1986

INTRODUCTION

Although Lee Lozowick had talked about the need for a spiritual master to say "Follow Me" if his Work was not to be lost to subsequent generations, his students didn't know what this meant beyond what had already happened. But the statement took on new meaning when Lee made an announcement after having quietly made a few trips to the Southwest. He said that he would be moving to Arizona and that students were invited to move with him and deepen their commitment to spiritual life by living together on property that he and his wife were purchasing for an ashram.

In some ways, Lee had prepared the group for the upscale that had been coming, but it nonetheless came as a shock. Moving to Arizona and leaving the familiarity of family and surroundings was a stretch for all concerned. Students would practice together and live a kind of new life that was unknown and directed by the guru. A few students went out ahead of the group with instructions from Lee for caretaking the property. Then Lee led a caravan of four cars across country from New Jersey with most of the twelve students who had made the decision to move in July 1980. It was of course unusual for the funds for an ashram to be provided by a guru or his immediate family. One of the first priorities for the Community was to figure out how to support itself. The limited amount of money that students had was pooled, and people began to work cleaning motel rooms, waiting tables, landscaping in the rocky high desert, working at K-Mart, and weaving cinches for horses, which was a departure from any kind of work that anyone had previously engaged on the East Coast. Lee transferred the names that he had given to the two households in New Jersey, Arrakis and Secundus, to the two houses on the new ashram. His reliance on God and his humor provided the teaching for students who struggled with the many aspects of adjustment.

Between 1980-1985, after dinner talks were given twice each week with satsang or *darshan*[54] on Sunday nights. Over time, a daily schedule evolved which included communal meals, meditation for fifty minutes in the morning followed by *arati*,[55] and the day spent working, caring for the children, growing a garden, and attending to the property. At one point the *Guru Gita* ("Song of the Guru," a Hindu scripture) began to be sung several mornings a week, and a teaching meeting, facilitated by students, was started on Sunday mornings.

Celebrations were held three times a year, with meals served under an outdoor tent in all kinds of weather. Lee and invited guests would sit at the head table and volunteers would attend to washing stations for clean up right after the meals. Celebrations allowed students to share the intentions for work on self and provided communion with the sangha, aiding in their desire to align with the Influence of the guru.

After a few years, during one of the celebrations, Lee quietly organized the setup of a devotional evening space designed to replicate the form of a middle eastern party. The basic setup was not taken down, became a permanent fixture of the school, and came to be referred to as the "Tavern of Ruin"[56] out of Lee's consideration that "The Only Grace Is Loving God."[57] Though there was no intent for the space to last for more than one night, the impact of the evening was so tangible that Lee maintained it and students began to gather each night to consider

54 Divine vision (Sanskrit); literally, the sighting of the guru. In 1981, formal gatherings in Lee's company began to be referred to as "darshan."

55 Devotional Hindu ritual in praise of the guru which includes chanting and the waving of a lighted ghee lamp to symbolize the removal of darkness.

56 The "Tavern of Ruin" was a gathering place, similar to a prayer space in the Sufi tradition, where the mood of loving God was considered.

57 The title of a book written by Lee, published in 1982, which detailed a distinction between the Will and the Whim of God.

the mood of love as described in the Sufi tradition. Sometimes these gatherings, imbued with a longing for the Beloved, went well into the night after Lee had left the Tavern.

Over time, a glass-display-case business became a source of Community income, with Lee cutting the glass (often imperfectly) that was assembled on wooden bases and sold to protect and exhibit Native American kachina dolls and other collectibles. A bookstore named "Mudra," where spiritual literature and weaving supplies were sold, was opened on the main street in town. The Community sold food and lemonade at an annual Fourth of July fair, which became group work, with students involved in food preparation tasks, paying attention to the needs of the space, and serving customers, while Lee directed all the activities in the booth. Though few students were athletic in any way, the Community joined a local softball league with a team named "The New Nuclear Family," and became known for the enjoyment it had despite continuously losing games by wide margins. Lee and a few students took a karate class several times each week, led by an impressive black belt instructor who worked those in his classes in a way that none had ever experienced before. At one point, Lee took on the Prison Library Project, which involved corresponding with and sending books to prisoners. And, of course, there was the game of bridge with Lee at his kitchen table whenever there was a free evening. Bridge was played for enjoyment and practical work-on-self. Lee's attention, consistency, and efficiency was a marvel to students preoccupied with self-meditation as he moved through environments of inner and outer chaos with ease and punctuality. Every circumstance was an opportunity to live the teaching and learn from what transpired in relationship to him.

Lee sent a few students to do outreach in Boulder and northern and southern California around 1982-1983. In the few years that followed, he made regular visits to these outposts, and teaching lessons occurred wherever he went. He made contact and established friendships with teachers from various traditions and brought back considerations for practice that were shared with the Community by students who had accompanied him. During his travels, Lee was available to others from any path or walk of life who were interested in help or dialogue, such as a *Penthouse* magazine writer with whom Lee maintained a friendship and who had a spiritual perspective.

There were those, of course, who had a negative assessment of Lee even if they had never met him. On one occasion he expressed an interest in attending a public event sponsored by students of another teacher and was stopped at the door and screened to make sure that he would not cause trouble. He appeared interested in the experience of the communication of other teachers and in being invisible and unrecognized when possible in attending talks or seminars that they gave. In one instance, Lee learned that Werner Erhard, the founder of the est training, was giving an unorthodox ministerial workshop to a small group of clergy. He applied to attend as the director of a spiritual community and attended with a few of his students. Lee seemed to have no concern for his reputation. On a few different occasions over the years, he had satire issues of a Community magazine published, which poked fun at the spiritual scene but also at himself and the Community, complete with pictures of himself that did not reflect the prevailing concept of a spiritual master.

Around 1985, the Community became involved in a business that made public-space art, started by a student from California. At one point, Lee even went on some sales appointments. He was a businessman and completely able to navigate and function in the world in practical ways. Toward the end of 1985, he asked a few students to perform music at a wedding, which led to musical projects becoming a central part of his teaching Work over the coming decades. Even in the early years of the Community, Lee had a propensity for writing lyrics that were occasionally put to music by students. But particularly noteworthy was that, unbeknownst to others, Lee wrote poetry throughout the early 1980s that he sent by mail to the Beggar-Saint of south India,

Yogi Ramsuratkumar. He later said that, when he realized that Yogi Ramsuratkumar had been his master throughout lifetimes, the form of his poetry began to change and become more personal. But his process was internalized, and he did not make it known to others at the time. By 1986, he was planning another trip to India, and life in the Community was about to change again.

APPRENTICESHIP

(September 14, 1980)

Apprentices Help Free Up the Master

Both the spiritual master and the community need apprentices.[58] Without apprentices, the spiritual master's Work would not be communicated or passed on. Without apprentices, the community would have no possibility of gaining any kind of higher knowledge. It would just be a bunch of people that got together for a common goal. It would just remain "oatmeal," as Jean Shepherd[59] used to say about his audience.

Apprentices are the lifeblood of the community because the gap between the understanding of the master and that of the candidates for apprenticeship is so far apart. If the master was going to train students with no help whatsoever, he would probably blow his brains out in frustration or jump off a cliff. He would never have time to do his own work. Most apprentices probably consider their understanding of spiritual life to be minimal at best. Yet, compared to someone just coming in, they practically appear to be masters. Even so, that maturity is almost nonexistent compared to possible maturity.

The apprentice's skills are important to the master because the more skilled the apprentice becomes the more the master is freed up to do other things besides train apprentices. For example, if a master sculptor spent all his time training apprentice sculptors, he would never get any of his own work done. There are a lot of works of the old masters—

---

58 In this context, apprentices are students dedicated to learning the Work through practice and on-the-job training with a master. Those approaching the community as new students are considered to be "candidates for apprenticeship."

59 A radio host and storyteller on WOR radio in New York City from the 1950s-1970s.

Da Vinci, Michelangelo, Rembrandt, and so on—that are supposedly painted by students. The style is so similar that only an expert can tell the pictures painted by the students from the pictures painted by the masters. The apprentices are the lifeblood and a necessary part of a master's Work, but only part of it. Another part of the master's Work is his own work. If the master is an artist, sculptor, or painter, there are always certain projects that the master must do himself.

Master artists and craftsmen in the sixteenth century were supported by wealthy patrons. A patron would commission an artist or craftsman to do particular work for him that was also a contribution to art. From the perspective of the artist, the patron didn't know anything about the master's craft; the patron was just rich. The patron didn't have an artist's mind but could recognize artistic value. He didn't have mastery of an art, but he did have money and could use his money to further the creation of art. That is also true of unions and management [which may have none of the skills that workers have]. Apprentices are the lifeblood of a union, because management has nothing to say to a person that really wants to be, for instance, a skilled mason. Someone that wants to be a mason can relate to a mason, not to management.

In the same way, a spiritual apprentice is the lifeblood of the community because people can't relate to the master. He or she is too arcane, too esoteric. In some cases, he or she is totally distant. As the spiritual master, I don't have any of the skills I am suggesting that you develop. I am just management. But for new candidates for apprenticeship, senior apprentices have something tangible, real, and visible. If people approaching this school were honest, they would recognize that they are attracted to you, not me—at least initially. Once they understand to some degree what you are doing, they begin to be attracted to me through you. Sometimes people see my picture and they get zapped, but nobody develops real devotion by looking at me. They begin to develop devotion through you. Eventually, that devotion becomes real.

If there weren't any apprentices in the community, there would be no possibility of furthering the lineage. Likewise, if there were no apprentice electricians, in a couple hundred years we would have to figure out how to do what electricians do all over again. If all of the master masons died out and there were no apprentices, we would have to learn again from the beginning what to put in the mortar, how to lay the stonework, how temperature affects the process, and all of those little tricks that a mason learns through experience.

An Apprenticeship Program Is a Program of Doing

An apprenticeship program is a program of experience—of doing, not book-learning. When you apprentice to fly an airplane, for instance, you have to become a mechanic, a weatherman, a radio-operator and any number of other things. You read and study, and they give you a written test after so many flight hours. You may do pretty well on the test, but there is nothing like being in the plane, doing your first takeoff and landing, and then parking. The first time the flying instructor says, "Taxi it in!" and you've got about six inches of wing room on either side of the parking space, your heart is in your throat. But you learn by doing. Apprenticeship in spiritual life is exactly like any other kind of apprenticeship. You struggle and struggle and one day you come to a point where something clicks.

When I was taking flying lessons, I was very scared to apply gas to the airplane at first because I had the idea that the engine was too powerful. One day the instructor and I were coming in for a landing and he said, "You do it." I was very gentle with the controls because I was scared to just punch it. "You will never learn to fly that way," he said and took the controls to show me how to do it. "Your turn," he said. I swallowed and pulled myself together, eased back on the throttle, and made a perfect bank. "Now take it in for landing," the instructor told me. I whipped in, full throttle. He laughed because he flies like that all the time, full throttle. Until I learned that it was okay to do that, my apprenticeship in flying wasn't going well. Every week we went up he gave me the same corrections, but I didn't get it until the day I got it.

It's the same thing in other areas. Once you get a certain principle about your apprenticeship—really get it—there is breakthrough. You only get it by doing, and sometimes you have to be told again and again. In any apprenticeship program, what the master does seems formidable. If you don't have any of the talent and all you have is a desire to apprentice, you look at the master-apprentice or journeyman and you can hardly imagine doing all of that. But sometimes you are in there just doing it very quickly, like nothing. It becomes second nature. But you have to *do*. You can't possibly develop as an apprentice without *doing*. That applies to spiritual apprenticeship as well—you have to *do*.

A spiritual community, like a nation, has a very real need for defense and production. What does a spiritual community need to defend against? White sheep![60] If a spiritual community gets too watered down, it can lose its purpose and lose touch with its foundation or essence. Apprentices are those people skilled in defense and production. An apprentice who runs a study group is skilled in defense because people that don't belong in a given lineage are a danger to the lineage. They are a danger to the students, to the other apprentices, and to the teacher. If you get enough of them, they can literally eliminate the communication of that particular community.

Likewise, if a country loses all of its skilled apprentices, it loses contact with the modern world. Now that wouldn't be so bad if the modern world would leave the poor country alone. The problem is, if that country has oil in the ground or good soil for growing coffee or

60 The term "white sheep" refers to people who are not ready to become apprentices, and whose approach to life is a buffer to seeing the cause of suffering and the need to work on self. Some adopt a new age philosophy and become spiritual tourists.

sugar cane, the modern world won't leave that country alone. A modern nation is not satisfied to do its own business; it's got to do everybody else's business. You know what that costs if you read the newspapers. It costs money and lives. It's not a law of nature that history must repeat itself. But it does because we are so damn stupid. It's not that we are too stupid to learn from history, it's that we are too invested in chief feature to do anything about what is obviously going down.

Apprenticeship takes a man with two left feet and says to that man, "You can be a skilled draftsman." He says, "That's ridiculous. I can't even draw a straight line!" An apprenticeship program will show that person experientially that they can be a master draftsman—even if they are unable to draw a straight line at the beginning. There are a lot of people who could be real master craftsmen given the right apprenticeship program. But there is a difference between someone who has skill as a master craftsman and someone who can teach that skill. A person might have a talent to relate to a deaf child, for instance, but they wouldn't necessarily be able to teach the deaf. In India there are certain spiritual masters who just can't communicate their spiritual mastery. When people attempt to relate to this kind of spiritual master as a teacher, they end up making idols of them because these masters are unable to communicate their mastery.

Mastery Means Much More Than Technical Perfection

Production is needed [in a community] to sustain its environment: housing for students, a place for prayer, a dining room, in some cases a printing press. There must be apprentices, and candidates for apprenticeship, or there is no production. You could take two dozen people in the world who had credible skills—a mechanic, an electrician, a gardener, a cook and so on—and bring them into a spiritual community and there would be no production. To use the prodigious talent that you have *in the right way* you must be in an apprenticeship program. Someone might be an excellent musician, but there is a difference between being technically perfect in playing a guitar and playing a guitar in a way that communicates something more than technique to an audience.

When we consider the ultimate utilization of any given talent, technical perfection may be a part of mastery, but mastery means much more than technical perfection. What is the difference between something Frank Lloyd Wright designed and something that any straight-A drafting student could design? It's the difference between mastery and simply having technical skill. I would much rather see an apprentice have context first and then develop the skill. There is plenty of time to develop the skill. The idea is to have the skill *and* the context.

Breakthrough by Shock or Frustration

It was actually fear that got me to bank that airplane correctly. I didn't want my instructor to start doing loops. We had fifteen minutes left to the lesson and he had already done a role-over. He said, "This is what you have to do." It was fear of what he was going to do next that actually got me to use the throttle properly. Then we spent the rest of the time banking, instead of flying upside down, so he knew I had really gotten it. It's very much the same in the apprenticeship program in the spiritual community. It typically requires a tremendous shock to push you over the line. Sometimes you get pushed over the line by frustration. Some of the greatest breakthroughs come when people get to their wits' end, spiritually and otherwise. Some people will come into the Community and immediately start getting shocks. Somebody else will be sitting there thinking, "I wish Lee did that for me!" Other people are not moved by that kind of shock. They may have to wait and wait and be frustrated in every single attempt at higher work. The pain of that frustration finally pushes them over the line.

That's what happened to Gautama Buddha. He sat down under the bodhi tree and said, "I vow not to move from here until I achieve enlightenment." And he sat for forty-nine days. But you have to really want it. Buddha really wanted it. Buddha had exhausted all his other possibilities. He had tried every spiritual path offered in India at that time. He mastered them all and he still hadn't gotten his answer. You can't simply walk around feeling a little frustrated. You have to recognize, in your heart and soul, flesh and bones, that there are no alternatives to the spiritual work you have engaged. When Buddha sat under the bodhi tree it was enlightenment or death. Until he was twenty-one years old, he had everything the world could offer: the most beautiful wife and child in the kingdom, wealth, and power. When he wanted to leave the kingdom and become a monk, his father offered him the most beautiful dancing girls, the best masseuses, the finest cook to give him a new meal every night. None of it could dissuade him. Buddha had really come to the point when it was enlightenment or death.

You have got to come to your wits' end. You've got to sit for ten years and have nothing happen and exhaust every possibility until there is nothing left but what's on the other side, and you can't keep going the way you always have. That is the hard way, but some people require that way. Some people would love shocks. But they would just recover quickly and go right on and think they were doing a lot of work and would not be doing any. What people require is a matter of tendency. Some schools only provide shock. This isn't one of those schools. This is the frustration lineage. The master and the students just sit and sit. When we are at wits' end, we upscale.

Paying Your Own Way

As an apprentice becomes more proficient, he becomes more productive and begins to pay his way. An apprenticeship produces benefits for both himself and the master. The apprentice benefits because he has increased capacity and potential, and the master benefits because the apprentice can now do some of the work that has to get done which is too basic for the master. It's the same in the spiritual apprenticeship program. The master is always doing basic work that is really unnecessary for the master to do, but which has to be done. When an apprentice gets to the point where he can do that work, the master is freed up to place his attention elsewhere.

Upscaling in the Work is a function of how available you make yourself to feed what it is or who it is that is using you or would like to use you for food in a spiritual sense.[61] The more you are able to pay your way, the more service you provide to the universe.

The artists of the sixteenth century would never have produced as much work as they did if they didn't have apprentices to do the basic steps: to crack the stone properly, to select the right piece of wood. Da Vinci, for example, was a rare human being, an incredible artist and craftsman. He painted, sculpted, invented mechanical equipment, and wrote. Everything he did has his texture, his stamp, but he had a lot of apprentices that helped him. He just didn't have enough time in the day. It was to the benefit of the world that Da Vinci had apprentices.

In the same way, if the master has to do every step himself from beginning to end for the life of the spiritual community, very little work will get done. But if apprentices can do some of the basic work that the master is not needed for, like making the teaching available, the master can go on to produce more work. It is to the benefit of the Work that there are apprentices in a spiritual community. There never would have been a Christian church if Jesus didn't have apprentices. Why do you think he sent his disciples out to heal in his name? When he met them later on, he would say, "How did you do?" One of the disciples would say, "I did pretty good *here*, but not so good *there*," and Jesus would say, "Okay, we need a little more work *there*." That's what he did.

---

61 See the following talk on "The Work" for more about this principle.

[*Lee delivers an exaggerated sales pitch:*] The apprenticeship program at Hohm is designed, ladies and gentlemen, to create the ability in you to pay your own way with twelve easy lessons—all of which come on handy cassette tapes with essays with each one. You too can learn how to pay your own way and support the universe! [*Lee is referring to the twelve-week Study Course, including cassette tapes and written material, which has largely been reproduced in the "Basics" (Part I) section of this book.*]

A research scientist will be much more productive to a company doing pure research than training a lot of other scientists to do research. It's much more likely this one genius will come up with the next billion-dollar idea. A company could start to use apprentices to clean the lab and do some of the other basic jobs this research scientist needs to have done. An apprentice pays their way by freeing up the master. But that usually takes a while. No company will let an apprentice into a top-secret laboratory where they can steal ideas unless that apprentice has proven himself.

Yes, the more valuable you become to management, which is a function of management's investment in you, the more critical your service becomes, and the more demanding management becomes about keeping you. To use a worldly example, if you join a certain company and they think you have potential, they may send you to graduate school. The company is going to be justifiably bitter if they invest a lot of money and time in you and some competitor hires you away for a larger salary when you complete graduate school. That's why companies keep giving more and more fringe benefits to employees to entice them to remain. There are companies that build their employees whole towns—with houses, shopping centers, transportation, bowling alleys, and movie theaters—because companies make more and more of an investment in apprenticeships.

It is very expensive to support people, practically and spiritually, in an apprenticeship program. You might need six to ten years or more of training. The parallels between the world and spiritual culture in this regard are exact. Because the parallels are so exact, sometimes a spiritual culture that begins with good intentions will start to become worldly and not even notice it. We need to be very careful in this regard. Both teacher and student can never rest on their laurels. If spiritual teachers rest on their laurels, they are dead. Temporarily dead if they are lucky, but dead. A teacher may have the possibility to be a real spiritual force but if he rests on his laurels, even for a minute, that's the end. The teacher is like a generator for food. Sometimes a teacher will need a certain foundation from which to go on, and when that outcome is achieved he or she will think, "Now I've got what I need." The minute the teacher thinks that, it's the end. Even to rest for one day—assuming that something has been completed—kills it. And it might take years to get it back again.

No spiritual master will allow an apprentice to take on certain obligations if that apprentice hasn't proven their commitment. Because if the spiritual master gives an apprentice an obligation he can't fulfill, the spiritual master's Work is hurt severely. That is why to get [Work] obligation, rather than responsibility, you've got to be deep into the apprenticeship program. Otherwise you don't get obligation, you get higher and higher levels of responsibility. Leading a study group is not an obligation; it is a responsibility. Writing articles for the dharma publication is a responsibility. As you fulfill your responsibility properly, you get a higher level of responsibility.

Ultimately, the process is one of devotion, surrender, and obedience. The student cannot do any of those things without a profound appreciation of the master. The master is not going to give obligation without an equally profound appreciation of the student. So, as the apprenticeship program matures, mutual respect grows. Ultimately, the moment of surrender in which Divine Influence moves you in an irreversible way is more important than the entire apprenticeship program. But it is the apprenticeship program that is the vehicle to develop that mutual respect.

Two Kinds of Enlightenment

You actually have to be enlightened to get obligation. There are two kinds of enlightenment: one is the enlightenment that is always already present, and the other is that moment at which it is impossible for you to ever go back to anything that is not spiritual life. The final point is the only point at which you know that you can never go back. This is a great spiritual secret, and a trick besides. What the spiritual master does is get you to consider the second kind of enlightenment so deeply that you realize that there is no way to conclusively know whether that is where you are or not, because the horizon is endless in front of you. You can't tell that you can never go back unless you are looking from the final point. If you consider this deeply enough, it will lead you to the first kind of enlightenment, which is true enlightenment. The second kind of enlightenment is academic or dualistic enlightenment. But you can basically only get to the first kind through the second kind. This is probably one of the most secret spiritual things you will ever hear, so don't tell anybody!

Qualifications for Apprenticeship

There tends to be a tremendous feeling of elation and freedom when you first enter a spiritual community. You start to lead a pure lifestyle, eat clean food, exercise and do yoga regularly. You've got more energy than you ever had before. But you don't know what it costs, in a literal sense. If your body is present in the school and you are not working, things get really tough. You walk around filled with tension, reactivity, and various negative emotions. You think, "What am I going to do?" You could decide to enter the apprenticeship program at a later time, after you have been around for a while. But then a much higher level of intensity will actually be given to you intentionally. Better to walk in with your eyes open and enter the program to be a candidate for apprenticeship to begin with. What does that require? Study, exercise, meditation, and disciplining yourself in terms of any exercises you are given. Very simple.

It makes plain common sense to plan for your future. You've got a long future—not just the next fifty years. It pays in a very real sense to plan for your death and after. Not by getting yourself a mausoleum somewhere. That is not preparing for what happens after you die. It would serve you well to plan for the future that you're going to have with the body and also the future you're going to have after the body turns into fertilizer. The things that you are asked to do are absurdly pleasurable, but you refuse to do them. You refuse to work in a way that brings you joy. God only knows why. You meditate and exercise for a day and you feel better than you've ever felt. Why don't you do it every day? It's simply a matter of seeing what you have to do and doing it.

In worldly terms, as an apprentice, the best employment security is skill and knowledge. How do you develop skill and knowledge? Work. What work do you do? Whatever work your teacher supports you doing. What are the qualifications for apprenticeship? Well, in spiritual terms you must have some part of you that is not completely dead. For some of you that is a glimmer, for others much more of you is still alive. There are a lot of people around who are literally dead. They need a Jesus. They need someone that can raise them from the dead. An apprenticeship program does people like that no good.

The second qualification for apprenticeship is to have an aptitude for working with your hands. That means you have to be willing and able to work in the way that the master asks. You have to be willing to be active and you have to have the strength or energy to be active. Some people don't have that.

The third thing is confidence in your own judgment. In a spiritual sense, having confidence in your own judgment means being able to recognize the difference between what the master says and what you are saying in reference to what the master says. You have to know when it is you speaking and when it is your teacher speaking. A lot of you speak as if it was me speaking when it is far removed from what I said or meant. Having confidence in your own judgment means having the clarity to know when you are speaking and when you are communicating something exactly in the way it was said. That is a tricky one.

The fourth thing is that you must be willing to learn and to apply what you learn. Most of the people that approach spiritual communities don't have the least willingness to learn. A capacity, interest, a felt need, yes. But most people have almost no willingness to learn whatsoever. The second part of the fourth qualification for apprenticeship is to be able to apply what you learn. If you consider your own experience, it's likely you have seen that applying what you have learned is a whole other story. You apply certain things very easily and readily; other things you learn over and over and will simply not apply. If you don't have a willingness to learn and to apply what you learn, then you can't be in an apprenticeship program.

You must have perseverance, ambition, and initiative. Perseverance is obvious. It means exercising, meditating, studying every day, staying on the diet and so on. Ambition means the willingness to recognize how necessary you are to the evolution of things. Initiative doesn't mean making a lot of surprises for the journeymen or the master. It means, if you come up with an idea, you present the idea to the people that are responsible. Then you work with them to complete the idea when you are given the go-ahead. If somebody knows what they are not supposed to do and they get permission for doing it in a way that justifies their actions, that is not what is meant by initiative. Instead, you find out exactly what can be done, you take charge of it, and you do it exactly in alignment with the wishes of whatever governing body (the school, the teacher, the household) is responsible for that particular initiative.

THE WORK

(January 4, 1981)

The Realization of Freedom by Sacrificing Mastery

I have a couple of things I'd like to read. One is a quote from an article written by Henry Miller on water-color painting, which was a hobby of his. Then I have something from the last issue of E.J. Gold's *Secret Talks*[62] called "Journeys to Inaccessible Monasteries." First the Henry Miller:

> *The greatest joy, and the greatest triumph, in art, comes at the moment when, realizing to the fullest your grip over the medium, you deliberately sacrifice it in the hope of discovering a vital truth hidden within you. It comes like a reward for patience—this freedom of mastery which is born of the hardest discipline. Then, no matter what you do or say, you are absolutely right and nobody dare criticize you.*[63]

The realization of freedom is only possible through mastery. At the same time, the realization of freedom is the *sacrifice* of the mastery that many times has cost a person a lifetime to obtain. Mastery has to be sacrificed to find freedom. To use somewhat of a poor analogy, I might not have been the best Silva instructor in the country, but I had certainly mastered my craft. I was very close to being able to do all the yogi tricks, like stopping the breath and so on. But I made up my mind not to use those powers. I decided, for instance, not to heal myself. And I don't

---

62 A publication containing talks given by E.J. Gold to his students on principles of the Work.

63 Miller, Henry. *Sextet*. New York: New Directions Publishing Corporation, 1977, 94.

"charm" people anymore. I agreed with myself not to use powers in that way. The doorway to the next level was the sacrifice of that kind of mastery.

So, what does someone who has perfected the ability to create objective art[64] do next? Do they sit in their studio and create more and more works of objective art for coming generations? No. Whoever discovered how to build the hanging gardens of Babylon never built anything like that again. When the ancients mastered the ability to code a work of art, making it objective, they sacrificed that mastery for freedom. Paradoxically, the freedom they found created objective art all over the place. But that was not their intention. The mastery of a craft precipitates the knowledge that to turn out perfect works of art is not the goal anymore. That becomes completely incidental.

My parents had an art store. It was not uncommon for people to come in with a napkin that one of the artists who were famous at the time—like Picasso, Chagall, Miro, or Klee—had scribbled on in a restaurant. They'd reverently give it to my parents to frame. Well, when someone masters their craft, anything they do has value. Of course, these people saw the value in terms of how much money such an item would be worth someday, not in terms of mastery. But everything a master does has value. It's not a function of technical mastery anymore; it's a function of the freedom of that human being's sacrifice.

The Greatest Moments of Creativity Come When You Forget What You Know

The utilization of powers always gets you all of the things that chief feature desires—and more as a matter of fact. But it does that in an interesting way. It does not get you the things that chief feature is afraid

---

64 Gurdjieff made a distinction between subjective and objective art. Art that is objective requires at least flashes of objective consciousness. The artist knows what he or she wants to convey, and the art produces the same impressions in everyone.

of, even if those things are the obvious extensions of chief feature's principal desires.

The kind of mastery that supports chief feature will never teach you anything. It will not allow you to get into a position where you will be shocked into seeing yourself more clearly. You will maintain a life of comfort and positivity. You may be envied but you will not advance beyond the mastery of a particular quality—which is always a function of knowledge, even if that knowledge becomes automatic.

If you ask anybody who does something well and has a particular expertise, they have a lot of knowledge about it. But the greatest moments of creativity come when you forget what you know, because you become so involved in what you're doing that the mind is gone. Then, for the dancer the dance is transcendent, for the musician the music communicates something it never communicated before, for the weaver the weaving looks the same, but it *feels* different. Undeniably. So, there is a step beyond mastery which is the freedom that is achieved by surrendering or sacrificing that mastery.

Real life is not a matter of knowledge. Mastery is a matter of knowing perfectly what you are doing and being able to duplicate what you're doing in a technical sense. Freedom is not a matter of being able to duplicate a perfect creation in a technical sense. Freedom is putting your heart and soul, body, mind, and emotions into what you do. Picasso could scribble something that looked like nonsense, yet it made a communication of creative freedom because of his spontaneity.

Some Zen paintings are examples of that. The monk sits with a brush and paper and waits for a moment of satori. When it comes, he quickly paints until the satori stops. Have you ever noticed that every Zen book has a picture of a circle drawn with brush and ink? It looks like anybody could pick up a brush and draw a circle like that. What's so good about the circle? It's how the circle is drawn. It is done in a moment of satori so it embodies a certain freedom. Even people that don't know they have the capacity to empathize with that freedom get it. Do you think that all the people that are moved at the opera or the ballet have the sensitivity to perceive feeling? Most of them haven't felt a thing in their lives. But they'll sit and be moved in a vital way by the right performer—even if they never admit it.

If you are even minimally curious, you will wonder why you were touched by a performer. At the very least you will appreciate being touched—so much that you become hungry to be touched in a real way again. If you have more sensitivity, you go about investigating *being what it is* that touches people that way. If you have the ultimate sensitivity, at that point spiritual life is the real teacher that puts your nose to the grindstone...or your pecker to the lathe—the spiritual lathe, of course. Most of us think that it would be a pretty good deal if the lathe would enlarge it instead of sanding it down. Women worry about breast size. They don't have to, but it's so engrained in our culture that most of them do. They're either too big or too small or they hang too low or any number of things. Men worry about pecker size. It hardly matters how much Gestalt practice you do. You can sit on the hot seat and free yourself up so you're as centered as can be and you'll still think about your pecker. You'll wonder what it would be like to have one that was twelve inches long and six inches in diameter.

Being Called to Master Sacrifice

What is it that you are called to master? Some of you are pursuing your own particular form of work. But what you're called to master in your spiritual life is this thing called "sacrifice." Now it's certainly possible to do that through ballet, weaving, music, or something else. In some communities, you're asked not to do whatever you're good at. I think you should enjoy and pursue what you're good at. I don't think that most of you will achieve mastery in any of those areas—although it's possible. You don't have to be a master in the eyes of those who conventionally appreciate your particular art to achieve personal mastery. The world might look at Rembrandt, Gauguin, or Rubens and think, "Ah, these were master artists!" But the world hasn't judged Henry Miller's watercolors in the same light as it judged Rembrandt or Gauguin.

When I was fifteen, I went to Europe with my mother and my aunt. We visited every museum in France and Italy. I don't think we left a museum untouched. The galleries of these museums were filled with the works of Rubens, Rembrandt, Titian, and so on. In the first museum I was kind of awed; in the second museum less so. By the twelfth museum, I was drawn to certain pictures and the rest were just more Titians, Rubens, Gauguins, and Rembrandts. When some artists reach mastery, either everything they create becomes a work of mastery and is publicly recognized, or nothing they do is publicly recognized after a certain point in their lives. Their biographers talk about how, after they had created so much incredible work and contributed so much to humanity with such a gift, something suddenly seemed to break and they went downhill into insanity.

Nijinsky, for instance, is more recognized for the dancing he did than for his writing. If anything could be more than his dancing, it was the writing he did when he was in an insane asylum. His writings are somewhat well read, but nobody remembers Nijinsky as a mystic. They always remember him as *the* greatest male dancer, who was also somewhat of a spiritualist or mystic. But he was principally a mystic. If I can interpolate, his mysticism was a result of his freedom—not his dancing. Nijinsky's dancing was his mastery, which led to freedom, which freed his mysticism. He had a very clear realization of reality, but it took madness to achieve it. Many people that achieve a great vision of reality are considered mad. Some are put it into mental institutions, some aren't.

In our own lives, our level of mastery is a function of the mastery of *this*—whatever *this* is. [*Lee seems to be referring to spiritual life.*] If some form of art happens to be a particular passion of ours, then we can master *this* through the art. But many of us, myself included, will never master an art. Those of you that have read my unedited writing know I'm certainly not going to master writing. But you can master *this* directly though the work that is provided for you. You can make any form of art tangible and practical. Some of *this* you can't make tangible or practical. Some of *this* is so paradoxical, even nonsensical, that it's hard to make *this* your form of mastery. But you can. Whether you're involved in an art form or not, *this* [spiritual life] is the form of mastery you're called to realize.

Student: How does mastery come about in a student's relationship to you? How does a student know what progress is being made in terms of that mastery?

Lee: You never know in the heat of any mystic experience, because all you can see is the truth of that experience. You don't see it in relationship to anything. When you're awake, you're awake. You don't see that you'll be asleep tomorrow or that there's more work that goes on after awakening. When you see that there's only God, that's all you see. You're lost in the vision that there's only God. There are no distinctions. There are moments when people are awake. But when that moment is over, there is a tendency for it to take years before admitting that they are not awake anymore or that there is something more to be done. We can't rest in one moment of satori. We have to keep working. That's why help is needed—no matter what level you are at.

Duplicating the Master

Even Gurdjieff needed help. Even Ramana Maharshi needed help. Even Jesus Christ needed help—and probably had it if the stories of his travels in India and Tibet are true. So, you tend to realize mastery after the fact, rather than before the fact. The thing that serves you here is the graceful Divine Influence that permeates our lives together. This guy [*meaning himself*] might be an organic work of objective art, but most of us are not serious enough students to want to decode that. Acting *like* me is not decoding that. But it can serve. For instance, if you listen to the seminar that two of my students gave, you'll see that two things are happening. They are becoming more themselves, but there are also times when they are exactly like me. This is true for many of you at times. If you were self-observing at such times, you would probably feel like Lee was speaking—like you didn't exist.

There is a very valuable esoteric key in that experience of duplicating me that is important to study and pierce. There is a difference in doing that with *me* versus doing it with anybody else. The difference is in who is "assuming" you [opening to a real master begins a process of being transformed into who the master is, or of realizing one's own true nature] and why you can be assumed in that way. It's not because I have any power. You're assumed in that way because you're willing to sacrifice to the person who assumes you. When you do that with me, you're not just assumed by my chief feature, which is what happens when you do it with anybody else; with me you get graceful Divine Influence. If you understood the key, you could study me very closely and then consciously and voluntarily attempt to duplicate me in yourself. But without understanding the key you're simply acting out a role. If you study closely enough to understand the key, then you have something very valuable.

Decoding Objective Art

It's the same as decoding a work of objective art. The difference is, when you decode a work of objective art you get whatever has been coded into it. Most works of objective art have specific communications coded in them. Many have been coded with vast panoramas of information that have been destroyed to some degree. So, the entire body of knowledge coded in the Great Pyramid does not exist anymore because of robbers, weather, erosion—any number of reasons. It still holds a vast amount of information, but not all of the information it held when it was built. When you go to any museum, you see that a lot of artifacts are damaged. Usually, the damage affects the information. What you get is a partial communication; rarely do you get the total communication.

There are some incredible works of objective art in the caves at Ajanta and Ellora in India. One is a very large, magnificent statue of Brahma with heads facing the four directions. But part of the knowledge that was coded into the art has been lost. When a museum curator takes an artifact into the museum lab, nicks the rock, puts a bit of it under a microscope, and makes a little sign to say who it is—that detracts from the communication of the artifact. We don't know this since the communication of objective art is not contemporary knowledge. We want to preserve the artifact for the future. And we do preserve the outward form, but sometimes in preserving the outward form we muddy, confuse, and even occasionally obliterate the esoteric communication that an artifact has been created to communicate. The thing you get here in my presence is the influence of a living, breathing, expanding, communicating, organic work of objective art. That's encouragement for you to realize mastery.

The Cellular Communication of the Master

There is a story about a Sufi master [Mansur Al-Hallaj] who said, "Ana al-Haqq!" ("I am the Truth!") He was seen as a heretic and a troublemaker and was called up before the caliphate. The caliphate decided to lop off his head. The Sufi master was very well known, so when he came to the scaffold thousands of his supporters were there. The executioner asked, "Will you recant now? You have one chance." The Sufi said, "No. Ana al-Haqq. Ana al-Haqq! I am the Truth. I am the Truth!" So they cut off his head. The story goes that he stood up and held his severed head in the air, and that the severed head said, "Ana al-Haqq! Ana al-Haqq! Ana al-

Haqq!" Of course, the crowd went *wild*! The executioner was converted immediately and the story lives on until this day.

The cells themselves communicate when a work of objective art is organic. The force of evolution that allows the guru to continue to evolve is like a broadcasting station—except with a lot more than fifty-thousand watts. It pulses the Influence to anything in its environment. The guru can create an artifact with intention—which is what prasad is—or the guru can withhold the communication to some degree. It's completely different than the power that is taught in courses like Silva, because it is not a function of mind. Mind is one of the aspects of the process, but it's not a function of mind. It is not a matter of knowledge of some kind of technique. It's a matter of sacrifice in any given moment.

The guru could go around organically coding everything with the Influence. Most of what he or she could code would never be used. But some of it would be, in an absurdist way. In fact, some of us are here because of just such an absurdity. Anybody that listens to this tape someday, even five hundred years from now, can have a connection as strong as some of you. It will simply be a function of this kind of communication. But before you can communicate in this way, you need to go through a process of acquiring some kind of mastery.

Learn to Follow What Feels Right

Student: Is Grace a factor in whether or not someone can use an encoded communication?

Lee: Whether you *can* use it or not is a completely graceful event. Whether you *will* use it or not is totally your personal responsibility. Some people can't use it; others can. You have nothing whatsoever to do with that. You couldn't even begin to hope to have anything to do with that. If you think you have something to do with that, you're just fooling yourself in the worst way. I can hardly think of a worse way in which you could be fooling yourself. On the other hand, it's your choice and entirely your personal responsibility to use the communication or resist it, ignore it, or pretend that it doesn't exist. There will come a point when you're so deeply involved that you can't choose anymore; you've got to pursue your raison d'etre.

To bring the consideration a little further... The first thing you must do is learn to follow what feels right—with a little consideration (but no regard) for chief feature. Every one of you has probably fallen in love numerous times, and you have known—even when you were a teenager and had never heard of spiritual life—when a love affair was right or wrong. I don't mean right or wrong in a moralistic sense. You knew in your heart that you should be with this person, or that being with that person was a whim or a fancy—that (as men say) the "pipes needed cleaning." That knowing applies to food, living circumstances, the car you drive, the clothes you wear, the work you do. Sometimes you need to do work for one reason or another that is not appropriate for you. In that situation, you do the work you need to do. But don't be swayed by your conditioning. Don't be swayed by personality tendencies. Our body runs us, our emotions run us, our desires run us. But our principle focus should be what is appropriate in line with the Work.

You can have resistance up and down the line, but follow what you know. You know what feels right and what doesn't feel right. You can apply this to anything. You know what's appropriate for you or not.

Student: When you said that we all need to acquire mastery, were you talking about mastery of a particular form?

Lee: One of the reasons that I am interested in some of you learning a craft is just to communicate a certain principle to you. If we spent twenty years at a craft or skill, I doubt that more than three or four of us in the room would master it. If you're going to master something you have to have one-pointed focus. If you read about some of the incredible austerities engaged in by someone we would call a "master," you might wonder why they did that. It was because mastery was more important than anything else.

Human communication becomes important *after* mastery. Before mastery, it may make your life more or less easy, but it doesn't mean anything. After mastery, then human communication and living with people really means something. Because then you can free people. Before mastery, no matter how much you appreciate them, you're not going to free them. You're not going to let them do what they have to do—whatever that is. You're just not.

Maintaining a Vision and Communicating the Possibility of the Work

[Lee reads from Henry Miller:]

> *Today I see that my steadfast desire was alone responsible for whatever progress or mastery I have made. The reality is always there, and it is preceded by vision. And if one keeps looking steadily the vision crystallizes into fact or deed. There is no escaping it. It doesn't matter what route one travels—every route brings you eventually to the goal. "All roads lead to heaven," is the Chinese proverb. If one accepted that fully, one would get there so much more quickly. One should not be worrying about the degree of "success" obtained by each and every effort, but only concentrate on maintaining the vision, keeping it pure and steady. The rest is sleight-of-hand work in the dark, a genuine automatic process, no less somnambulistic because accompanied by pain and aches.*[65]

Henry Miller is communicating from his artistic vision exactly the process that the spiritual student takes on the path. When you allow

---

65 Miller, 95.

your vision to be clouded or distracted, you don't threaten the ultimate realization of that vision; you simply slow it up. Slowing it up can mean lifetimes—thousands of years. If you've got a particular vision, it is essential to maintain that vision in the face of all the other stuff that goes on.

When you meet somebody that does something well and who has some degree of mastery in your field, you really flash on them. If you're completely honest, you see that mastery is attractive to people who are, in various ways, pursuing mastery themselves. Eight or nine years ago there were a lot of people I really wanted to meet. Now I have no more interest in meeting them than in just walking down into the barrio and saying hello to the bums. As you master your own way, you outgrow your awe or reverence for levels of mastery beneath your own level. For example, there are probably friends you miss, who you were drawn to because of your conditioning and circumstances. But somehow it isn't like old times when you get together with them again. Even a little bit of mastery will separate you from most people. What you want to do is be with people who are at a similar or higher level of mastery so you continually evolve.

As you advance spiritually, you exclude the mass of humanity from any conceivable relationship—up to a point. It's a funny paradox, like an hourglass. Down at the bottom of the hourglass some people turn you off, but you're pretty easy-going; you get along with just about anybody. When you occasionally meet someone in the world who is a devotee of any kind, you can get along very well with them. Or you are attracted by people who have developed a higher degree of mastery in something other than your degree of mastery in spiritual life. You like them, are interested in them, want to talk to and spend time with them. When you get near the middle of the hourglass there are only a few people that you really feel like you want to be with. Then you reach the turning point [of the hourglass] and start going back again. More and more people become interesting. By the time you get to the top of the hourglass you're actually interested in the rejects of humanity. It's an interesting paradox how you rise up out of the murk and depths of the swamp and you end up bringing light back into the very depths and swamps that you rose out of to begin with. That's exactly what spiritual life is all about. Some of you are probably expecting to go to heaven. But it's *hell* you end up in—not heaven, you see. Heaven is after the swamp is all cleaned up and there's a nice development on it with half-acre plots, and every house has a little pool, and there's a nice food co-op that serves the neighborhood. Then you get to go to heaven. But at this point in the game, you go to hell when you get realized—to fulfill the Work. You drag some of those creepy crawlies, alligators, snakes, and swamp worms out of there. Lighten them up a little bit!

Student: Is the tipping point in the center of the hourglass the point at which you want to share God with other people?

Lee: It's not that you want to share God with other people. It's that you become interested in communicating the possibility of the Work. If even one person can lead a life that is not filled with suffering, then it makes your work worthwhile.

Just Sacrifice Your Peanut Butter

Everybody knows we're at a crossroads now—whether we're in spiritual life or not. Old people, young people, middle-aged people, even the most unconscious person on the planet. But people are tormented and sick about it because they are not willing to do what has to be done to break the cycle. But they know it must be broken. You are to some degree doing what has to be done. Whether it gets done or not, you must work for that because you know what you feel. But because of the nature of the mind, people are just "waiting for the rapture." It's not going to happen. "Well, I know there's an oil shortage and a food shortage, and a peanut shortage…" People are not willing to take thousands of clues and indicators and do what must be done. We will not eat something besides peanut butter. We'll complain, fight, and suffer incredibly, but we will not do without peanut butter. That's what it's all about. You might laugh, but this war that we are going through within ourselves is all about peanut butter. You know what we would do if we had to do without peanut butter? Complain about it for the rest of our lives. We would tell our grandchildren, "I remember when we had peanut butter." If our grandchildren asked us, "If I had three wishes, what should I wish for, Grandpa?" we would say, "You should wish to taste peanut butter."

We'll never give it up. God, The Work, chief feature, ego—forget all of that stuff. Just sacrifice your peanut butter. Just drink water for a couple of days if you run out of milk. Use oil if you don't have any butter. That's what spiritual life is all about. When you lie down at night on your futon and put that little roll-thing under your neck instead of a pillow, with your little prayer table next to you with a candle, just be happy that you're alive. Be thankful that you're blessed enough to be healthy, with a bed to sleep in, and able to fall asleep. That's what spiritual life is all about.

By the way, this is all for the benefit of our guest. [*To the guest:*] This is the first time we've laughed in about two months. I'm not kidding. I don't want you to be under any illusions. It's not always this fun. This was just for you. That's compassion—to laugh for a new student.

The Invocation of Entities

On to *Secret Talks Volume 4* by E.J. Gold.[66] You'll find this interesting.

[Lee reads from E.J. Gold:]

Some entities we are able to feel all the time if we become subject to their influence.

---

[66] Some of the excerpts from Mr. Gold's *Secret Talks, Vol. 4* appear in Gold, E.J. *Visons in the Stone.* Nevada City, CA: Gateways/IDHHB Publishers, 1989, 130-133, 172.

E.J. Gold and I have very different styles. By the word, "entity" he doesn't mean ghosts. We wouldn't use the word "entity" and personalize it that way. We would say that graceful Divine Influence includes all entities. E.J Gold distinguishes between various degrees of entities.

[Lee continues reading from E.J. Gold:]

A book, if written consciously and with knowledge is an invocation. When used in an exact setting—such as the seance atmosphere—with a candle and no electrical apparatus, it can function as a key to certain artifacts inaccessible in any other way.

To get the entire communication of an artifact—like every one of our books—you need to read it in the exact proper setting. Some people accidentally make themselves available to a certain aspect of the communication, but not all of it. So it is worth a little experimentation. There are a number of aspects that apply regarding the setting—one of which is the mood with which it is read.

[Lee reads from E.J. Gold:]

Thoughts evoke emotions; emotions evoke a general totality of mood. Mood can be an offering which invokes an entity. An exact mood must be aroused and maintained between members of a work group.

Your criticisms of one another are true, but to use those criticisms as a way of personally "righting" yourself by "wronging" others invokes an entity that is simply not beneficial to your work. The devil has just as much power as the archangels—simply on a different end of the scale. Then there is God, who is the ultimate power. But there are entities that have tremendous power to move, transform, and generate. The entity that you invoke by the general mood you carry around is not hurting you, but it could. You all have been very fortunate because the entities you have invoked have been neutral. It's very possible to invoke negative entities—but you haven't. You've been Graced. That's why we're still here and working hard. A negative entity that we wouldn't want could be invoked if the group became so business-oriented that we totally forgot about spiritual life—if our entire aim was to propagate the existence of the corporate entity called Hohm.

Every group has an entity: the women's group, men's group, study group, core group, the group as a whole. You must make your group attractive to the entity that is going to give you what you need for your work. You'll get it if you make yourself attractive to what it is or who it is that needs you for higher purposes. I can assure you that you're not going to get it by gossiping about and criticizing one another. The entities that can upscale you are waiting. They need your participation. You're valuable to the cosmic evolution of existence itself. You're needed to be bodhisattvas. You're not needed to be devils anymore. You've come a long way from that.

You've got higher entities interested in you because you can be used in a way that benefits all of mankind. But you must make yourself attractive to those entities or they will not use you.

Student: It sounds like whenever we get together a new entity can be invoked. Is that correct?

Lee: Every single time you get together you can invoke a new entity. That's why you get a certain feeling at some meetings and you get a different feeling in others. Sometimes you invoke an entity that stays with you for a long period of time, and sometimes you invoke an entity once. When you've been used for the purpose that is needed by the entity, you're not needed anymore.

Student: Can one person make a difference in the entity that is invoked?

Lee: One person can always make a difference. If one woman were to make a difference in the woman's group it would cost her, but ultimately the payoff would be a thousand-fold. There is an immediate cost but an eventual payoff that makes any immediate cost worthwhile.

Student: Is the principle the same for attracting entities individually?

Lee: The principle is the same, but the value isn't the same as when two or more are gathered in my Name. One person can invoke entities that are valuable for their personal enlightenment, but not for the Work. Personal enlightenment commits one undeniably to the Work anyway.

[Lee reads from E.J. Gold:]

> *"To write an exact text to call down an entity," he continued, "requires exact knowledge."*

You can intentionally write something that will communicate exact knowledge if you have exact knowledge. But it will very rarely be in the form of a technical treatise. There are certain works of literature where the author knew full well what they were communicating. If you look at Dante's writings and at Swedenborg's writings, you find communications that elicit very similar entities. It's much more possible to get that entity from a piece of literature than from a technical text on yoga or spiritual development.

If any of you are really curious about this, take *Laughter of the Stones* [Lee's third book, published in 1979] and read certain of the essays. Try to figure out in a group what kind of an entity is invoked by each essay. "For the Love of God" invokes an entirely different entity than "The Divine Path of Growing Old." There is a significant difference in the impression one receives from each of those. Forget how the essay is written or if the grammar is a little off; just read it for the mood.

Student: Do human beings read literature or dharma to call down negative and/or positive entities?

Lee: Yes, people are drawn to particular forms of literature for that reason. Someone who reads the *National Enquirer* is drawn to a different entity than someone who reads *The City of God.*

[Lee reads from E.J. Gold:]
When a group reads to understand data the ideas are of only minor importance. They serve only to direct the other parts of the organic whole toward the 'invoking mood and views.'

The rhetoric only serves to orient your heart. It doesn't matter what the ideas or words say; they're irrelevant if an eloquent piece of writing invokes a mood of devotion. What's relevant is the mood that's invoked. If you read *Layla and Majnun* by Nizami, you don't have to look for esoteric clues in the language. "What's he saying here? Is this a parable? Is this a metaphor?" Read it and allow what it organically creates in you to communicate something. Study your body. When you get what your body is telling you, you won't have to decipher the esoteric clues. "As below, so above" [a saying which communicates that what happens on higher levels of reality also happens on lower levels] is true on all levels—even the organic level of flesh and blood. That's the way to work with study.

[Lee reads from E.J. Gold]:

Our own work has a very small part in the Work as a whole...You may not know very much just yet, but you can 'smell' the necessity and benevolence of it.

The Work with a capital "W" includes all of the real Sufis, Christians, Buddhists, and Work teachers in the world. There are pockets of spiritual students all around the world. At this time, there are many in America that are important to the Work at varying levels. But in terms of the

Work as a whole, you as an individual are insignificant. The Work as a whole is made up of an entire network of little cells feeding the great beast, so to speak. You don't know until the end whether it's the great beast or the divine angel that is being fed. It happens to be the divine angel, but when it eats, you are devoured just the same by the angel as by the beast. The only difference is in who and what gets served.

[Lee reads from E.J. Gold:]

> *...man is an exact model of the cosmos as a whole... But for specialized entities which are not like man, it requires several—and sometimes eight or more—men to make a manifestable formation for an entity of higher formation just because these very specialized entities are not exact models of the cosmos as a whole.*

For those of you who have come from traditional religious backgrounds of Christian and Jewish origin, think of some of the rituals in your religion that require a certain number of people to perform the ritual. For instance, when someone dies in the Jewish religion, ten or more adults are required to "sit shiva" [Shiva Minyan] for seven days. So, these ideas are still around—often in very diluted and misunderstood form.

[Lee reads from E.J. Gold:]

> *Some entities are so specialized in their formation and so different from the Great Cosmos in body and psychological type that they require many thousands of men for their organic manifestations on planet Earth.*
>
> *For this purpose they inspire—and then use for their own aims—concerts, religious meetings, political rallies, wars, marches and riots, and so forth.*

Have you ever felt the energy of a riot? Or of a certain kind of rock concert? Unbelievable! You wouldn't think that there are entities actually using the Earth to create a certain type of energy and force for their own needs. That's exactly what happens during war. Who are we to think that war is not necessary at some time? A quantity and type of energy is released in a war that has a certain utility. Krishna wasn't against the war [described in the *Bhagavad Gita*]. He simply told Arjuna, "Think of me and fight."

[Lee reads from E.J. Gold:]

> *Entities benevolent to the Work are by definition against Nature although only impartially and without malice. They are not, unless provoked, disruptive to Nature.*

Nature is just another big machine. Nature is not God. People go out on a spring day, look at the flowers blooming in a green sea of grass and think that nature is God. But nature is just another big machine. God is God, nature is nature. This machine, nature, doesn't always serve God's purpose. Entities benevolent to the Work are interested in consciousness. Nature is just another big machine which will do as much to avoid its own realization as this [human-biological] machine will do to keep from its realization. There are entities that will disturb nature, to the point of producing raging storms, hurricanes, tornadoes, volcanic eruptions, and earthquakes, if nature gets in the way of the Work. If it's necessary that nature be shocked, nature will be shocked. Entities benevolent to the Work are only interested in the Work.

Student: Is this the same principle as when we experience reactivity to one another?

Lee: No, that's a different principle. That has to do with psychic inter-reaction between one machine and another. What we're discussing here is the inter-reaction between context and content. Entity is context, machine is content.

Student: There are things that go on for us that seem to have to do with us and things that go on for us that are just to serve the Work.

Lee: Right. And much of what we think has to do with us does not.

[Lee reads from E.J. Gold:]

A small group will, even if operating without real knowledge, only be able to contact more or less harmless entities. Once there is a group of more than eight, there is danger.

Any eight people of like mind become extraordinarily powerful. Eight people like you have phenomenal power for calling entities. There's a certain part of the psyche that is not accessible when the conscious mind is in control. That's why Gurdjieff used alcohol. Alcohol breaks down that barrier. Then, certain entities can be called down that can't be called down without the alcohol. It's not that they couldn't be in theory, but in practice there is armor that prevents this from happening.

[Lee reads from E.J. Gold:]

"Learn to adopt postures which draw work entities." (G. demonstrated by calling attention to how he was standing, hands in pockets, one leg slightly forward.) "This posture is very uncomfortable for me," he said, "but I remain in it for drawing down. We can with experience recognize an entity by its 'signature,' sensing, mood and mentation. We must pay with hanbledzoin;[67] I have an enormous amount, almost a bank."

---

[67] This term was used by Gurdjieff to refer to the substance that is gathered, particularly from intentionally-made being efforts, which can be used for work.

Some of the kriyas that people [manifest] call down definite entities. If you can maintain the position of a certain kriya for one to three minutes without moving, you will see something significant that you should pay attention to. The person who experiences the particular kriya isn't the only one that can try this. The postures invoke entities. So, if you were to regularly sit in a posture that you knew brought down certain entities, you would bring to yourself a reminding factor or an influence. The more you did it, the more it would continue to work. The "prayer of the heart"[68] works on that principle.

Hanbledzoin

"Paying" with *hanbledzoin* means that the posture you choose will either fill you with energy or make you very tired. It doesn't mean that hanbledzoin is exclusively a function of your physical energy, but sometimes they synchronize. When you are in a certain posture, it can dramatically affect your general energy. Certain Sufi dancing will give you all kinds of energy. If you're tired and you do a certain dance—even alone—you'll be filled with energy. Some yoga asanas can do the same thing. Other postures will exhaust you. Both being filled with energy or exhausted are paying with hanbledzoin. You need to develop hanbledzoin in order to invoke higher entities that serve the Work.

Student: What is hanbledzoin?

Lee: Personal power, psychic energy, life force. None of those [definitions] actually fit, but it's [close to] that idea. Sex is the best possible way of developing hanbledzoin, but the circumstances must

[68] "Lord Jesus Christ, Son of God, have mercy on me a sinner" is a short prayer often associated with the Orthodox Church. It may have originated with the Desert Fathers and Mothers around the fifth century.

be just right. Like kundalini, sex can trigger very powerful energy. It's nothing to fool around with. Besides sex, some other ways to develop hanbledzoin are through the right use of stress, prayer, meditation, and work. You can also get hanbledzoin while you are sleeping, which is a nice way to do it. We develop it all day long and then typically piss it away. We sleep it away, argue it away, and jealousy it away. If we could just stop wasting the hanbledzoin we get without even doing anything special to get more, we'd have plenty of it. Part of our study is to learn how to conserve and develop hanbledzoin and use it to pay for the help we get from higher entities.

The reason it is so improbable to have sex work with any consistency as a way to develop hanbledzoin is that you have to be absolutely impartial. If any factors such as jealousy or worry about whether you are satisfying your partner are involved, you tend to undermine the process. Almost anybody can get hanbledzoin from sex randomly, when you just accidentally happen to hit the right circumstances and conditions. But to duplicate that voluntarily and intentionally is less likely. You've got to know what to do with it once you get it. It can take twenty or thirty years in the Work to even begin to use sex in the proper way.

Sex is the procreative mechanism in the human being. But mystically, procreation has to do with the evolution of existence and not the continuation of the species. If we procreated with our noses or our lungs, then breathing would be the way to develop hanbledzoin. If you do certain breathing techniques, you can develop a lot of it. But if you don't know how to use those techniques, then they become more detrimental than valuable. That is why I have been very slow to talk about breath practice.[69] It's better just to learn simple, deep breathing than to play around with tricky techniques, because if you trigger the right *nadis* [Sanskrit: energy channels] and nerve channels, you can

69 Lee gave specific breath practices in later years.

really get blasted. Usually people don't get hurt, but they get scared. That can sometimes close off an area of work to you for a long time.

A teacher gets hanbledzoin from his students, which he uses to draw down higher entities for the students themselves. A teacher knows how to use it, so he'll take it from students and give it to higher entities for the students. To do that a teacher has got to have a lot more hanbledzoin than his students. Anyone who has taken on obligation for other people has got to have a lot more energy. The more people a teacher takes on obligation for, the more energy or hanbledzoin he's got to have. Energy is a little misleading, because hanbledzoin is a lot more than energy.

[Lee reads from E.J. Gold:]

> *You must decide soon whether the Work is very important, or only a little important to you. If it is very important, you cannot allow negativity.*

Negativity is one of the principal ways of wasting hanbledzoin, besides degenerative orgasm. Sometimes negativity will actually waste a lot more hanbledzoin than degenerative orgasm. It doesn't necessarily hurt you, but it continually uses up your store. At the end of the day you have zero in the bank when you should be developing a nice little savings account with interest.

Student: It seems that the process that you describe of getting hanbledzoin should be a selfless one. At the same time, I have the sense that the drive or motivation to get it is selfish and self-oriented.

Lee: You simply won't be able to get hanbledzoin consistently if the motivation is selfish. Maybe you'll stumble on it randomly, but that's about it. You've got to be impartial—meaning selfless. And to will impartiality is not true impartiality. Actually, it's as partial as you can get.

Everybody gets hanbledzoin and everybody spends it. It's not particularly rare. Basically, if you breathe you get it. A spiritual student begins to see what hanbledzoin can be used for other than being a high energy person or keeping our biological organism alive for a certain number of years. When you begin to see what other value it has and how you can increase or decrease your attraction of it, then it can begin to be used. Some people, without even knowing what they are doing, attract and develop a lot of it. They may have a tremendous amount of power at three o'clock in the afternoon, but spend it drinking and sexing at night. You all are beginning—even unconsciously—to want more of it to use for yourselves. At this level of the game, most of you could still be magicians. You could figure this out and, boy, what you could do! A little further on, you won't be able to. Academically, technically, you'll be able to, but you'll be too committed to the Work to use it in a magical way.

[Lee reads from E.J. Gold:]

> *...by working in this way, our emissions become stronger and eventually we will develop a working magnetic center; then who has this special need will be drawn to you like bees to nectar.*

When each of your [outreach] groups is able to call down higher entities, those who need that kind of an Influence will be drawn to the group like [bees] to honey because there are people out there that need this. I'm talking about people that have some sensing of the Work. The average person's reaction to this comes from personality and fear of having to do anything. They don't see the benefit. Their initial reaction is to the suit of armor that will be destroyed instead of seeing the benefit that comes afterward.

When we start to get this power [to accumulate hanbledzoin], we're like a kid with a new toy on Christmas. For instance, when they came home after the first trip to India, people were just exuding power. We had been to shrines every day; we meditated, we studied, we enjoyed one another's company. There were very few outlets for wasting the hanbledzoin that was developed. When you maintain your practices with discipline, a tremendous charge is built up. That's why many real monks have tremendous clarity. You can see it in their eyes.

Student: Is there any possibility that there are negative entities involved in any of our practices?

Lee: Anyone that develops power becomes just as valuable to negative entities as positive ones. We have positive entities using us, but negative entities are like hyenas. The hyenas just stand around when a lion makes a kill. The lion has got to watch out because every once in a while, the hyenas run in and try to get a nip. So, there may be negative entities waiting and hoping that positive entities will go to sleep so they can close in. We've got a tremendous amount of power. The power is impartial and is of use to different entities. You must always pay attention to your work. If you get sloppy, you could be sorry. There may be negative entities just sitting and waiting, biding their time, hoping somebody falls off the wagon. But you can always resist them if you're conscious. If you're not conscious, then you can get trapped. That's why attention is necessary. You must always remember God. Be angry, be jealous, do anything you want while you're getting rid of all your garbage, but remember God. If you remember God, then the negative entities won't have a foothold. They'll be absolutely outshined. Darkness and light cannot exist in the same place. All this talk about entities is a matter of context. I'm not talking about beings or ghosts in the sense that you understand those things.

Why the Work Is Necessary

The more we get into it, the more we recognize why the Work is necessary. It's not a matter of fearing what happens to us if we don't do it; it's a matter of recognizing that the Work is the only alternative to a life of unconsciousness, negativity, pain, and mortality. By the time you get to a certain point in the Work, you can't do anything else because anything else is hell. The Work is your chance at transcendence, transfiguration, transformation, godliness. Years ago, you could live with what was wrong. Now, some of the things you could live with then—your jealousy, envy, vanity—are maddening. Then, you could say, "Everybody's got their thing." Now, it's not good enough that everybody's got their thing. When you get to the point when it burns too much, you'll drop your "thing" like a hot potato. But to get to that point takes a lot of hanbledzoin.

The power that you have is neither good nor bad. It's a matter of whether we serve people with the power we have. If we draw people to us that can be served, then it's very valuable. If you don't draw people that can be served, then we can continue to build power together. But what do we do with it? Go visit other communities and leave them in awe? That's not good enough. That doesn't serve the Work, that simply perpetuates a myth and makes for good spiritual literature. Better to serve the Work and forget the spiritual literature, except for a random work of objective writing now and again.

So, have you re-committed yourself to the intensity of the Work that you were just thinking was getting too intense?

DIVINE MADNESS

(January 20, 1981)

Divine Madness Is Being Given the Ultimate Responsibility

Any discussion about divine madness treads on very dangerous ground because many among the common masses would love to give up all responsibility for their lives. One of the ways of giving up all responsibility is appearing to be divinely mad or drunk with God. This kind of person would love to come to our ashram and walk around the property naked, saying whatever they feel like saying at any time with complete disregard for any consideration of service, sacrifice, surrender, devotion, obedience, or any such thing. They'd love to wake up when they feel like it, recite poetry at the dinner table, maybe start a food fight or play music like they were being really free and spontaneous. In most cases this is simply aberrated behavior.

Because of the pressure of the modern world, the common man loves to hear the good news of radical spiritual life. They would like to come to the monastery and act crazy. But that's not divine madness. Divine madness is not being relieved of all responsibilities. Divine madness is being given the ultimate responsibility. Even though you are lost in God, even though you are drunk with the Beloved, the Sufis would say that you become truly responsible for who you really are. To suggest that divine inebriation or divine madness is the way to live requires a tremendous amount of strength and confidence in your own understanding of what that means.

If you're a common man or woman you can have some degree of integrity. You can be responsible for yourself and your family. Then you'll be looked upon by your neighbors as a very responsible person. If you are still reading the newspapers (in complete contradiction to my recommendation), you probably read about a man who lived in a very wealthy neighborhood in Virginia with a quarter-of-a-million-dollar home [home values have gone up a lot since 1981], a very beautiful wife, and several beautiful children. He was a pillar of the community, but it turned out he made his living—millions of dollars a year—as a common burglar. When his wife went to sleep at night, he would get up and go to "work." He'd rob three or four houses a night, then come back and stash the loot in his basement. He told his wife he was an antique dealer and she believed him. He and his family lived like royalty. When the police finally raided his basement, it took them weeks to catalog all the stolen stuff they found—jewelry, watches, silverware, furniture, art. For four years he was robbing three or four houses a night. The police had seven hundred people on the case and no leads.

One night he got surprised by the owner of the house he was robbing, and he shot the guy in the chest. The guy drove himself to the hospital and died when he got there. But on the way to the hospital, the guy sees the thief running down the street, so he runs him down with his car. When he gets to the hospital, he's able to tell the police where to find the thief before he dies. The police find the man, not hurt but shaken up, sitting on the sidewalk where the guy ran him down. The cops say, "Who are you?" He says, "Boy, are you going to be surprised." All his neighbors were shocked because to everybody that knew him, he was responsible. His lawn was manicured, his children were taken care of, his wife always looked beautiful, and he was always ready to lend a helping hand to others. Conventionally, that's what we think responsibility is. If we take care of ourselves and our family adequately, then everybody says we're responsible. If we're always on time for appointments and put chains on the car to drive safely in the snow, we're responsible.

To the common man, the pressure to be responsible in this way can be devastating to the soul. Who can be responsible to a family that sees you as a possession, like another comfy chair or a good dining room table? How can you be responsible for parents who've taken your life-force as a child? Now the responsibility for them is yours and it's a heavy responsibility. You smoke, but when your children come home smelling of cigarettes, you expect them to listen to you when you tell them not to smoke. When the spiritual master says "come and be divinely mad in my company," you jump at the chance. For some people, that's the straw that breaks the back of conventional responsibility. They come to the ashram and act completely out of line, aberrated, clinically insane. They should be put in a mental institution and they think they're being spontaneous, natural, free, divinely mad.

That's not divine madness. Divine madness gives you responsibility a thousand times greater than responsibility for your family. Divine madness gives you an ultimate obligation, because who are you organically but the human race? It's not good enough anymore to defend your wife and child against whatever you think you have to defend them against. You have to defend the entire human race from its own stupidity. The human race is mired in a swamp that is almost impossible to be extricated from. But you've become personally responsible, obligated, to extricate the entire human race from that swamp. Not only are they stuck in it, there are landmines around them and you're like a bomb expert. You've seen the way people's minds react. If you touch the bomb the wrong way once—boom!

When you are divinely mad, you're like a demolition expert. You fly around in ecstasy touching people on the head, glancing into their eyes. You take on the ultimate obligation. Who in the world would want that? Nobody wants it. Nobody is running to surrender to divine madness. It is the most ecstatic, the most exquisite, the most magnificent conceivable life, but nobody wants it. Our conventional mind recognizes the obligation that is required, and it is already bent over double from our dinky everyday responsibilities. We can't imagine that kind of obligation. So, what happens is that we refuse to be divinely drunk. We refuse to be inebriated by the elixir of God because we aren't willing to surrender. We don't have the faith to recognize that if we did surrender and drink this elixir, the obligation would be nothing. It would be like the weight of a flea. It might look like we felt it, but we truly wouldn't even feel it.

When You Surrender to God, the Outer Form of Your Life Is Irrelevant

The Tibetan yogi Milarepa did his sadhana in a cave out in the wilderness where there was nothing to eat but nettles. Nettles are a plant that has pods with spines on them. That's all that grew on the mountainsides, and all he ate was nettles for seven years. He turned green from the nettles—his skin was green, his intestines were green, even his hair was green! One day his sister happened to find him. She'd heard that Milarepa was a great yogi now, living in a cave. He called to her, "Sister, come in," and she recognized his voice. She went into the cave and when she looked at him, she said, "Huh? This isn't my brother!" It had been seven years since she'd seen him and now he just looked like a skinny green madman. She said, "My God, I've got to get you something to eat! What do you have to make broth for soup?"

"There's only nettles so you'll have to make a nettle broth," Milarepa replied.

"I'll need spices and salt," his sister said.

"There's only nettles so you'll have to make nettle salt," he told her.

"I'll need some meat for the soup," she added.

"There's only nettles so make nettle meat," Milarepa responded.

"Well, okay," his sister said. She picked some nettles for nettle broth, and some more nettles for nettle salt. She used nettles again to make nettle meat. They sat down to eat and after Milarepa's sister ate a few mouthfuls, she got sick and threw up. She couldn't eat the nettles. Meanwhile, Milarepa was salivating. He took a taste and said, "Boy, this food is great!"

But she said, "You can't live like this!" She goes down the mountain to a nearby village to find some flour and a piece of meat—something good for him to eat. To Milarepa, nettles were fine. That's all that was there, so he ate nettles. He was divinely mad but he looked awful. He was emaciated—every part of him was green from eating nettles, even his teeth! He looked in the worst condition and he was in ecstasy all the time. Outward appearances don't mean anything when you've surrendered to God.

When you surrender to God, the outward form that your life takes on is irrelevant. When Hazrat Babazan [the Moslem woman saint who awakened the Indian master Meher Baba to God-life] kissed Meher Baba on the forehead, he went into an altered state of consciousness for many months and banged his head on a stone every day. Every day he'd bang his head on the stone until he bled. Meher Baba's family, which was caring for him at the time, tried to stop him but they couldn't. So they put bandages around his head to protect it. But he wasn't sad when he was banging his head; he was happy. You can't judge from outward appearances. He was completely gone—he had no semblance of ordinary consciousness. When he came out of that state, he couldn't remember any of it. He had no idea if a year or twenty years had passed.

Then there was Nityananda, who behaved like a madman. He lived in a tree for years. His devotees would bring him food and he would just grunt. People would come from miles around and sit around the tree—not right under it for obvious reasons—to get his darshan. Then there's this guy, Poondi Swami, twenty miles outside of Tiruvannamalai. He's always lost in samadhi and people come and treat him like a lingum stone. They do Hindu rituals to him like are done to a stone idol in a temple. They take the cow urine and yogurt and pour it on his head. They paint symbols on him and pray to him. He just sits there during all of it. That's all he does all year long. He has to be force-fed because he won't eat. They open his mouth and put some food in there. Then they massage his throat to get him to swallow, like you do to a snake to get them to eat. Poondi Swami transmutes the food they give him into some cosmic substance; he never goes to the bathroom. People come every day to bathe him and dress him in clean clothes, and he's perfectly happy.

When American seekers like us see these divinely-mad swamis, we think it's just awful. We want to get the welfare department to come in, rehabilitate them, and give them all their own apartments with running water. We don't know that many of them left fabulously wealthy families to live this way. Anandamayi Ma was a very saintly woman from a wealthy upper-class family that went on pilgrimages to various ashrams and religious festivals throughout India. She was a strikingly beautiful woman when she was young. God knows why she wanted to dedicate her life to God! (That was just a joke to see if all the liberated women would get their hackles up.) And Tara was one of these Tibetan goddesses that went out and meditated in the mountains with no clothes on. So it's true that outward appearances mean nothing. If someone is turned to God, it doesn't matter what the outer appearances are. When you're divinely mad, God gives you the outward form you're best suited for.

Divine madness is not a matter of giving up conventional responsibilities and letting the ashram take care of you as you wander around naked. Some of these guys that wander around naked in India are on a big ego trip. They've completely abandoned their conventional responsibilities, but not because they are divinely mad; they're clinically insane. They are manifesting an aberration of divine madness. Anyone can say, "I'm God," but if you look at their lives it's obvious they're not God. To say those words and know the truth of that organically is different than saying "I'm God" because you heard it was true. It was very hip in the early days of the Community to go around saying, "We're all God." It's not a casual thing, but it's also very important not to think, "Man, this obligation is so heavy! What am I going to do?" Then you're thinking with conventional mind, and when you surrender to divine madness it isn't the way you think it is. When you actually surrender you find something that's different than what you thought.

When we were in India there was a *mast* [one who is intoxicated with divine love, entranced by internal spiritual experiences, and cannot function in an ordinary way] whose family clearly thought he was insane. He just stood out in the yard of the family home under a tree, yelling the Name of God. Nobody answered until I saw him out the window of our hotel and started yelling back. When I yelled back at him, he got so happy. He had figured he was all alone in the world, but finally there was somebody else who understood him. When you find God, whatever that means, you realize you're all alone. He had just been alone too long. He was sad and ecstatic at the same time. Then his wife came out and yelled at me because she thought he was going to have a seizure. Soon his whole family came out, worried that somebody was communicating with this guy in his own language. They just thought he was crazy. It made them feel good to take care of him, very responsible in conventional terms. If they had the chance to give up that responsibility and melt into the flavor of this guy's madness, they wouldn't do it. They got angry at me and thought I was a crazy Westerner.

It was probably the first time in the guy's life someone talked to him in his own language. He got so happy he was dancing around clapping his hands, like children do when they get so happy they don't know what to do. If I'd been down there when his family came out, they'd have beaten me with sticks because I was getting this guy happy. All they could see was that he was going to mess his pants and then they'd have to clean it up. Obviously, he was insane and couldn't take care of himself. They should have opened the gate and let him walk around town yelling the Name of God. Then he would have had a big following and gotten all his devotees to give him money and his family would have been comfortable the rest of their lives. But no, they wanted to keep him locked behind a fence and take care of him. It would seem that this family was being responsible and earning the good graces of God by taking care of this poor insane head of the household.

Transcending the Cultural Vision That Surrounds Us

We have to be willing to transcend the entire cultural vision that we've surrounded ourselves with. It's like we're on a stage with the scenery completely around us. We can't see the audience. We're penned in and there is only scenery everywhere we look. We don't know that we could rip the scenery apart and look out and see that: *My God, there's a world out there!* And when you see the world, then what is there to be responsible for anyway? When you think about divine madness, when you consider being inebriated with the wine of God, don't think about it in conventional terms: "Things will be even harder. I'll have so much work to do. I'll have to be responsible for all these creeps I live with. They don't even put the top back on the tube of toothpaste!" But you need to look at what the world really is by punching holes in the scenery and realizing it's only scenery. That may be a dramatic metaphor, but don't worry. There are no Milarepas in the world today,[70] so you won't be put through the kind of trials he was, or endure what he did to get the teaching. There are no Marpas [Milarepa's teacher] in the world today either.

This is the age of Kali. We're not heroes, we're suckers. We're running scared. The most we get to do is a little heavy sadhana. We get to confront our lust. We get to "Ram" our beads [repeating a name of the Divine while using prayer beads] every day or give the guru some of our hard-earned money—real heavy stuff, you know. But there are no Milarepas today. Look what people like Milarepa have done and they didn't even know they were going to get God! For twelve years all Marpa did was get Milarepa to build houses and beat him for one reason or another. He'd give Milarepa one paragraph of poetry and Milarepa had to work a whole year on practicing and piercing that. Milarepa's example is very inspiring.

---

70 A reference to a statement made by a Tibetan lama whom Lee had visited in New Jersey.

You don't have to worry about those kinds of challenges. There aren't those kinds of teachers and there aren't those kinds of students today. We're just carrying on the lineage until the next age when those kinds of students show up again. Some of you may have been those kinds of students in the past and might be in the future, but there aren't those kinds of students in the world now. It's miraculous that the people sitting in this room are here. You've made some sacrifices for this Work and even in this day and age that's something to celebrate!

THE FAILURE OF PURIFICATION TO ENLIGHTEN YOU

(December 2, 1984)

Seeing What We're Up to in the Games We Play

There is a game called "Dungeons and Dragons" where you select a character and go through all kinds of adventures. If you observe the choices that you make with your character, it's amazing how clear the dynamic of ego becomes. It's literally like a map of ego—not essence. The game shows you your disposition and the particular kinds of gestures that ego makes. Many things that we do, that we take to be very innocent, can be a tremendous magnifying glass in focusing awareness on our own dynamics. It is so easy to see other people's numbers and so difficult to see our own. The clarity with which we view ourselves is really heightened by the kinds of things we take seriously when we are playing.

Psychologically, we know that when people say "I'm just kidding," they are more serious than if they say something without that disclaimer. Many people don't know how to be honest, or they don't want to hurt somebody's feelings, or they are embarrassed or shy. If they have an issue with another person, they will say to them, "Man, that's an ugly shirt! Just kidding. Haha!" It is as if that form of communication is just a friendly, humorous interchange. Almost invariably, when people say "Just kidding," you can be sure that they are very serious; they just don't know how to say it seriously.

The games that we take seriously are tremendously informative about our own dynamics. It's one of the reasons the game of bridge is so valuable. If you really pay attention to your relationship to the other three people, especially if there are a couple of criticizers, or your friends are around and everybody is looking over your shoulder nodding or making comments, your reaction to the dynamics in the game can really map out pretty clearly or at least point you in the direction of recognizing your own egoic tendencies. Those tendencies will come out in any game that we take seriously. Games and jokes are a very good way of recognizing our own egotistical foibles, so to speak.

There are a lot of opportunities for this kind of self-observation. At the Fourth of July show booth this weekend, where we sell fry bread every year, there were really long lines. Everybody was working very hard. Nobody really had time to even eat. We ate before eleven and then didn't get to eat again until closing time. Every once in a while, we would stuff down a bite of something as we worked. Throughout the afternoon, people were saying to the person taking orders at the window, "I bet you'll be glad when Monday comes!" or "I bet you'll be glad when this show is over!" We were all really having a good time, but we have this habit of complaining. When people working in the booth heard these comments, they would say, "Yeah, it'd be nice to get a chance to eat something or go to the bathroom," or some other negative comment. These comments were not said to me, so I didn't say anything. But my thought—which was relatively true for everybody—was that I wouldn't be doing the show if I was glad it was going to be over on Monday. We work like this while the show is on and then relax. It's a tiring process, but the busier we are the better. Today was absolutely the way I love it. It is awful when you stand around and the fry bread gets warm and soggy because you cooked too many. Today there was no fry bread left over.

We are generally pretty careful in our interactions within the sangha. But when we get into a situation where we are just socializing with the general public, it's amazing the clarity with which we can see our own dynamics, our own process of ego. These kinds of circumstances are very valuable for a spiritual student. Some students have seen this value, appreciate it, and like to engage in such situations for that reason. Other people just like to work hard. There are a lot of reasons why people who do the [Fourth of July] shows like to do them; the benefits for sadhana are really exceptional.

Interactions with the public are a good way to see what we are doing. It's not that we should dwell on the idea of seeing what we are up to. You could very realistically spend your whole life seeing what you are up to because you are always up to something—even when you are functioning from a disposition of enlightenment. Then it will have a different quality to it, a different tone or feeling. But you'll still be up to something. We could spend our whole lives observing what we are up to and not recognize the principles of the divine process. There is the divine process, and then there is all of the content that we identify with: our likes, dislikes, behavior patterns, psyche, motivations, physical posture—all of that. You can continue to have deeper and deeper insights for a lifetime.

Almost Anything Can Trigger the Fear of Extinction

The dynamic of mind, of ego, of psyche is like this... A child suffers some event that causes him to believe he is not going to survive. It could be anything—not being nursed quickly enough, a dream of falling, or mommy tripping while carrying her baby and even though she catches herself the child telepathically feels the danger. It could be any one of a thousand events. When the child feels that it is not going to survive, it imprints at a level of instinct all of the stimuli and feeling that arises in the moment. Using that same example, where mommy is carrying baby and trips, even though she regains her balance, there is a moment of instinctual response where the survival mechanism is triggered. The child isn't sophisticated enough to reflect upon the survival mechanism and know that mommy only tripped, and that baby is fine as soon as mommy catches herself.

The child is telepathic with mommy, and the survival mechanism triggers the possibility of extinction. The child imprints everything in that instant—all the stimuli within its perception. Suppose mommy is wearing a red blouse and a white skirt, and the room is painted yellow.

There is music with violins playing on the stereo, and the temperature in the room is sixty-eight degrees. The child had just finished nursing and still had the taste of milk in her mouth when mommy tripped. It is theoretically possible that any one of those stimuli—red, white, yellow, sixty-eight degrees, violin music, that particular taste—could trigger the same feeling at any time for the rest of that child's life. For those of you who think you have free will, pay attention to this example.

Let's say it's a year later. The child is in a room and the temperature is sixty-eight degrees. The memory of that moment when survival was triggered is touched by the temperature and the child experiences primal fear again. Now, suppose the child is wearing blue pants and a green shirt and is playing in a crib looking through the bars. There is a cat walking across the room, which is lit with fluorescent light. Suddenly a car horn blares outside, frightening the child. From then on blue, green, fluorescent lights, a cat, a car horn, sixty-eight degrees, violin music, and the taste of mother's milk can trigger survival. If we extend the example to every time one of those stimuli triggers the original feeling, all the additional stimuli in the environment of that moment add to the pool of stimuli that can then trigger survival. Although the process is random and arbitrary, by the time we are adults we are locked into a psychological dynamic whereby almost anything can trigger the fear of extinction. We are not free beings.

There are people in mental institutions who are driven into a kind of catatonia as a way of avoiding the trigger and response. They have shut down all systems so that the fear of extinction will cease to be triggered in their lives. But for the ordinary person, just about anything at any time can be a survival trigger. You can see that working on ourselves, at that level, is an absolutely endless process. Imagine trying to clear the psyche of all of the things that could trigger the fear of extinction. You would hardly know where to start, except on the grossest level.

Transcendence of the Mechanism

Maybe as an adult you recognize that you are claustrophobic. Every color, sound, smell, and feeling that was present every time you were ever in a closed space is now a trigger—even subtly—for the feeling of claustrophobia. Many people walk around feeling a vague fear. There is nothing outwardly wrong, but they have a sense of foreboding and they don't know why. It's because any one of countless stimuli can trigger the fear of extinction at any time. There is value in recognizing survival as the principal dynamic of ego, but it's an almost impossible task to try and clear the psyche so that all of those things that create reactivity or recoil in our lives don't anymore. Some things are regular triggers. We could probably trace down those things, but it wouldn't clear the psyche by any stretch of the imagination.

The focus needs to be transcendence of the mechanism itself, not transcendence of the particular stimuli that trigger survival. The mechanism needs to be transcended into a condition of Organic Innocence.[71] When the survival mechanism is *needed*, the condition of Organic Innocence has the intelligence to trigger it.

There are some people who don't feel pain. It is an actual but fairly rare medical condition. A person who doesn't feel pain could get a very serious burn and not know it, but they would still go into shock and suffer all the bodily responses to organic trauma. That kind of condition does not happen when you transcend the mechanism that triggers the fear of extinction. You can only transcend the mechanism into a condition of Organic Innocence, which is directly aligned to the Great Process of Divine Evolution.[72] The Great Process of Divine Evolution

---

71 A teaching phrase that Lee used to describe the essential intelligence of being or existence and of living from the instinctual freedom and knowledge of the body.

72 A teaching phrase that Lee used to refer to the Will of God, the evolutionary force of Creation.

has a kind of benign intelligence that is aligned to the instinctual process of the body. One of the instinctual processes of the body is to maintain its existence: to jump out of the way of a car that is speeding toward you, to brace yourself when you fall, to instinctually protect your face, to blink when something comes toward the eyes.

Those kinds of mechanisms will not be transcended because they are genuine survival mechanisms. They are distinct from the mechanisms that trigger when *ego's* survival is threatened. Even in our Community, where people are intimate friends with a common agreement to develop a culture of compassion and care, and to be direct and honest and real with one another, we can observe what goes on when a primal issue like power is triggered. Our high ideals go out the window! Imagine a twenty-six-year-old guy that manages a Kentucky Fried Chicken and pulls rank on the four high-school-age girls that work for him—he's a maniac for power. Then consider the kinds of excesses that probably take place within a large corporation when billions of dollars, tens of thousands of employees, and sometimes even life or death are at stake.

One of the things that we need to know is that the labyrinth of the mind is intricate beyond our imagination. It's more intricate than any computer we could ever imagine. To try and purify on that level is an endless process. The nature of our purification is not arbitrary, and neither is it rational. As spiritual students, the nature of our purification follows a law of spirit and not a law of logic. Because we are under the Influence of the Divine, we are not purified in a linear, psychological way. There are many holistic health processes that purify and balance people in a linear logical way that moves you back through deeper and deeper levels of the psyche and through early experiences. Those things all have their place. They are fine if that is your destiny. Doing that kind of purification is better than living out your life as an animal, but it is not the point in this school. Not only is it not the point, it is not what happens here.

We Get What We Need to be Submitted to the Will of God

It is true that some people remember events from their childhood very clearly; some people remember certain experiences from inside the womb. It's not that we don't purify from those dimensions, but the purification is not a logical, rational process. We purify according to the law of Divine Influence. Each of us as a unique individual—given the influence of the stars, our birth, tendencies, disposition, and dynamics—will get what we need to be submitted to the Great Process of Divine Evolution. We purify exactly in relationship to that. We are not subject to an overall psychological law that is the same for everyone. Because each of us is unique, each of us purifies in a unique way that is directly in relationship to what is needed in order to be submitted to the Will of God. Through the Divine Influence that permeates our lives, we are all submitting ourselves to the Will of God. Different facets of the psyche will be purified for each of us. So, everybody doesn't go through the same thing. We each go through purification around whatever particular obstruction we have in relationship to the Great Process of Divine Evolution.

That is the way it works. When you recognize that principle in your own lives, you won't knock your head against the wall attempting to manifest psychological purity because we don't have to mature linearly. All we have to do is be submitted to the Will of God, to the Great Process of Divine Evolution. That is the beginning. Then we start to work. How to get to the point where we are so committed to the divine process that no matter how it manifests in our lives we can't go back to being unconscious again? In traditional cultures, the end has justified the means to get people to that point.

It should be an easy enough matter to remember, even if it requires some effort of will, not to get wrapped up in or fascinated by the linear purification of the psyche. There is so much fascination with how our childhood and infancy affect our functioning as adults. The purification of those levels can be discomforting, but also tremendously fascinating, interesting, and enlightening with a small "e." There is nothing wrong with those kinds of memories when they arise, as they naturally do, as long as we don't get trapped by or distracted with that kind of realization and mistake it for sadhana. Sadhana is the transcendence of the never-ending mechanism of stimuli triggering the fear of extinction [survival] into Organic Innocence [instinctual freedom]. Remember to focus on the process of transcendence through the help of submission to Divine Influence, and not on being fascinated by the process of the psyche.

Student: If the idea is not to get fascinated with psychological purification, and if all of that stuff is illusion anyway, why are dreams important in our sadhana?

Lee: The imagery in dreams is mostly subjective—even archetypal imagery can show up in a subjective form—but information, direction, and hints can also be communicated to us in dreams. Dreams can be of some value in giving us clarity regarding sadhana.

Student: How about the life-level conditions? For me they serve a process of linear purification. Do they also support non-linear purification in the way you have been speaking of?

Lee: All of the conditions—diet, exercise, study, meditation—serve to align the biological organism or make it optimally responsive to the influences that interface between the chemistry and spirit. The purification that I was speaking of before is purification of mind or emotions, but it shows up in the body. Many of you have trouble making this distinction. For instance, people will ask me to tell them what exactly they are resisting. It is really unnecessary to know that. It's fine if you discover it. Just remember that there is resistance, and the process itself will take care of addressing the resistance. A lot of people want it in black and white; they want a map. They say, "Show me where I am resisting, and then I am going to work on it." When I look at students, I don't look at them with the idea of seeing where particular pockets of resistance are. I may know someone has trouble with diet or trouble with studying, but I don't look for that kind of thing.

Student: For me it brings up doubt. Am I in the right place with the right teacher? Maybe by the time I find out I will be entangled and trapped—a spiritual slave.

Lee: You have to trust your own intelligence and self-esteem so that you don't get psychologically trapped. Watch me and see if I am trying to trap people psychologically. If I am, question that. But I think you'll find that you won't get psychologically trapped. You might get trapped in a spiritual sense. If you do, that's great—for you.

Celebration tent, Arizona ashram, 1986

A NIGHT WITH THE GURU AND HIS FRIENDS

(June 23, 1985)

Liberation Defines a Game with Unbreakable Rules

I was listening to a tape by a Buddhist teacher and a man in the audience said, "I think it's all 'play.'" The teacher said, "It *is* play, but to know what that means, first of all you've got to know the game, and second of all you've got to know the rules. You can't play the game if you don't know the rules."

If you don't know the game, all of this nonsense about being free and spontaneous is a bunch of garbage. Life *is* play, and the most ecstatic and delightful aspect of life is play, but you can't play if you don't know the game. And you can't play the game if you don't know the rules. The thing about the rules is that they are the *rules*. When you play the game, whatever game you're playing, you have to follow the rules or else you're not playing the game. The context of playing the game is that it doesn't matter if you win or lose. What matters is playing the game.

The content is, if you're going to play the game, don't sit around and be a tepid schmuck. Throw yourself into it! If you're playing tennis, go for blood. Whatever you're playing, throw yourself into it like it was life or death, like nothing else existed in the world but that game. Not cutthroat, but with passion. When you play a game, play it to the limit, with as much passion, power, and energy—not aggression—as you can throw into it. It doesn't matter if you win or lose. That's totally irrelevant, but the irrelevancy of winning and losing is not the point. Most games are competitive, and the idea is to win. So, if that's one of the rules of the game—that there is a winner and there is a loser—you play to win. And if you don't win, it doesn't make any difference. If you lose so bad that you'll never be able to live it down, it doesn't make a bit of difference. What matters is that you play by the rules and throw yourself into it 100 percent—*more* if you can. With every ounce of energy and enthusiasm and mastery you have, throw yourself into the game. That goes for *every* game.

If you're playing *this* game—I'll call it "the ashram game"—you should throw yourself into it if you're going to ultimately benefit. I don't know how many of you are still looking for liberation, but liberation defines a game that is absolute, with rules that are unbreakable. A lot of people think, "Oh, when I get liberated, I'll go to this *loka* and that *loka*. I'll visit Venus and see what's cooking and check out this and that other realm." It's not like that. When you get liberation, you move into a game in which you can't break the rules—not upon pain of death! It's not like some horrible thing will happen if you break the rules; you *can't* break the rules. Liberation means you're in a game in which the game is obvious and the definition is clear. Liberation is not, "Free at last! Now I can be immortal, I don't have to pay attention to anything, and everybody will honor me. I won't feel pain ever again and isn't it wonderful?" That's not liberation. That's certain types of heavens, which are basically at the same or at an even lesser level than we're at because we have a better opportunity to realize.

You have the greatest opportunity to realize God when you live in a world that is essentially a play of opposites. When you live in a world in which there are no opposites, which is defined by one particular end of the spectrum—when you don't know that there even are opposites or you think that you've left opposites behind—you don't have much chance to realize yourself. You're locked into a static dynamic. The fact that human life is so full and absolutely rich with the play of opposites—pleasure-pain, dark-light, etc.—is why the opportunity is so great here.

Machine Problems Never End

[Lee switches gears to read from E.J. Gold's *Talk of the Month* titled "Conflict Management":]

If the attention of the essential self is focused on machine problems, one set of circumstances will occur, and one set of results will obtain, and conversely, if the attention of the essential self is focused on transformation toward becoming a necessity to the Work, then the Work will somehow, through coincidence control, arrange your transformation, and at the same time, the life of the machine will change, right back to the moment of conception.[73]

You know the est[74] statement: Problems will "clear up just in the process of life itself." If you recognize a certain essential quality, you won't need to intentionally resolve, rearrange, or fix anything. As the saying goes, "If it's not broken, don't fix it." So, if you are not going to take personal responsibility for seeing something accomplished, leave it alone; it's none of your business. If you're going to take personal responsibility for something, then see it through to completion to the best of your ability. Not just until it gets a little frustrating, because it *will* get *damn* frustrating. The whole world doesn't want it—whatever *it* is—done properly, including *this* world here on the ashram. If you don't have the ability to see a task through to completion yourself, that's perfectly all right. Nobody expects you to be super-human. Seek help if you need help, but don't give up.

If you focus the essential self on the problems of the machine—your conditioning, education, psychology, prejudices, fears—you'll never eliminate them. All you'll do is uncover pocket after pocket of problems. In *lifetimes* you wouldn't begin to scratch the surface. There is an analogy that's used of "polishing the mirror of enlightenment." When you get the

---

73 Gold, E.J. (circa 1981). Conflict Management. In School Conditions: Six Talks by E.J Gold. [Online] Nevada City, CA: Gateways Books and Tapes, 7. [Accessed March 2021].

74 An organization founded by Werner Erhard that offered seminars from 1971-1984 aimed at transforming one's experience of living.

mirror polished, remove all the dust, and look in a clear mirror—that's enlightenment. The only problem is that the dust settles again when the mirror is left unpolished for a very short period of time. Machine problems never end! Never! At the point at which the machine begins to mellow out, then you deal with the problems of old age: eyesight and hearing fail, you've got digestive problems, and on and on.

You can deal with machine problems somewhat successfully as a young, strong, healthy individual, but you're going to get old and die sooner or later. You're going to have sagging coopers and a flabby ass. Your hair's going to start to fall out, and either the wife or the husband is going to look twenty years older than the other one. You've seen couples where the guy looks forty and the woman looks fifty, or the woman looks forty and the guy looks fifty, and you say, "What are they doing together?" That's the way it goes. The machine never runs out of problems! You can be dealing with machine problems forever. However, if your focus is allowing the machine to be a transformational apparatus, "...the life of the machine will change right back to the moment of conception." In our language, the only way to deal with life is to transcend the cramp of duality. Then all of the problems of the machine will cease to control you. They won't stop coming up, but they won't control you anymore; they won't bind you organically.

How the Work Can Provide for Our Transformation

[Lee reads from E.J. Gold:]

> *Of course, your work to prepare yourself for the Work is still necessary...because without the chemical and psycho-emotional foundation, all your efforts towards transformation will be as if nothing.*[75]

[75] Gold, ibid.

You might wonder why you have to do the life-level conditions if there's only God. You must do the conditions to prepare yourself for the work of transformation. Because if you move into a space in which the machine is functioning as a transformational apparatus, but you haven't prepared the groundwork, then all the products of your alchemical experimentation will go to waste. That's why we do the conditions: to prepare to do the Work when we're given the Work to do. Jesus said that nothing will grow if you throw seeds onto barren ground. We've been lucky enough to have been blown by the wind onto fertile soil. When you were born, the dispositions of your father and mother were ingredients that went into the kind of plant you are. Speaking very honestly, some of you are still vegetables, but we're working on it.

[Lee reads from E.J. Gold:]

> *...but we can make ourselves so indispensable to the Work, even now, in sleep, that the Work is forced to cause our transformation...*[76]

Don't *try* to wake up the machine. That's very difficult to do. It's easy to wake the machine up for short periods of time, but not permanently. Make yourself, "even now in sleep,"[77] so indispensable to the Work that the Work itself will take care of your transformation naturally, easefully. Easeful to the Work...it might not be so easeful to you. So that's a very serious consideration. How can a sleeping being be indispensable to the Work? Well, [chuckling] keep spreading your spiritual legs, as they say in some circles. That's the answer if you're a woman. If you're a man, make sure your spiritual "leg" doesn't go limp at the wrong time... spiritually speaking, of course.

[Lee reads from E.J. Gold:]

---

76 Ibid., 8.

77 Lee and Mr. Gold seem to be referring to the state of "sleep" as self-meditative, mechanical life.

> *...provided we prepare the ground, sow the seeds, add nutrients, water regularly and constantly watch over and cultivate the garden as necessary. This more or less accurately describes the process of what is called work on self.*[78]

Student: Would that be defined in our language as "doing the conditions"?

Lee: Right. If you are not prepared, if the garden is not properly tended, the Work won't cause your transformation; it will just blow you up. Why don't we all wake up tonight? Because the Work, Divine Influence, is very selective. The ground needs to be prepared for all eventualities. The Work will be forced to provide our transformation if we prepare the ground, sow the seeds, add nutrients, and water regularly.

Some of you have been awake for a week or weeks. That in itself is a part of the preparation. Waking up for three weeks is like developing a hybrid strain. The hybridization of corn makes it resistant to insects like corn caterpillars that eat corn and make it unsellable. The hybridization of a human being also makes it resistant, but to the things that take the human being, the machine, away from the Work—like pride, jealousy, anger, fear, doubt, envy, greed, and lust. If you think about it, you will recognize that certain experiences in your sadhana have changed your relationship to some of those things.

Like lust, for example. Ten years ago, some of you would get it anywhere you could, under any circumstances, just being careful not to get disease. Even then, if you were hot enough, you'd throw all caution to the wind and say, "I'll take my chances!" And what some of you have seen is that you've been hybridized. You're no longer willing to use sexual energy in that way. Even in a committed relationship, you're not

78 Gold, ibid.

willing to just piss it away anymore. So, when you wake up for three weeks, that awakening is like Divine Influence experimenting on you. We're all in a laboratory and Divine Influence is experimenting with us. The nice thing about this laboratory is that Divine Influence doesn't make mistakes. In a sense there's experimentation, but in another sense the end result is guaranteed. So, when we're hybridized by Divine Influence, we get to be like the ultimate consumer item. We get to be absolutely what is best, what the consumer wants.

It's an ongoing process; you don't do this in one moment. The first thing you have to do is make sure that the garden is tended properly. Basically, you take care of the soil, the light, add nutriments and water. Then, when the garden is fairly well prepared—meaning when your discipline is at an acceptable level—you consider how to make yourself, even in sleep, so indispensable to the Work that the Work itself will provide your transformation. Before that point, there is no need to consider the question [of how to come into the waking state]. Because if you come up with an answer, you'll probably try it out, and then more than likely you'll be *expressed* from the Work. Divine Influence is also a great pimple popper. If you make the wrong move at the wrong time, you'll get all pus-y and sore and then the Work will *[makes an expelling sound with his mouth]* … Goodbye!

Well, tonight is rich with metaphors!

You Can Blow a Very Delicate Alchemical Experiment in an Instant

If you aren't in control of your emotions, you can't control your chemistry. When you lose your temper, you can blow a very delicate alchemical balance in an instant. Lose your temper and there's too much heat and the alchemical experiment is dead. You can spend *years* preparing a very delicate alchemical experiment and blow it with one loss of temper. You have to be very sensitive to your own emotional moods. It's been my experience that emotional moods are like an epileptic seizure; you can feel them coming on. Usually, we feel ourselves getting angry and we just say, "The hell with it, I'm not going to stop it." But you can. There's a lead-in in which you know it's coming, and you can stop it or mute it so it doesn't blow the experiment. We all need to learn to do that. Divine Influence provides the proper catalytic function at the proper time.

Most people are on the path of machine life and want to end up benign quiet individuals, basically healthy, serving their friends and being good moms and dads and having good kids and not worried too much. That's fine, but it has nothing to do with the Work. That's the way to remain on the wheel forever and get some good karma so in your next life you'll have less struggles. If you want to wake up, you have to stop being consumed by the life of the machine, or the alchemical reactions necessary to awakening won't occur. It's just a matter of law. It's purely organic, nothing mystical about it. No matter how much white light we see, if our focus is on solving the problems of the machine, we will not enter chambers[79] in which higher work is going on. Why would we? The life of the machine has nothing to do with higher chambers. The life of the machine is purely automatic. It's a perpetual-motion machine.

The Guru-Devotee Game

[Lee reads from E.J. Gold:]

> *All you have to do is go through it, learn how to work, if possible, and don't hurt yourself or anybody else in the process.*[80]

---

79 Spaces where attention is focused, and a mood of communion and receptivity is present. In a chamber, one may find oneself in the waking state for a period of time.

80 Gold, 9.

You can't learn how to work from me—it has to be experiential. Not hurting yourself or anybody else should be common sense. There are some levels of meaning to that. Don't give yourself or others more karma than necessary, don't [negatively] affect other people's participation in the Work. Those kinds of things.

[Lee reads from E.J. Gold:]

> *Pass on what you have learned but only after you understand what it is that has happened to you,* and very strongly disallow in yourself that first tendency after your transformation to gather people around you to touch your robe.[81]

Very, very important. Most of you have met people that have had a very real experience of awakening but have taken that to mean that they're done and should now be doing the ultimate teaching work, gathering people around them to "touch their robes." Sooner or later, those people always come to bad ends. If you look at many teachers, they are more than willing to have students teach within their essential matrix, but not at the same level of responsibility they've taken. The biggest mistake I could ever make is to fail to continue to remind you not to lose a sense of yourself. Within the domain of robe-touching, it's very easy to lose a sense of yourself. And I have to be careful because this is the form [that of being a guru] that we will continue to pursue. I have personally transcended it; you need to transcend it. This game is defined by the guru-devotee relationship, and there are certain rules to that. We need to play the game completely, but not get trapped by the game.

A certain kind of holding on to my robe is trying to win the game, not realizing that it doesn't matter whether you win or lose. Winning and losing the guru game isn't at issue. Being the guru's favorite is

---

[81] Ibid.

ostensibly winning the game. Losing the game is, "He never gives me any attention!" Throw yourself into the game with every ounce of passion you can muster but realize that winning or losing the game is not what's at issue here. My communication is made whether you win or lose this game. So, play to win, but play to win from the context that, in your relationship to me, winning or losing is irrelevant. There is a game here, the rules of the game are obvious, the conditions are established, there are several thousand years of traditional information that define this culture. Play the game, pay attention to the rules. Winning or losing is not at issue. That's the context.

When you wake up, realize that you are being hybridized. Don't take your waking up to be a sign that you should go out and gather people around you to touch your robe. That's always the first inclination because one of the rules of the Work is that you must pass on what you've learned. You will be moved to pass on what you've learned, but you must be careful not to gather people around to touch your robe or your feet...or something else, which is a masculine tendency. "I'm awake now! There are a lot of lucky women out there that should be initiated." You have to be very careful not to follow your first inclination to spread the wealth in a way that reinforces ego. You should share what you've learned but in the appropriate form.

Editor's note: *At this point a student is taken by helpless laughter, undoubtedly in response to Lee's comments. Lee encourages the student to let go...*

If you're going to lose it anywhere, this is the place. [*Student is laughing and trying to hold it back.*] When she's passed the point of embarrassment, she is going to wonder, "Wow, where did that come from?" That could be a form of enquiry under very exclusive circumstances when you have a free moment that surprises you—the mature form of enquiry. We'll start with "Who am I kidding?" ...Hey, we're developing a nice system here... Then in the mature stages of practice we'll move on to the "Where did that come from?" form of enquiry. "Who am I kidding?" is applied everywhere. Then, when you've matured to the point where you've freed certain levels of your being so essence can peek its little head through, then you can use "Where did that come from?" We've discovered something here!

[Lee reads from E.J. Gold:]

> *In order to help somebody else to achieve the same thing, you* must first understand *what has happened, and how it happened.*[82]

In the beginning of my teaching Work, I understood *what* had happened, but I didn't understand *how* it happened, which is why my expectancy was frustrated. I literally expected people to just duplicate what had happened to me, immediately. I imagined that I would tell them, and they would duplicate it. As I began to understand how my shift of context had happened, then I was able to communicate the teaching in a more usable fashion. In the beginning, there was nothing usable about the teaching, although it bonded people to the Work. Now there's a lot of usable communication because I also understand how it happened. And to tell you how it happened is to probably guarantee that it will take you twice as much time to get there. So, understanding how it happened is also, in a sense, frustrating because I have to communicate that experientially—not by *telling* you how.

---

82 Ibid.

Choosing Between What the Machine Wants and What the Essential Self Wants

[Lee reads from E.J. Gold:]

> *It is an inevitable that the machine will go through a certain amount of suffering if we are to have the transformational effects.*[83]

If the body is going to be evolutionarily transformed, there's going to be some organic pain. There's got to be some suffering. The same is true on the levels of emotion—that's what the "dark night of the soul" is. The dark night of the soul is the inescapable suffering that arises out of evolutionary changes in the machine. There is some pain involved in a transformational shift in the body. When the cells change, there's some suffering that goes along with it. But it's not the suffering of the life of the machine, and it's not *felt* like the suffering of the life of the machine.

[Lee reads from E.J. Gold:]

> *Many times it will become necessary to take a direction that doesn't make any sense from the machine's view. We can either have what the machine wants or what the essential self wants. We can* never *have both at the same time. Never, ever.*[84]

At some point in your life you have to make a choice between what the machine wants and what the essential self wants. I had an argument with a friend of mine who said that I wasn't leading people into spiritual life with their eyes open. I was making *unconscious* artifacts. Trapping people, in a sense, into the Work. This man could not be convinced

83 Ibid.

84 Ibid.

otherwise. But in a sense, people *are* trapped into the Work, onto the Path. Then, when it's too late, if they're sensible, they stop fighting it and just throw themselves into the life of the essential self—which is focusing on the machine as a transformational apparatus. At that point you couldn't choose that form of machine life if you wanted to. Isn't that nice to know? It should be nice to know. For me it's comforting just to know what I have to do.

Hilda Carlton told me many times that once in the Work you're a slave to it. And I would say "No!" I was holding on to an image of there being no bounds and no limits and being able to do anything I wanted. If you follow the life of the machine, that's true up to a point. But if you follow the life of the essential self, it's simply untrue. And so, we should be very happy to be given our limits. When you're given your limits, the sane thing to do is to simply move within those constraints. You can fight city hall all you want, but you can't change it. City hall is city hall. The army is the army. Spiritual work is spiritual work. Why fight it? You know what the game is, you know what the rules are. You aren't going to change the rules of *this* game. So, you ought to start playing by the rules.

[*Lee narrates what is going on in the room at the moment, for the benefit of anyone listening to a recording of the talk:*] Shakti is moving one of the devotees into a strange position of apparently carrying a tremendous burden, with rounded shoulders, bent back, twisted neck, and a look of extreme pain on his face.

That's the way it'll look if you keep fighting this—spiritually, emotionally, physically. The rules are obvious; play by the rules. Why bother playing if you're not going to play by the rules? You can't fight the rules. Moods of depression, loneliness, anxiety, and frustration hit you in cycles because you're not willing to be responsible for the fact that you're in an airtight game and you don't want to play by the rules. You want to try and change the game. You can't change the game! Believe me, I'm telling you from experience. If the game could be changed, it would already be different. The game cannot be changed.

Everybody that encounters a real school will have to make the decision to give priority to the essential self and its work with the machine. To quote E. J. Gold, "Let the chips fall where they may in the life of the machine." Suppose, academically, it is to the essential self's benefit to move to the ashram and live here. Then, to let the chips fall where they may might mean you have to make some very difficult decisions—like leaving a job that you love or giving up certain comforts you enjoy. For people that come to this Work with children, your child has a relationship to the Work entirely independent of you.

Wanting your child to be in the Work is the same thing as wanting your daughter to be a virgin 'til she gets married. Let *them* choose whether they're going to be in the Work or not. If this is where they belong, they'll show up here.

You must at some point take a vow with your own conscience that you're not going to compromise by being consumed with the life of the machine. For many of you, the suffering in your life is caused by the fact that you've made that vow and you are not letting the chips fall where they may. It has nothing to do with me. If you want the suffering *I* can provide, you've got to honor that vow.

[Lee reads from E.J. Gold:]

> *Your remaining here in this community is your way of saying, "Let me have... whatever is necessary."*
>
> *Your continued presence in this community is implied consent to this.*
>
> *You must ask yourself:... Are you willing to work to be in the Work?*[85]

[85] Ibid, 10.

Nothing should create an argument in you, because your continued presence here is implied consent that I am obligated to provide for you, and I *will* provide for you, whatever is necessary. My job is not to pussyfoot around and treat you with kid gloves. You're giving me permission to do my job and you should understand that. Your questions should be: Do I want to realize love? Do I want to be a real human being? And am I willing to submit myself to whatever discipline is necessary to *be* that? If you realize love, you may find that love is not necessarily what serves your satisfaction, happiness, amusement, and pleasure. As those of you with children know, love is sometimes something else entirely.

[Lee reads from E.J. Gold:]

> *There will be only one topic of conversation in this community from now on, if you understood what I have just said: "How are we going to get these damn machines into the waking state? How are we going to activate them as transformational apparati?"* This *is the kind of gossip and conversation I expect to hear... not machines chattering endlessly on with their petty considerations and preferences... let's hear a little* essential *self gossip!*[86]

Look, the gossip that goes on around here is either gossip about one another or gossip about machine problems: your diet, the tea you're drinking, your relationships, your dreams, your intuitions and visions. You can't imagine how boring all that stuff is to me ...and aggravating, annoying, and infuriating. The people that live with me don't see my inner life; my inner life is masked. I want "essential self gossip!" Let's talk about God! Let's talk about the Work! Let's talk about transformation! Not raw food, tea, and ginger baths.

Editor's note: *The same student who was laughing earlier and trying to hold it in is still laughing. Lee calls back as he leaves the room:* "Ho, ho, ho..."

---

86 Ibid.

TO BUILD CASTLES ON SAND

(August 20, 1985)

Editor's note: *Lee begins this talk with references from two different books—one on Zen practice, one on Baul practice. Then he speaks on his main topic, "to build castles on sand," and weaves principles from the readings into the main theme and in answering questions in a characteristic free-ranging style of teaching.*

Zen Practice

Since it's come up pretty consistently lately, I want to talk about ritual, form, rules, and hierarchy. But first, this is from a book called *The Mind of Clover* by Robert Aitken:

> *Practicing compassion goes hand in hand with practicing realization. On your cushions in the dojo (the training center), you learn first of all to be compassionate toward yourself. I can recall occasions when I sat in zazen with my mind a turmoil of murderous thoughts and feelings. Perhaps you have had such experiences also. We vow to save all beings, but how do you save the roughnecks in your own mind? Treat them as neighbors who come to the door when you are meditating. Take a moment to acknowledge them. They are closer than neighbors, after all.*
>
> *"Oh, there you are, you violent thought." With this recognition, you are ...at ease with yourself because you are no longer blindly responsive to your thinking and feeling—and thus no longer at the mercy of your karma. Then when your boss or somebody else takes up a role in the old family play that formed your life, you can exclaim, "Oh, I remember you!" and the pain will be reduced. You will be left to deal with circumstances, which might be difficult enough without clouds of childish emotions to confuse them.*[87]

[87] Aitken, Robert. *The Mind of Clover.* San Francisco: North Point Press, 1978, 18.

This passage is an answer to several questions. Those of you for whom the shoe fits, wear it! Rarely does anyone approach me with a serious question about what circumstances are providing. The question is almost always about the clouds of childish emotions that arise coincidently to the circumstances. So, deal with the clouds of childish emotions. Acknowledge them: They are there. They've arisen. They're in your stream of consciousness, and they'll be gone soon enough. If you're hungry enough, they'll be gone as soon as the meal bell is rung.

[Lee reads from Robert Aitken:]

> *This Bodhisattva practice has its source in zazen where you discern the power of a single unacknowledged thought… and the importance of seeing through it.*
>
> *Thoughts and feelings conveyed from our grandparents and beyond, disrupt our families and set the stage for the continuation of subtle and even overt violence in the future. With awareness, all this can change.*
>
> *"I should not have said that or done that," you can say to your spouse or child, and the damage is repaired to some degree, perhaps without a seam if it is caught soon enough. Compulsion is weakened by such correction, and next time perhaps the error will be milder. This too is Bodhisattva practice. Complete freedom and devoted compassion are the same in the Buddha-mind, but even Shakyamuni had to work at it. He did not experience true nature as soon as he sat down, after all…*[88]

> *The practice of peace and harmony is peace and harmony, not some technique designed to induce them.*[89]

---

88 Ibid., 18-19.

89 Ibid., 23.

If you want to know how to be in relationship, *be in relationship*. There is no technique to teach you how to be in relationship. The technique for being in relationship is to be in relationship. Did you get that? (loudly) *The technique for being in relationship is being in relationship!* (even louder) THE TECHNIQUE FOR BEING IN RELATIONSHIP IS BEING IN RELATIONSHIP! DID YOU GET THAT? (The group responds with multiple "yeahs!") Good.

[Lee reads from Robert Aitken:]

> *Male and female have different perspectives. Children and adults live in different worlds. Without falling into a kind of pernicious equality, in which all views are equally valid, you can play with views and see what happens. If I am anxious to protect myself, then I will kill your views. If I practice giving life, then I will offer you the scope you need… Even deeply held convictions can melt in the dynamics of give and take where male and female, adult and child, friend and friend, hold dialogue in a spirit of trust. Easier said than done, to be sure, but the path of lazy retreat leads inevitably to suffering.*[90]

It doesn't matter whether views are right or wrong. Even if you think others' views are wrong, you still do violence to someone by attacking their perceptions, by failing to acknowledge them.

[Lee reads from Robert Aitken:]

> *"Pots and pans are Buddha's body," announces a sign in some Zen Buddhist monasteries, reminding the cooks just as they are. Zafus and blankets, hammers and shovels, all are Buddha's body. I confess I am often offended when I see zafus left every which way in the hall,*

---

[90] Ibid., 23.

and when I see someone straighten his cushion with his foot, when I see tools left in the rain. Things are altogether faithful. They follow the rules with precision. We owe them benevolence in return.[91]

In other words, a hammer is a hammer. It does what it's supposed to do, especially when you use it properly. But even if you don't use it properly, it follows its nature perfectly. It's heavy and hard. If you use is improperly, it will still do what something heavy and hard is supposed to do. Therefore, it's owed benevolence in return. For a hammer to do what it's supposed to do properly means that it shouldn't be covered with rust. It should be clean and well-taken care of. The same is true of your clothing and the zafus you sit on for meditation. Things do exactly what they do without complaining. Your zafu never complains. It does exactly what zafus are designed to do and should be treated with respect and benevolence, not kicked to the back of the hall or thrown in a messy pile.

Baul Practice

There are some things in the book *To Live Within* that relate directly to what I want to speak about tonight. The book was written by Lizelle Reymond and is an account of her time spent living in India as the student of the Baul monk and scholar, Sri Anirvan. I'll read and comment on some excerpts, then go into what I wanted to talk about with you all tonight. This is a quote from Sri Anirvan:

Remember that our understanding of life progresses at the speed of a bullock cart. The impatient man runs, greedy for conquest. Our mind has wings and can soar over difficulties, but we have a fine pair of feet to keep in touch with Mother Earth. We have to plow

91 Ibid., 34.

> *through it and often stumble over roots and stones. Then comes the time for sowing. Our feet dance in joy and this spontaneous joy is the daughter of our soul. Remember that all the real things in life are in accord with a very slow rhythm like the changing of seasons and the coursing of stars. This work in depth is done in darkness, without sound.*[92]

The way I read this it takes so long to concretely manifest real change beyond the possibility of reversal that it's essentially like working in darkness. There's no illumination in it. It happens so slowly we can't track it. It's like watching a child grow. When you see them every day, you'll occasionally notice they've had a growth spurt. But you don't notice it every day. It happens "in darkness, without sound." It doesn't broadcast itself. One day the child starts to talk, or to know the alphabet, or begins to read. But the development of that happens so gradually, so subtly, that you don't see it. All of our work is like that.

We may be a hurry for what's called "realization." But it doesn't mean anything because it has nothing to do with practice. Practice is the only thing that matters. It doesn't matter how much you *know* if you can't *do*. Realization is the *embodiment* of the enlightened disposition from moment to moment. Maybe one of the reasons I've had a distaste for using the word "enlightenment" for the last couple years is that a lot of us think we're looking for enlightenment, and we shouldn't be. Enlightenment, as profound an experience as it is, is nothing but knowledge. As Werner Erhard said, "Understanding is the booby prize." Lizelle Reymond went to India, moved onto Sri Anirvan's ashram, and became his personal attendant. In the next quote she talks about how that affected her.

---

92 Anirvan, Sri, and Lizelle Reymond. *To Live Within*. Sandpoint, ID: Morning Light Press, 2007, 3.

Cracks in my outer shell were opening one after another, each time exposing some new zone of darkness in my understanding. At the moment I'm speaking of, all inner feeling being rejected, an extraordinarily dry period ensues, during which the Master's hand is indispensable. Discrimination gives rise to contradictions, in the midst of which one struggles; one lives without love, without patience. The vital attachment one had felt with those around one and the tasks undertaken lose their meaning; the aim, hitherto considered indispensable, becomes blurred. The imaginary ideal is broken. This is a cruel moment, but a necessary one, until there arises from the depths of one's being a new, more contained, though still eager, impulse.[93]

This experience will happen to everybody sooner or later. It's the point you have to push through. Almost everybody who leaves the school, after having been involved for a long time, leaves at this point. Some of you think you've hit it and you haven't. You've only hit a little ripple in the placidness of your lake of devotion and discipline. A quote from Sri Anirvan:

I could not bear Haimavati [a cultural center being established for translation] *to become a rendezvous. It must be a deep pool of life wherein one must plunge to live in death. And the work. This work is not a pretext to be taken lightly. It is a deep inner work in the rhythm of the heart of life.*[94]

Likewise, the ashram in Arizona should never become a rendezvous. Guests come and you sit and socialize. Your family comes and it's great. You take things lightly and easefully, the weather is nice, the food is

93 Ibid., 9.

94 Ibid., 15.

pretty good, and it's not a bad place to live if you're going to be on an ashram. But you can never allow this place to become a rendezvous. It must be a place where you plunge into the depths of life every moment. The mood of this place has to be, "Die before you die." It has to be passionate and vibrant. You must always remember that the Work that goes on here is as intimately symbiotic with the pace and the mood of the creative universe as could possibly be.

You must never think that we're somehow waiting for God's lightning bolt to strike us because then your work will become sloppy, lazy, and irresponsible. Obviously, Sri Anirvan said what he did because it's everyone's tendency to make a place like that: an ashram…a rendezvous. The teacher is there and is glorious and radiant. Visitors come from all over the world and it's exciting. The community starts to get large. Important people come to visit, which is a sign of success and respect, and you start to get lazy. Then the place becomes a rendezvous and the senior students can fall into the habit of becoming social directors. "Who's coming this week?" "So and so." "Oh, boy!" You dance around and make special plans. Never allow this place [the ashram] to become a rendezvous. It doesn't matter who comes and how important a place of pilgrimage it becomes; the ashram must always be place of work and vibrant expression of the depths of reality. Sri Anirvan says to Lizelle:

> *For the moment you can do but one thing—create in yourself respect for your own work, for your own effort, in silence, and with the discipline you are approaching.*[95]

Respect for your own work—that's it. Are you doing a good job? Are you working as hard as you can? Are you goofing off, hiding things from the teacher or being lazy about your work? Just create respect for

[95] Ibid.

your own work. That's all you can do. You can't be a bodhisattva, you can't save the world, you can't be compassionate, you can't help others, you can't serve. Just develop respect for your own work. That's what many of you should be doing at this stage of the game. Others of you have already gone beyond that.

Structure in a School Is Needed but Is Never the Point

One of the things that we're doing in our evolution as a school is to label, in a much more formal way than we have before, all of the particular manifestations, functions, and domains of the school as they appear. The dharma's becoming more sophisticated, the avenues of approach are becoming defined, and the structure of outreach programs is becoming very exact. Unfortunately, it's a necessary step. It's unfortunate on a couple of counts: one, because it is necessary and very few people recognize the necessity of it, and secondly, because those that don't recognize the necessity of it as a stage think that it's some kind of advancement upon the crudity of the school. At last we're becoming sophisticated! Now we're getting somewhere! Well, in a sense we are getting somewhere, because this is a necessary stage. But we're not getting somewhere in the sense that we're getting better. We're getting there in the sense that once this stage's lessons are learned, we will be closer to the ideal of community that the rhetoric espouses.

You must remember that you are the ones creating the structure of the school. We need it, but you must remember that the structure is a means to an end. It is never the point—never. The ritual and the structure are never the thing. Those of you that are creating it have to create it on a foundation of sand. There will come a day when we'll pull the rug out from under the formality and the structure entirely, and the castle better collapse. For ourselves. This will never happen for the school-at-large—it just wouldn't work. If the castle doesn't collapse, we will have taken all those years of spiritual work to make us mature students and built another artifice on top of it. So you must remember, as you create the structure, that it is necessary, that it will serve at this stage of the game, but that we must create it on a foundation of sand.

When it is time to pull the structure away, you need to let it go. You will see, if you haven't already, that some of you are very attached to the structure. The structure, when it's defined and enforced, can be a tremendous security blanket. It can make you feel really safe and taken care of. When you get up every morning and you know that at seven o'clock there will be people meditating in the darshan hall, chanting the same chant every morning, that can make you feel tremendously secure and warm. It's something you can count on. You have to realize—freely, open-eyed, no distinctions, no hidden meanings—that we are creating a hierarchical, defined, formal structure… on sand. So that when it's time for you to move into what's *really* going on, we can pull the rug out and the structure will collapse, and you will be left free. You don't want to be trying to hold the castle up while it's collapsing: "Don't let the arch fall! Get the gate!"

Flowing Freely in All Domains Based on the Needs of the Moment

One of the things that I look forward to is just sitting around with friends. It would be wonderful to just sit around and be together in a beautiful environment like the Tavern that is softly lit, with nice music, eating and talking and enjoying the space. The people who were at the early meetings in New Jersey had boundless enthusiasm without being sloppy about it. I never had to tell people to calm down. You can safely get away with things when there's a certain kind of naivete. That's what we were doing in the early days. We were in communion at a certain level, but we didn't touch a lot of other domains. Now we're in an entirely different domain. To be in communion in *this* domain is different. In those days we didn't realize we were organically connected.

We were in the blush of an amazing infatuation and it lasted a long time, but we never organically realized the truth of our being together. We didn't realize that if we were serious about what we had committed ourselves to we would reach a point of no return.

There was a tacit understanding of my place in everybody's life. We were friends together, unfolding the most exciting drama we'd ever come across, looking forward to every new revelation with enthusiasm and excitement. No fear, no problems, no purification, no contraction—although we used that language all the time. We were big on contraction, but nobody had any. We were just moving through it as fluidly as can be.

True community is community in which there is a tacit recognition of the role of the wise man or village elder. There needn't be any uncomfortable or nonessential ritual in relationship to that. There are rituals to establish a certain mood, but not because they are necessary and not because people must treat the wise man in a certain way. It's because we haven't realized ourselves. But the more ritual or form a school defines, the easier it is for people to become "guardians of the flame" where everybody has the idea that a spiritual master's space is sacred and if a guest puts their foot in the wrong place they're lucky if they don't get it chopped off.

Instead, our mood needs to be like it was whenever we had new people come to the groups in New Jersey. We didn't panic over little intrusions upon certain forms of protocol in relationship to me. We functioned in a domain of superficiality, but the form was perfect. Now we function in the domain of great depth and sensitivity, profundity, sanctity. But we also need to return to that sense of innocence. We need to just be a bunch of friends sitting around enlivened by the majesty of the Divine—tacitly recognizing it and intuitively responding to the mood of whatever space we're in without doubt, considerations, contractions, or negative emotionality.

Ultimately, I see us as a bunch of friends sitting around, free with one another, in communion—not at a superficial level but at the ultimate, essential depth of our beings. Essentially functioning with freedom of movement at every level of psyche so that no domain is foreign, no domain is fearful, and no domain produces crisis in us except positive crisis—such as sorrow over the death of a loved one, a genuine teacher in the world, or a real devotee in another school even if we didn't know them. Having a kind of world compassion. Freely flowing through all domains purely based on a response to stimuli in the environment or to the need of the moment…tacitly recognizing every aspect of protocol, distinction, and consideration in any given circumstance, and living freely in every domain with each other.

On the other hand, there will always be the extended school with ritual, formality, and routine. We can't help that. People don't move, just like that, into a space of maturity in which they're capable of moving through every domain of their being freely. The rhetoric says that problems are illusory; just be happy, just surrender. The rhetoric is great, but it doesn't work when we're trying to be happy in the midst of conflict. It's not as easy as it seems. But we've all randomly been in circumstances when one mood arises unmotivated out of another and completely and instantaneously eclipses the previous mood. We didn't do anything to make it happen and if we try to maintain it or make it happen again it doesn't work.

Self-Importance Is Based on the Wrong Facts

We're in a place in our sadhana as a Community in which we need to consider our creation and context of ritual very carefully, because it can be a tremendous trap. There's a certain positive, valid food that many people get by managing structure. But we don't want to slip into the feeling that we're important because we're managing the structure. Our importance is the degree of freedom we have in our practice. If our practice is to maintain structure and we're free in that and good at it, then that's what counts—not the structure itself. It's crucial that you don't develop an exaggerated sense of self-importance because you're managing the structure.

You *are* important. Who else could manage the structure? But an exaggerated sense of self-importance is based on the wrong facts. If you feel important based on what is true, your importance will never show. It won't be exaggerated. You won't call it *self*-importance. You would call it your role in the Work, your value to the Work, your work as a student. It can be a gigantic trap when a school begins to structure and define itself. People get handed important jobs for managing other people and creating the forms that other people will have to apply themselves to. You have to be very careful. One of the big conflicts for outreach leaders is how much leeway they have to run the groups in their own way, versus manage the groups in alignment with what the ashram decides. That will be resolved as they make the groups successful based on their own energy. They'll instinctually realize the degree of leeway that they have.

Somebody came into the Tavern the other night, felt uncomfortable in the circumstance and later said to me, "I had to leave. There was nothing else I could do." To my way of thinking, there certainly was something else they could have done. They could have looked around, recognized what was uncomfortable, shrugged their shoulders, and taken a position in Tavern that was unusual for them. It could have been no problem whatsoever. If a conflict arises, it should only last for an instant. Then forget about such considerations and go back to your business. Walk into a space, instinctually recognize the appropriate protocol there, and abide by it. Recognize a space as quiet or loud, serious or humorous, ecstatic and joyous. Don't start cracking seventh-grade dirty jokes when you move into a space that's radiantly joyous, romantic, and sensitive. It's very simple really. Intuit the space you're in and be there.

The Mystery of Creation Never Gets Tired

At some point there will be no ritual for the core group. It needn't apply when you have a tacit realization of what is. There may be a prayer over a meal or a toast with an aperitif on a special occasion, but a million rules won't apply. We'll get together and do our practices. We'll meet with one another as friends and enjoy the ecstatic mystery of creation together. Because that never gets tired; it's always new, fresh and vibrant. There's always a blooming rose. And when a blooming rose isn't around, then there's a snowstorm. And when the snowstorm isn't around, there's a hailstorm. And when the hailstorm isn't around, there are orange, red, and yellow leaves falling from the trees, or a new cloud formation in the sky.

There are always new people approaching the school. You'll never end up being bored in communion. There's always a visitor or guest to be interested in and excited about, and new friends to be made. For the rest of your life there will be new friends to be made. Good friends, heart friends, forever. We can sit around in Tavern every night and enjoy the magic of creation because everybody's unique and we have an untold number of new friends to make. My God, what an unbelievable, unimaginably vast possibility life is! That's my vision of things.

Embodying Realization Through Practice

We've reached a point of maturity where we can't go back to the way it was in naiveté. We've learned too much. The next stage is about how to use what we've learned in a way that does not create obstacles for us. The first thing is to instinctually feel when a certain protocol is required and do that. This may sound contradictory to what I've told you before, but it is by an effort of will at first. There are certain spaces in which the value of the space is the tension there. Most of us will move into a space like that and the first thing we'll want to do is get rid of the tension by cracking jokes, making noise, acting like a clown, whispering to the person next to us. How many times have you come into a circumstance where something is going on and you started whispering to the person next to you, [*Lee whispers:*] "What's going on? I just got here. What are we supposed to be doing?" It's obvious that to answer you would not only disturb the space but also break the person's attention on what is happening.

When you move into a space, you will typically either respond spontaneously or habitually. But a third option is to intentionally *not do* what you would habitually do. If you have to exert an effort of will to not do what you would habitually do, that's what you do. That's the way you begin embodying what you have already learned. You have all had enough realization to last the next ten years. Half of the people in this room could write a book as an "anonymous Western mystic," with a ghost writer, because you've had the experiences. You've had enough realizations, but to embody them is another story. What's needed is diligent practice. The Buddha supposedly said on his deathbed in response to the monks asking for his final offering, "Work out your own enlightenment with diligence." The monks all gasped, "Oh, no! What about the Buddhist lineage?"

We're at the stage of working out our own enlightenment with diligence. You have had realization as deeply as you are ever going to have it. When you have come to me knowing who I am, it's been real. It can't get any more real than real. You have already seen what there is to see as profoundly as you are ever going to see it. You can have those same realizations over and over for the next twenty years and it won't make any difference. We're at the stage where we have to work out our own enlightenment with diligence. To work out our own enlightenment with diligence we have to pay attention and remember. In order to do that, it's just practice, practice, practice. It's very significant that the gift that we've been given is the Bodhisattva of Compassion from a Japanese temple.[96] We have been given an artifact that reeks of practice.

---

[96] Lee is making reference to a thirteen-foot oak statue that had been hand-carved by Buddhist monks and had been an artifact that Swami Rudrananda

This artifact is going to remind you to practice if you are sensitive to its life force. That's what we need to do to embody our realization.

You have climbed up the mystical ladder and climbed back down again. You've been given gifts, *prasad* [a gift or offering from student to the master, and from master to student, that is symbolic of the spiritual exchange between them], and you've brought them back. Now the thing to do is to display those gifts as forms of your being. Not to put them in a museum and say every once in a while, "Gosh, I'd like to get that back again." Don't put your realization in a museum. Embody it. Become a living artifact. That is what we should be immersing ourselves in as a consideration together. How do we do that? Practice. If you say, "I'm not sure how to practice," then meditate, follow the diet, study, and exercise every day. Make your practices more consistent. Pay attention to the subtle things. Be on time; don't interrupt people when they talk. You have to start somewhere. You don't start with practicing the enlightened disposition in every moment.

Structure as a Means to an End

If you work out your own enlightenment with diligence you will also realize that what you're trying to get from me is not what I provide. I'm not your daddy. I'm not the lawmaker. I'm not where the buck stops. I'm none of those things. You will coincidently realize who I am, which will continue to deepen your relationship to me. When that perspective matures in the sangha, then we can sit around together in the Tavern without artifice. We'll create and structure the community-at-large, but we need to realize that structure is only the means to an end.

What I'm looking for is a group of people who have no pride, greed, fear, or contraction, who are full of charity, and who are not dishonest or

---

(1928-1973) had for years at his antique shop in New York City. Through a series of interesting circumstances, it had been donated to Lee for his ashram in 1986.

violent in any way. So, the Work is a continuing and ongoing experiment that does three things: it allows those who are moving toward that ultimate space [without pride, etc.] to become trustworthy; secondly, it attacks the pocket of pride, self-importance, or arrogance in us so that we get a chance to see and respond to it; and third, it sets up a certain field that some people, who would not be attracted in any other way, will participate in. It also eliminates people that would have otherwise participated.

Student: So, the structure is like monkey bars to exercise on, which we will eventually outgrow.

Lee: Exactly. That's a good way of putting it.

Student: What about people who come along who are more mature and have perhaps engaged in practice elsewhere. How do we handle that?

Lee: The outreach people make it a point to recognize someone who's done the monkey bars already, and approach that person personally as an exception to the rule.

Student: You said we want to be sure the structure is built on sand. Is that something we have to continually check?

Lee: Absolutely. We should be checking regularly to make sure that the people involved haven't gotten carried away.

Student: The structure seems to me to be an illusion that you have to see through.

Lee: Yes, but the structure also needs to work. The structure needs to have a workable kitchen, plumbing, electricity, bedrooms, a living room. It's not just a facade like in Hollywood. It's got to be a real structure… on a foundation of sand.

Student: I've had a notion that part of the way that can be done is to keep the form from being dependent upon any one individual. In that way, the support of the structure is not dependent upon personality. It's objective to a certain degree. Is that part of it?

Lee: Yes, that's one of the factors. If you can define the structure in a way that allows people to move in and out of jobs without the structure being affected, that's wonderful.

Intention Is the Secret to Success

Student: But we often assume our identity based on the job we have. It's really kind of backwards to how it should be.

Lee: When I was in training to lead the Silva course, there were people who openly laughed in my face and said, "What are you doing here? This is not a place for people like you. You should be doing something else." Later, those same people considered me to be one of the best teachers in the country. I had nothing going for me but a desire to do the job right, and I learned. I am of the opinion that most people can learn—even crucial roles—given the right teacher and the right circumstance. If you have reminding factors, you can learn to do any job effectively. Actually, the right aim or intention is more important than the teacher and the environment. Intention is the secret to your success.

Student: There have been periods of time where the practices have been very consuming for me. Then, in the middle of the stretch of time in the early morning hours that would include all the practices, you would ask me to do something for you. I would generally do what you asked me to do, but I would be in recoil over the timing, forgetting that serving you is the most important practice for me.

Lee: That's a good example of what I was talking about earlier when I said that form is security. Having everything timed perfectly, even practice, is very secure.

Student: The practices are real for me. The benefit is real. They're part of my life *and* I make them something they're not.

Lee: A testimony! When you mistake the form for the thing itself and the form becomes your life, then if anybody interferes with the form you forget your essence. That's the structure of ego. That's how we become identified with the body as if that were all there is. You've literally described the dynamic of separation. That's what we do organically.

Student: What can I do about that?

Lee: Don't identify.

Student: Don't identify?

Lee: When something arises that interrupts the structure and you feel recoil, do the thing and then go back to your practices the next morning as religiously as you do them every morning, remembering your intention to not identify with the form.

Student: I get annoyed because I imagine my practices are more important than being interrupted by you—or anyone for that matter. Castles seem to be created as fast as things arise from a true context.

Lee: That's true up to a point, but when you reach "majority vote"[97] then you start catching the castles before you build them and observe the identification before you make it.

---

97 A phrase used to refer to the state when one's internal or work-balance has tipped so that the intention to live from essence is more important than the need for ego to be in control.

Student: Even though I don't want to respond to you or others in a prideful, impatient way, it keeps happening.

Lee: That's because you don't pay attention and remember. You may catch a thousand of those triggers a day. That's a drag, exhausting, boring, and annoying. But the next day only nine hundred will affect you that way, and next day only eight hundred, then seven hundred, and pretty soon only one hundred of them will affect you. Before you know it, you're free of it.

Student: That's an interesting twist because the nature of pride is to not desire to catch yourself building castles.

Lee: Of course, you have to trick it. You have to talk to pride like a spiritual teacher talks to a beginning student because your pride is like an adolescent. So you say, "Listen, you have no idea the wealth of experience that awaits you if you grow up. Let me help you eliminate your adolescent manifestations so you can have that experience." You have to trick it. It's just like the new student who doesn't want to be different until they are tricked into it. Before they know it, they're not themselves. They're an essential being, and by that time it doesn't matter. Why would you want to remain a bundle of recoil and pride?

Student: It seems like you have to get into the habit of paying attention. It takes intention. It takes something more to remember in the beginning.

Lee: Yeah, it does. You don't program attention by an effort of will, like positive thinking. You can program it by an organic desire.

Student: That organic desire has to be strong enough to direct attention. We have to realize that it's important to work, to surrender, to remember so that we start paying attention.

Lee: You may decide to change things, but those kinds of decisions are never effective. You have to make an organic decision to be different. You only do that when under great pressure. What changes carbon to diamond? It's not time, it's pressure. You could be in a school for a lifetime and nothing will happen if there's no pressure. But it's a positive pressure that can speed things up. You can't ask for more pressure than you can handle, or you'll shatter or melt. But you can gracefully move through your life free of a lot of the recoil that arises. You can hold the tension or crisis in a constructive context.

Student: So, thriving in adversity or stress becomes a certain kind of food?

Lee: Yes.

Student: When you say we can be free of recoil, do you mean not manifesting it? It doesn't seem possible to not have reactivity.

Lee: Yes, I'm talking about the expression. Having recoil is just what the organism does.

Realizing That Love Is Not Scarce

Student: When you say it's possible to hold things in a different context, is that the same as changing an attitude?

Lee: Look, there's only one thing going on. To reference Werner Erhard's work, all recoil and resistance is based on a feeling of a scarcity of love. We can be very sophisticated about it, but that statement says it all. Werner's use of the language of scarcity works perfectly. Recoil comes from the feeling that love is scarce. That's the bottom line—despite the intricacies that we weave based on the dharma. If you can develop respect for your own work, that's the beginning of realizing love is not scarce.

You may want more attention from another individual than is reasonable, but that has nothing to do with love. "If my partner loved me, they would always be paying attention to me." That's not love, that's recoil. All failure to live life to its fullest—richly, passionately, profoundly, sacredly, under all circumstances—is based on the contextual feeling that love is scarce and that you can't or won't get enough.

I wouldn't want to argue this philosophically—I'd probably lose because it's a sloppy analogy—but we could say that to shift into a context that love is available is akin to waking up. It is your job as students to move into a context in which love is not scarce. Then you will cease to resist my help. You will cease to argue with me about the things you think that I would do if I were working freely and how you couldn't live under those circumstances.

Nobody knows what I would do if I was working at one hundred percent.[98] But anyone could live under those circumstances if they lived from the context that love was not scarce. Then everything I did would make available the domain in which love could be tangibly recognized and communed with. It would be obvious that love was present no matter what I did. Without exception, the presence of love would be felt under any circumstance if I were working at one hundred percent.

98 At times, Lee spoke about his need to work well below his capacity in order to match the capacity of his students.

STUFFERS AND REALIZERS

(October 29, 1985)

Conflict with the Activity of the Master

There is an interesting process that seems to take place when people approach the school. The way people usually enter this particular stream is that they are initially attracted by the dharma. The argument of the teaching makes a point with them. As they get more involved, they end up connecting secondarily at the heart. They experience certain moods of ecstasy or elation, or moods of abject agony and suffering. They say, "Oh, the spiritual master really gave me a jolt of ecstasy yesterday. He is so loving!" Or, "The spiritual master pierced right through my ego today. He is such a fire of transformation!" Or they might say, "The spiritual master is so enigmatic. You can never tell how he will show up from one day to the next." All of that has to do with the heart. What they end up doing lastly is coming into conflict somehow or other with the activity of the spiritual master. Some people don't, but most do.

In my case, people tend not to come in conflict with my activity as much as my lack of activity. The most common conflict in this Community is not about what I do; it's about what I don't do. Why am I so patient? Why am I so quiet? Why am I so benign? Why don't I bust the asses of people that are always goofing off? Why don't I run around the ashram raging and making great teaching lessons for people? Why don't I use alcohol and drugs and sex and violence? Why, why, why? That is what people want to know. So, it's most common for people not to have a conflict with my activity as it manifests, but a conflict with my activity as it *doesn't* manifest in the way people think it should. That is nothing new because everybody thinks they've got one up on God. They are more than willing to give God advice—if not to the person of the spiritual master, then directly through prayer. People are always telling God what to do in the silence of their meditation or contemplation. I suppose it's to be expected in a culture as immature as ours. But it happens even in mature cultures because people are not terribly good at "eating humble pie," as the saying goes.

Generally, people hear the teaching and that draws them to the group. Then they have some kind of interaction with the heart and that usually creates certain questions, considerations, or assumptions. It will create assumptions like, "Lee is so loving. Gosh, isn't it wonderful? We're so lucky." But you don't know that yet from your being—it's from your psyche. And anything you know from your psyche you can't say you know. At best, you can only be lucky enough to have a kind of sympathy or similarity with what is actually true. Some of you happen to be on target, but in the wrong domain or from the wrong context. Then people will question either verbally or to themselves, "Why do I feel that way? Why does Lee create this in me?" And all those responses will arise in contrast to what attracted people at first, which is the dharma.

The Dharma Is the Sounding Board to Gauge What Arises for You

The dharma explains everything and generally attracts most of us, but not all of us. Some people are attracted to the heart first and some to the body first, but those are the exceptions. Generally, we are attracted to the dharma first. We may feel something beyond the language of the teaching, but it is the mind of the spiritual master that first intrigues and captures us. That was the case for most people here even though some of you are definitely not mind-oriented. People will be attracted by the dharma and will study it, but they will tend to forget to use the dharma as the magnifying glass or critical razor by which to judge everything else from then on. The dharma never ceases to be of value. It is the sounding board by which you should gauge what arises for you as you mature. When you find yourself considering the heart, what you should do is gauge that consideration based on what the dharma says about it, because the dharma has all the answers. But we tend to forget the dharma exists when we are in a mood—any kind of mood, high or low. The dharma is the critical factor of consideration in viewing all activity.

With everything that arises you can do three things: you can enquire of it, you can assert,[99] or you can resort to the dharma. We can equate Enquiry, Assertion and the critical use of the dharma to the three types of yoga: karma yoga, bhakti yoga, and jnana yoga.[100] Some people tend towards bhakti by disposition, and they tend to use Assertion. Some people tend towards karma yoga, and they tend to use Enquiry. And some people tend towards jnana yoga and they tend to use the dharma. Any of those forms of relationship with the teaching is fine. It depends upon your disposition and what is most easeful for you in terms of practice. One is not better than any other one.

Walled Off from Vulnerability

We enter the Community on a wave of commitment and enthusiasm because we have heard the truth of the teaching. It resonates with us—no question about it. Then we encounter the heart and we are thrown into a consideration of vulnerability and vitality, which we are absolutely walled off from to varying degrees. Some people are very sloppy—kissing, licking, and drooling over everything. Some people are just the opposite. They are very cold in the sense that they analyze everything and have no emotions whatsoever. Somebody dies and they just analyze it and allow themselves to feel nothing. Then there are the vast majority

99 Assertion (a specific practice that Lee gave to acknowledge the reality that is tacitly obvious in every moment) and Enquiry obviate the mechanics of the mind. Twenty years later, Lee identified them as two of the three "core practices" for students. The third core practice is the Heart Breath.

100 Karma yoga is the discipline of selfless action or work, bhakti yoga is the path of love and devotion, and jnana yoga involves the practice of discrimination, using the intellect to transcend the mind's identification.

of people who are in the middle. If we really see that we are emotionally sloppy, we get to consider that we are essentially prostitutes to our emotions. Someone else may have to consider that they don't allow themselves to feel at all. This is a very harsh consideration because it's like being in a steel straightjacket and can be very difficult and painful to work out of. People in between get to consider they have never really loved before. That's their favorite insight when they need something to get bummed out about.

There tends to be a crumbling of confidence, because we begin to see that we are not perfect, and we need to throw ourselves at the mercy of Benediction [Divine help]. Who knows what will happen? Maybe our hard hearts will crack. Maybe our masks will be broken and that will entail some degree of pain. The mask is only plaster, but we think it is skin. You can just smash the thing and nothing will happen. But we are like a patient sitting in a dentist's chair. Nothing has happened yet, but we grip the armrests and anticipate pain when the dentist walks over. We tend to anticipate how painful it will be to become real, when it needn't be painful at all. We create this passionate wealth of anguish over nothing.

Listen, there are two kinds of people and you are either one or the other. You are a "stuffer" (I made up these words) or you are a "realizer." It is pretty easy to figure out the difference. Realizers are pretty rare. The human being that is a little bit enlightened is willing to open their eyes and check out the environment. Those that aren't—they close their eyes and pretend that they are in Paris or Rome. Stuffers say, "Oh, look at the beautiful scenery," but it's all in their mind.

When most people move into the second relationship to the Community, which is recognizing the spiritual master's heart, their original burst of enthusiasm and infatuation begins to weaken because they are called upon to be something they are not truly or essentially being. They begin to have considerations: "Is this my school? Do I belong here?" Then, when they begin to acclimate themselves and allow the Influence to unchain their hearts and free their vitals, they finally come into a consideration of the most paradoxical and enigmatic aspect of the spiritual master: his or her activity.

The clearest and most obvious communication of the spiritual master is the mind. That is something that we can understand. We all have minds. We may have to play around with the language a little bit, but that is something we can grok fairly easily. The heart is a little more difficult, but basically we all love, we all want to be loved, and we all want to feel. When we finally get rid of the plaster cast, it really does feel good to be in feeling-communion with somebody. So, although there is some difficulty with the communication of the heart, it is easier than the communication of the body and activity of the spiritual master, which is the most paradoxical, difficult, and conflicting communication. We look at him and we think, "He forgets things, he stumbles over words, he gets embarrassed, he is just a guy." Questions start to arise: "Why does he do this? Why does he do that? Why does he exercise and meditate? Why does he eat this way instead of that way?" We can't deal with the body of the spiritual master, and we end up undermining our original enthusiasm even more. That is what ordinarily happens.

Getting Through the Doorway to God

A program of approach for new students should be designed completely opposite to the way people usually enter. People should deal with the most difficult factor first and get it out of the way. Once they deal with the activity or the body of the spiritual master, they are in the Work and nothing is going to get them out of it. They should connect to body, heart, and mind of the spiritual master in that order—body being activity, heart being love, and mind being Truth. The activity of the guru is always the difficult thing.

Student: Our first connection is not with the activity of the spiritual master. It is usually something we read or hear in a study group.

Lee: But it needn't be that way. What we attempt to do when people approach the school is to make sure they understand the dharma. Most of our educational material and our emphasis is based on making sure people understand. We figure that if they understand the teaching, they will be able to use that as a kind of critical edge when they get into conflict. But as soon as they get into conflict, they forget about the dharma.

If we were to provide a similar education in the activity of the spiritual master—who he is and what he does—there would still be conflicts, but people would have a stronger approach.

Student: How can we convey who the spiritual master is without using the dharma?

Lee: Personal experience… We can always tell guru stories from the traditions, about Shirdi Sai Baba, Nityananda, and some of the wild Sufis. Those stories are very romantic, and people forget them as soon as they get here. The ideal way of integrating people into the Work is to first deal with the spiritual master's activity, which is the most paradoxical aspect. Like the statement of Mansur al-Hallaj and other Sufis, "I am the Truth." Get over that one and everything else is a breeze. So, first connect to the spiritual master's activity—deal with your questions, your conflicts, and your crisis, and become established in trust—then move on to the heart, which is love, and then to the mind, which is Truth. The ideal chain of connection would first be to body, then heart, then mind. People would come in and get rid of the major fears and conflicts first, and the rest would be a little difficult sometimes—but heartful. The main obstacle would be out of the way.

Student: What is the major fear we have about the activity of the guru?

Lee: It's a lack of trust. If most people were pressed, they wouldn't even be able to say what they are afraid of. They are just afraid of being taken advantage of. The dharma, the mind, is not about trust; it's about instinct.

Heart is not about trust either; heart is about communion. By the time you get to the activity of the spiritual master, you've connected to Truth and the heart, but you haven't trusted the one that you must trust to get through the eye of a needle. The spiritual master is the doorway to God. You're not going to get through the doorway no matter how much love you have and how well you recognize the dharma if you don't trust the one who is the doorway to God.

Student: So, the way to communicate about the activity of the spiritual master is through personal experience?

Lee: Yes, like communicating what happened to your fear.

Student: Personally?

Lee: Yes. What were you afraid of and did it happen the way you feared? Ninety-nine out of a hundred people would be able to honestly say that they were tremendously afraid but didn't experience what they were afraid of. What they got was whatever else it was.

Student: And the fears were dispelled…

Lee: You at least set it up for people to understand that they manufacture most of their struggles. And I think it would be very valuable to not lead people to think that they are going to understand my activity. This is not about understanding.

Making Distinctions Between Ego and Essence

There are basically two approaches to stimuli. One is the approach of the self, which is ego; and one is the approach of essence, which is a pure relationship to stimuli. The approach of ego is the relationship to stimuli based upon considerations, assumptions, thoughts, education, conditioning, and all the rest. The thing that we need to convey to new students, if possible, is that until we are able to relate to the spiritual master from an essential, non-biased space, all of our assumptions are at best good guesses. We may be fairly accurate, but we may be one-hundred-and-eighty degrees off. It is ridiculous to trust our own responses when those are responses of the self which we are entering this Work to transcend.

Everybody has a foundation upon which to be in communion with the spiritual master in certain moments or for certain periods of time. Sometimes even brand-new students will be in communion right away for a minute, an hour, a day. From that position we understand perfectly well. Nothing bothers us about the spiritual master's activity. There is no recoil to it whatsoever. It is all delightful; *everything* is delightful. Some things in life are difficult, some things are easy, but even the difficult things are not empty of delight. It would be invaluable to convey a sense of that dichotomy.

People always ask, "How will I know when I am in essence?" That is why we seek a teacher, that is why we seek a guide. That is why senior students are running outreach groups instead of beginning students. We have come to understand the pervasiveness of ego and the genuineness of essence. With experience, we can develop a taste for that, like the difference between tasting a fine wine and tasting vinegar. That is something we need to convey. Judgments may be right on target, right on the mark, but they are invalid because of their contextual basis. Judgments will arise in any case; just don't indulge them. Let them arise, note them, and go on. Don't give them credit or make an investment in them.

The Master's Criticism as Resurrective Surgery

My tone of voice when I criticize my students is often taken personally. That is the failure to make a distinction between ego and essence. If the person would understand that I am simply criticizing ego as it arises in his or her particular case, as it is likely to arise in *any* of our particular cases given certain circumstances, then that kind of criticism can be ultimately valuable. It can sever ego's death-grip on essence, on Being. For every one of you who give me the egoic stimuli to provide extraordinary teaching lessons, my criticism could be taken for what it is: lifesaving or resurrective surgery. But if it is taken wrongly, then it just feeds ego's story: "The spiritual master is just one more person who doesn't understand me. Why is the universe conspiring to hurt me this way? What have I done to deserve this?" For a mature student, those should not be the questions.

Of what value is a criticism from the spiritual master? When the spiritual master, like a Zen archer, makes a well-aimed and perfectly thrust criticism to a specific area, we tend to think our head has been cut off. "Oh God, he just told me I am an immature practitioner, just a beginner! Oh no!" A criticism like that should be taken with gratitude and grace but is often taken as a literal threat to personal survival. We are all subject to that kind of criticism until we stop being a "stuffer."

We typically have one of two responses when a consideration comes up with the spiritual master: we either want to continue the consideration to a point of resolution or we want to forget about it as soon as we can. A stuffer is someone who, when a consideration is broached and some recoil arises, wants to make it better. That is the first thing everybody wants to do. There is an instinctual urge to come back to center and re-establish equanimity. Jumping out of the way of a car is also an instinctual urge. If we are in the middle of the street and we hear a loud noise, we jump onto the sidewalk. We are fine once we are on the sidewalk and there is no danger. The same thing should take place with the instinctual mechanism that is triggered when the spiritual master criticizes us. Self-protection will arise as part of our wiring. But we should be able to immediately turn around, see that we are safe and that survival is not threatened, and then engage the process. A stuffer is someone who feels that urge and immediately avoids any consideration of it. A stuffer will push it out of their minds, read a book, sing a song, go to work, take a shower—anything to forget about it.

Student: I have been in the school ten years and just started not running away from criticism six months ago. I didn't even recognize that I had been running away from it; I just thought that was what you do. Does it have to take that long? Is there a way to make my experience available to other people?

Lee: Because you have realized a different focus now, you see how much more valuable the new focus would have been if you could have had it in two or three years. Your experience can be communicated verbally and in writing. You have learned this, and you can provide that value to others. It won't come through an airy consideration of rhetoric; it will come through you empowering that shift in context. The fact that you have realized it cuts the degree of practice time necessary for everybody that comes after you.

Realizers are those who are not willing to be distracted by the initial urge to run, to pacify, to just forget about a consideration and hope that it will go away. But if the consideration is with me, then it needs to be pursued until I am satisfied that it is resolved. If the consideration is with me, *I* end it, not you. As long as I am willing to continue the consideration, it is not over. As soon as I am willing to drop the consideration, it is over—at least for the time being. It may come up again, but it will always be different.

I don't track down stuffers. If a consideration comes up and someone wants to run away, I let them run away. I may track down a stuffer on rare occasion, just to break pattern, but generally I will not. If you tell me you are done with a consideration, fine. But if you want to continue a consideration so that it will never arise in the same way again, you have to pursue it until I stop it. Then you will have mastered it by another grade. Every time I drop a consideration, even if it is not noticeable, you have mastered it to another degree. If I stop it and you feel it is not finished, then what you are doing is starting a new consideration. Because when I stop it, the consideration is finished. You have gotten what you needed to get, and to stay on it any longer would just be a waste of time and redundant.

Nobody Who Is a Realizer Looks Like a Stuffer

I hope it is obvious that the same process can hold true if you are considering something with one another and can both agree that it is resolved. The resolution is not always a hug, a kiss, and a good feeling. Sometimes you both realize that only experience will resolve the consideration and that no amount of discussion will. You might be right at the peak of a hot discussion when you both realize that words won't do it. To continue until you get a verbal resolve may not lead to actual resolution. Most of you intuitively know when you've gotten to the end of it, but then personality tempts you to want to end it the way it ends in the movies.

If any of you have seen the movie *The Last Wave*, it has an ending that is not a Hollywood ending. That is the way many considerations end. There may be domains in which the consideration is totally unresolved, but it is resolved in the important domain. The main character realized what he needed to realize at the end of the movie. No answers were given; that was the end of it. The whole future was left hanging completely, but there was a real resolution. The main character's consideration was resolved—not that of the viewers of the movie or the rest of the world. That was it: the end. So, if you can recognize when a consideration is complete on those terms and end it, then you go back to just being friends and go on about your business.

You can observe yourselves over the next week and see whether your tendency is to be a stuffer or a realizer. Most people are stuffers. Some people are stuffers but try and look like realizers. But nobody who is a realizer looks like a stuffer; it doesn't work that way.

THE DANCE OF THE INNOCENT IS THE BLOOD OF GOD

(May 25, 1986)

Answers Must Be Realized Through Practice

A lot of data is expressed through our discussions, but the production of data is not my primary function. The data is fairly accurate and has some value, but you will be frustrated at some point in this Work if your relationship to the guru is based on data. You will expect data to answer questions that only your experience can answer. The essential function of the guru or Godman in people's lives is to be a force of Benediction. It's not to produce knowledge. The fact that knowledge gets produced is simply because the guru can observe his environment and can draw some accurate conclusions from circumstances. But that's just incidental.

The event of the revelation of essentially being a slave to the Will of God precipitated the formation of the Community.[101] It produced Benediction or the realization of blessing power. If your relationship to me as guru is not held in that context, if the context is that I'm an answer man, then sooner or later we'll run out of content. You'll get to a point where you won't get answers. There's a certain level of maturity where the necessary answers must be realized through practice. Those kinds of answers can't be verbally communicated. We can verbally communicate to a pretty refined degree, but that's never quite it. Ultimately, verbal communication can never satisfy.

In the beginning, a lot of data can be helpful. It provides mental food, but also stimulates certain activity. Satisfaction has to be in recognizing the context of the source of Benediction, in how you contact God directly. God is experienced through blessing. That's not

---

101 Lee is referring to his awakening experience in 1975 that he later came to describe as a "shift of context."

even a function. That's the primary process of the guru's presence in your lives. Most of you have heard of Nataraj, the dancing Shiva, the very popular bronze statue with several arms. Shiva is dancing on the body of the world. We used to refer to a lot of my interactions with people as a cosmic dance in the first year of the Community when there was a certain innocence. The verbal presentation was extremely articulate, if I remember correctly. But that articulateness was never taken as the point—although we recorded the data and made use of it.

In the early days of the Community, we were all in the initial blush of this consideration of enlightenment. Many people had never thought about this before, so it was very exciting. There were a few questions about data, but the most passionate discussions were about the primacy of God in our lives. "Is this really true? Can we really be surrendered to the Will of God?" All the standard questions on reincarnation and psychic and mystical phenomena were asked, but they were asked almost incidentally. They were asked out of a sense of curiosity; we were just interested.

There were two primary communications in the early days of the Community. One was the need to be a slave to the Work, to be a slave to the Will of God. I think that from the beginning we've grasped that first communication and are making some fine headway with it. The second communication was the need to practice—how practice is held, what practice is. In the beginning, we didn't have the matrix [the strength and capacity of the mind and body for transformational work] to hold that. We just didn't. We were childlike, innocent. That childlikeness wasn't interested in practice; it was interested in play.

Embracing Dance, Play, and Innocence

We're coming to a serious consideration of the Baul practice of the use of breath and sexual energy, and I think that we have the matrix to hold it. Now that we have the matrix, a real foundation, we need to re-enliven that sense of play, that sense of dance. Unfortunately, one of the things that has happened is that we've tended to grow up like most adults in the world. We've tended to lose our sense of innocence, of playfulness, of childlikeness. We need to begin to hold practice in the matrix that we have, to be serious about it. But if we only do that, we will not be making ideal use of the communication. We must also re-engage that sense of play, of innocence, so that my lessons can be made, but made lightly and pleasantly without eliciting reactivity. If you fail to see my activity as dance, the machine will kick in blindly. If you take the communication as dance, from the position of innocence, you'll be moved to pierce the cramp—not based on pain, but on the obviousness of the delight of a life in God. My communication will generate a sense of longing in you, not a sense of the need to eliminate pain.

Student: It seems that most of our education is not about dancing. We were raised in the world not to dance but to be serious and not to consider blessing…

Lee: We need to embrace practice as children embrace things—totally. If you give a real innocent something to taste, they just take it in their mouth and bite it. If it's awful, they spit it out. But they don't take a tiny little piece and put it on their tongue. They *taste* it! That's why you have to put fences around wood stoves when there are children around because if they feel the heat, they'll just go for it. That can be dangerous in some circumstances. But without a sense of innocence, you'll approach practice guardedly. You'll always miss some part of my communication because, when I talk about a practice, I'll lay the whole thing out. How much you get when I talk about a practice depends upon the degree of innocence with which you receive it. If you receive it innocently, you'll get the whole thing in one lecture. If you don't, I'll have to keep talking about it over a period of years and keep refining the initial communication. But the first communication will be all of it. Were we able to dance, we would get the practice and embrace it.

Student: You were talking before about how the machine will kick in and we'll just react to your activity if we can't see it as dance, as play. For myself, that's a very good description of what I've been experiencing lately. What can be done?

Lee: The only two ways of approaching resistance to the dance are study, which will at least dispose you toward viewing it differently, and deciding to engage an activity even if it doesn't make sense and there's a lot of resistance. Those are basically the only things you can do. Studying the beggar Sufis, the Crazy Wisdom tradition, Tibetan Buddhism, the Christian Fools for God, and Native American culture—which has a Crazy Wisdom tradition though there's not too much information on it—develops a certain disposition to the dance on at least one level. If you can develop some intention behind that, it'll spread to the body.

Transformation and Resistance

If you engage the dance, you are liable to be captured by it. Most of you know how it is to go into something not wanting to do it and realize in the midst of it that you're really having fun. In realizing you're really having fun, you're able to relax a little bit and finish it out with a sense of delight and enthusiasm—even when you enter it with a sense of morbidity or whatever it might be. I would highly recommend that you engage the dance, whatever that may mean, with the knowledge that I'm sure you have frequently had of being transformed in the midst of something—no longer standing outside observing it. Transformation almost always comes in the doing of something that you have resistance to or lack knowledge of, rather than from observing it and deciding whether you'd like it or not from outside looking in. If it doesn't work for some reason, then you leave with it not having worked. What harm has been done?

In some respected treatises on making marriages work, they talk about how sexual frustration can create tremendous problems.

They recommend that if you have certain fantasies that aren't life endangering—which some people have—that you do them, because frequently we don't really enjoy the things that we hold as fantasies all that much, but we want them for a certain reason. If we do end up enjoying them, that's fine, and if we don't, we figure it out. We don't walk around blaming our mate for being some kind of prude when most of the stuff we experiment with wouldn't be our cup of tea anyway. But we don't know that until we experiment.

There was a woman that we met in India. She was an Australian who had traveled though India for eight years. She was celibate during that time, had visited many ashrams and saints, and had lived with many teachers. She decided she needed something and went out and lived on the streets. And when she got what she thought she needed to get, she left that lifestyle. Once she got the flavor, that was enough. The same is true of many of the dances we do here; they're not meant to be permanent fixtures of your spiritual life. They're meant to make a certain communication. They have a certain impact, they give you a certain flavor. Take the flavor, taste it, and then go on about what are meant to be the long-term fixtures of your spiritual life.

The Feminine Will Teach How to Dance

When the dance is offered, engage it and do the best you can. The feminine will teach you if you don't know how to dance. It's not a crime to let the woman lead until you learn to lead. How's a man going to learn to lead except by learning from a woman? In terms of our discussion, it's not *a* woman that teaches you to dance—it's Woman, the feminine. Let the feminine provide the lessons in dance, not by making any one woman an example, not by watching *a* woman. The feminine will teach you to dance. Allow yourself to be taught by that. It's not the form that the feminine tends to manifest as; that's not necessarily the dance. It's how the feminine quality applies to any given situation and what the essential mood of the feminine is.

THE MONKEY AND THE ORGAN GRINDER

(July 31, 1986)

Creating a Work Body

Ideally, you create a "Work body" by the intensity of your sadhana. To whatever degree any of you have done that, there are inherent problems in looking to expand the Community. You have got to maintain some continuity amongst yourselves. If two hundred people moved on an ashram and you didn't maintain a sense of yourselves, those two hundred people would eat the body. So, you have got to protect what you have earned so far. On the other hand, other people have to do similar kinds of sadhana for a Work body to grow. That means one of two things. On a large ashram, where it's understood that people are going to make lots of mistakes, and you give them time to make their mistakes and learn from them, you're never going to have this kind of intensity. You have to look at the way this has been for you. You found the Community—maybe you moved into a household after a while and eventually onto the ashram. Occasionally, somebody just jumps in and moves right onto the ashram; there have been a few. But sometimes you move in, you move out, you move in, you move out. As the process escalates for you, so does your understanding that you need this.

If we can't somehow duplicate this kind of intensity, the Community will never move beyond the basic stages that we have now—except we will personally get a little more mature. But the sangha body won't grow, such that anybody that sticks around is likely to last, without constant heat. You have to maintain the momentum for each other *and* duplicate it for new students. That means that people that come to the school need to be cooked the way you have been cooked. The only way you can do that is if you function from the disposition of enlightenment. If you don't instinctually know when to lay off the heat and give people a breather, you'll just burn them out. A few will make it because they're tough and they want it badly. For this vision to be successful, you need to be able to create the same kind of circumstance for other people that was created for you. The way that begins is with me providing the circumstances and you monitoring it. You show any prospective new student or visitor that you're a normal human being and that you went through the same thing. You are friendly if they need someone to talk to. You put the circumstances into the appropriate context and draw them into real relationship.

Sooner or later, *you* will have to create the circumstances. In a small sense, that is what bordello leaders do.[102] So far, as a general rule, bordello leaders have based their relationship to people in bordello on the way I've been with them, which has been conservative. People in bordello still feel the heat. When the Community first began, as some of you remember, there were eighty people coming around. One night at satsang I made the simple suggestion that we should become vegetarians, and forty people stopped coming. It wasn't because they had so much integrity that they couldn't lie [about their diet]. Just the thought of becoming vegetarians produced so much heat that they didn't want to come around anymore. It was a fascinating response that I never expected.

To Be Transformed Requires Heat

People have to have heat on them because they won't break through any other way. Your communion—the brilliance of your devotion, expression of compassion, love and delight in life—is going to have to be the enticement for people. It's going to be pretty obvious to most people that they are never going to have the intimacy with me that some

102 "Bordello" is the name that Lee used for study groups in different locales. These were run by students who introduced visitors interested in spiritual teaching to the Work and the school.

of you have in the sangha body. They're going to have to understand, on some level, that an equal communion to the communion that you and I share is available to them through you. You will be my Influence for them. The ecstasy that is the delight of God-realization and God-surrender, and the obviation of self-reference, is literally as available to them through you as it is available to you through me. You will have to communicate that to people. If you do, most of them will take the heat. But the heat is the kiln. People will not be transformed if they aren't put into the oven. No matter how good they look, everybody has to get put in the oven.

Even Werner Erhard realized that despite the technology he developed, enlightenment doesn't live without a sustaining culture. There must be a support system or what you get [in the est trainings] dies. It's perfectly obvious that people really "get it" [a reference to the insight that participants get] on the last day of the trainings. Then two or three weeks or a month later, they don't have it anymore.

You have to have a radical understanding of ruthless compassion [a reference to the need, often described in Buddhism, to cut through obstructions in order for one's true nature to become accessible]. You can't do that effectively as an act of intelligence. You must be surrendered to Divine Influence or you'll make mistakes—a lot of mistakes. To be truly effective, you must be instinctually surrendered to Divine Influence. With some people, there's a very linear relationship between what they look like and their need to be "cooked." You can look at them and it's very obvious. Yet, with other people, what they look like is totally unrelated in any tangible way to their spiritual needs. They look great… or they look terrible. They may look like they'll never make any value of this [Work] in a million years. But all they need is just the right tempering and they'll make radical shifts. Other people will get the heat—they'll be put in the kiln—and come out looking pretty much the same as before, or maybe a little better. But *inside* is going to be different. Other people don't make radical shifts.

We recently visited a ceramic artist in Massachusetts who does one firing a year. His kiln is ninety feet long, and it takes ten days to two weeks to fire it. Somebody's got to be on duty twenty-four hours a day to feed the kiln enough wood to keep the heat up to the appropriate temperature. All year he does his sculpture and then he does one firing. If he blows it, that year is gone. In a sense, that's the kind of kiln we're building in this school.

This man makes natural-glaze pottery. The glaze is actually melted ash. The heat gets so high that the ashes, which get blown on the pottery from the logs that are used for fuel, melt onto the clay. That's how hot it is. The ideal glaze is a glaze in which the pot has been covered with various formations of ash which have melted on in a certain way that is not ordinary-looking. Sometimes the ash melts very smoothly and you have a pot that looks like it's been glazed in an ordinary way. That's not the object. There are mini-explosions in the kiln because of the heat, and sometimes you get a pot that has big knobs of ash that melt onto it in various ways that produce streams of colors that are created when the fire gets real hot. That's what they look for. A very small fraction of the thousands of pieces he fires come out that way. He can never tell if the exact explosions will happen to produce the glaze patterns he's looking for. It's unpredictable.

The Spiritual Master Is a Master of Timing

That's the way this process works. You develop the ideal heat and hope for the right explosion. When the right explosion comes, the spiritual master knows what to do with the end product. But you never know when the right explosion is going to come. The spiritual master is a master of timing, but he or she doesn't design the timing. The master waits and takes advantage of it when the right timing hits. There's no way of creating it. You keep refining the kiln, the heat, the wood, and the pottery in small ways so that, as times goes on, you get better and better at increasing the possibility. But you never know when the explosion is going to happen.

The Sangha's Need to Duplicate the Process for Others

A lot of you will be creating that kind of heat one day. It's the only way the culture will grow beyond our ranks. But you need to know when to turn on the heat. How you do that, obviously, is by being in a position of authority—*genuine* authority—and getting people to work. At first, it's physical work. There are lots of possibilities. That's the situation you have to look forward to—providing the kind of function for people that I have provided for you. It will be your job to fire in the way that you have been fired. The ashram is the kiln.

The sangha body will not grow beyond our ranks if we don't duplicate this process. This is the only way. It's the only way because everybody is born with the same equipment. There are certain givens about being a human being, and we need to deal with those givens. This is the way we deal with them. We have talked about responsibility and obligation. When you get into the position in which you are literally called on to be the one who manages the kiln, that's a point at which you're under obligation. Because the life of the Community, the life of the body, is in your hands. The body must continue to grow or it stagnates and dies. That's the nature of things. If growth becomes impossible, then survive at all costs. That is what underground schools are about. There's obviously a very rich spiritual history of that. Any genuine Christians had to go underground to survive during the Inquisition. Many real schools throughout history have gone underground, *way* underground, and survived because of it.

Father and Son: Yogi Ramsuratkumar and Lee, India, late 1990s

AFTERWORD

Lee Lozowick's emergence as a spiritual teacher on the East Coast in 1975 arose unexpectedly, perhaps as part of the growth of the genuine spiritual process in the West. As with every spiritual master, there were different chapters in the story of his Work. This book has been about Lee's early teachings in which the groundwork was laid for those who came in contact with him to practice the dharma in the West. It has not attempted to review the subsequent chapters of his Work, which would take many more volumes. There will undoubtedly be future books by students and people who knew Lee which will recount ways in which his teaching Work unfolded and how his life quickened the spiritual process for them and others. Nonetheless, a few words about the rest of the story seems in order.

In *The Only Grace is Loving God*, Lee had written in 1982 that loving God was the major aspect of his teaching Work and the particular message that he had to deliver. He made the distinction between awakening or surrender to the Law in each moment as the highest *destiny* of man, and loving God as the highest *possibility* of man. He asserted that loving God could only come about through the Whim of God, but that this epitome of human possibility could be *considered*. This was done every night in the Tavern space from its inception in 1983 through his death. At one point, he spoke about the consuming mood of total love written about in *Vallabhacarya's Commentaries on the Love Games of Krishna* as the most resonant metaphorical description of his Work.

In 1986, Lee made another trip to India, where he had traveled in 1977 and 1979, with a group of twenty students and a few children. When he visited Yogi Ramsuratkumar in Tiruvannamalai, the Indian master sent him away. This was a shock given the magical events that had transpired during previous visits and the poetry that he had regularly been sending, which others had not known about at the time. Upon his return to America, Lee began to speak about Yogi Ramsuratkumar as his master, and in fact said that he had regarded him in this way for several years and had realized the timeless nature of their relationship. He said that he would not go back to India in his lifetime since his master did not want to see him, but he never doubted their connection and continued to send poetry.

While in India in 1986, contact was made with Sanatan Das Baul, who visited Lee's ashram in America several years later. Lee began to speak about his resonance with the Bauls given an essential similarity with their practice despite cultural differences. In the spirit of the Baul practice of expressing the teaching through song (which had not been known about in the early years of the Community), he had sometimes written song lyrics in notebooks. While eastern Baul practice involved singing accompanied by a single-stringed *ektara* and *duggi* (drum), Lee wrote lyrics that students began to set to music with electric guitar, bass, and drums beginning in the mid-1980s. In 1985, the Living God Blues band, which was later renamed *liars, gods and beggars* (LGB), began to perform, with Lee as part of the band. Lee accepted an invitation to travel to Germany from a teacher he had met in India in 1986. While there, he met people who gravitated to him and became his students. A whole process of the formation of a European sangha was begun as individuals from France, England, and other countries found him—or perhaps were found by him.

In 1988, two years after Yogi Ramsuratkumar had sent Lee away, Lee received an invitation to attend a celebration in south India for the Beggar-Saint, who would not be attending. He immediately knew that he should go, and upon arriving was surprised to find huge outdoor banners welcoming him as the "Divine Effulgent Flame of Yogi Ramsuratkumar" and the "Spiritual Master of the West"—descriptions of him that his master had apparently made. He also learned when he got to the celebration that he was to be the keynote speaker at the event. Though Lee always appeared surrendered and "one with" the circumstances that presented themselves in life, he also seemed genuinely moved by the turn of events. He had planned to spend just one or two days in Tiruvannamalai after the celebration, just in case Yogi Ramsuratkumar wanted to see him. Upon arriving at Yogi Ramsuratkumar's doorstep, he was fully welcomed home in a way no one could have foreseen.

There are many rich stories of Lee's relationship to Yogi Ramsuratkumar as it manifested in the world until the Indian master's *mahasamadhi* in 2001. With the exception of 1990 and 1992, Lee visited Yogi Ramsuratkumar every year from 1988-2001, and the history of their relationship and the interactions between them is described in books including *Under the Punnai Tree*, *Only God*, and *Father and Son*, published by Hohm Press. Lee attributed his 1975 shift in context and all of his Work to the Influence of his master as the individuated divine expression of all that exists. On India trips that Lee made with students over the years, Yogi Ramsuratkumar was known to enter into ecstatic *bhavas* [states of ecstatic consciousness], blessing those in his presence and making statements such as, "My Father alone exists. There is nothing else, nobody else—past, present, future—here, there, everywhere! My Father alone!" Lee wrote over 1300 poems to his master which have been published in three volumes, and he said that the *lila* between Yogi Ramsuratkumar and himself had been engaged lifetime after lifetime. A particular aspect of Lee's work involved bringing the empowered Divine Name (*Nama*) of Yogi Ramsuratkumar to those in need of spiritual help in the West.

In 1991, Lee met the French spiritual master, Arnaud Desjardins, with whom he developed a strong connection. He would see Arnaud each summer when he went to Europe, and their relationship was particularly notable for the way each served the other's students. Lee continued to write lyrics for rock and blues bands that he created. He sang and toured with LGB (1985-1999, thirteen albums), Shri (1993-2017, which continued to tour Europe for seven years after his death, nineteen albums), and the Lee Lozowick Project (2004-2009, five albums). He founded two other bands that performed music set to his lyrics: Attila the Hunza (1998-2005, four albums) and the Denise Allen Band (2003-2019, six albums). He wrote lyrics for two rock operas (*John T.* and *The Nine Houses of Mila*) that were staged by the Baul Theater Company, a theatrical performing troupe that he conceived in 1986. He referred to the tradition that he established as the Western Baul tradition.

Around the time of Yogi Ramsuratkumar's death in 2001, Lee began to emphasize the non-linear transmission of sacred artifacts in his Work and he started a business named Vigraha that became a vehicle for his Influence during the last ten years of his life. He worked with students in selling artifacts imbued with the communication of devotion and practice that he obtained while traveling in India and Europe. Lee continued to work for Yogi Ramsuratkumar until his last breath, passing from this realm in mahasamadhi on November 16, 2010. He left a body of practitioners which he sometimes referred to as "the enlightened community" for the way that it embodies his Influence. Lee also left three ashrams—in Arizona, France, and India. As with all genuine masters, his Influence and Presence continues to be available through the sacred spaces and artifacts he empowered and through his students who continue the practice of the Western Baul tradition.

In the past century, there has been an influx of teachers from different spiritual traditions who have come to visit or reside in the West, including Hindus, Buddhists, and Sufis. Having been born in other parts of the world, the distinctive cultural elements that came along with them and the teachings added to the mystique about the spiritual path. There have also been Western teachers who have entered the spiritual scene who may or may not be associated with a tradition.

It is likely that, as in all times and places, some who have charisma, intelligence, and power have assumed a spiritual identity as a teacher while being out of touch with the underlying motives of a psychological shadow. Others have genuine experience and integrity and have offered teaching that can be useful to those with a developing spiritual need. Some rare few have been masters who have actually been transformed beyond self-identification by the Great Process and have lived as the Law of Sacrifice.

In the West, our attention is easily captured by the search for stimulation, novelty, and pleasure, that only suffices in temporary ways. We do not have a history of dedicated apprenticeship to the kind of spiritual knowledge about ourselves and existence that has been present in other places and times. But, if we sense the need for more than the passing satisfactions offered in a culture of material and spiritual consumerism and are not satisfied with the explanations of mainstream religions, we can be drawn by the depth and wisdom of spiritual teachings and traditions that address the root cause of suffering.

A feature of Western life is that, with the advent of internet access, it has become simple for us to download information about anything—including spiritual teachings—that in the past may have taken many years of effort to access. By incorporating a conceptual understanding of the dharma into our worldview, some may think that they have come to understand the teaching. After all, "what is" is always right here and now.

But it is helpful to realize that, if we have a thirst to know who we are beyond identification, to resolve or transform our experience of the human dilemma, the spiritual process has always involved experiential work which challenges the primal reactions of ego and the separate identity that we seek to maintain at all costs. In his life, Lee highlighted this in a discomforting way, with his surrender and presence, naturally shining unerring light on ego's motives. He seemed to be used by the

Process to bring about self-reflection through a unique teaching style arising out of tacit familiarity with Western culture.

Coincidentally, his compassion, freedom, and humor evoked a part of us that we had forgotten, an innate joy that seemed to be a memory from the distant past. Being around him was encouragement to persist and go deeper since, for students who worked with him, it was obvious that he was interested in working on a level of ultimate value. His life was about enlivening that which we are beyond the assumed separate self, establishing a community that would continue to practice in the West, and bringing the blessings of his master Yogi Ramsuratkumar into the world.

What attracted people to Lee was more than his vast knowledge of the context of human functioning; it was his being, presence, instinct, and continuous availability throughout his thirty-five years of teaching. It sparked something—commitment to a higher purpose, or the possibility of loving God—in all who were touched by him. And yet there must have been some sorrow when students were not available to the Gift that was offered through him. What was amazing to witness was the abiding way in which Lee was present and served the Work in countless circumstances that he interfaced with over the course of his life as a teacher. It seemed that he got his orders moment to moment, and that his life was a sacrifice for the benefit of all beings.

To have the experience of Lee's intention, compassion, fierceness, holy madness, and humor was to get in touch with our own inner calling to work, to the free movement of the Divine within ourselves, and to the gratefulness that can be stirred in us to share what we have received in the way we live our lives. It is hoped that those who have a sincere need to pursue the spiritual path will find Lee's words useful.

If you are interested in books, activities, podcasts, or further information about Lee Lozowick or the Hohm Community visit **westernbaul.org, hohmsahajmandir.org**, and **hohmpress.com**.

Darshan, 2010

APPENDIX

Already Published Excerpts of Transcriptions of Other "Commercial Tapes" in Books by Lee Lozowick

The Alarm Clock Fable (*In the Fire*, 177-188)
Bonding: The Human Mother as Goddess (*Conscious Parenting*, 126-130)
Concern is Your Concession to Unconsciousness (87-91, and "Cult of the Hero" 148-153, *In the Fire*)
Content versus Context (entire 3 tape set published as *Acting God*)
The Mosquito and the Windshield (*Laughter of the Stones*, 83-98)
The One and Only True Secret of Tantric Sex and God Forgive Me for Giving It Away So Cheaply (*The Alchemy of Love and Sex*, 168-171)
Sadhana of Separation ("Sausalito Dream," *In the Fire*, 92-98)
Sex: Its Transcendent Possibilities (*The Alchemy of Love and Sex*, 199ff.)
Shakti: The Divine Mother and Cosmic Oedipus ("The Alabaster Breast," *In the Fire*, 111-117)
Study Course Week 12 (section on "Life in a Goldfish Bowl," *Laughter of the Stones*, 61-63)

INDEX

J

K

L

M

N

O

P

R

S

T

CONTACT INFORMATION

Lee Lozowick (1943-2010) an American-born spiritual teacher taught thousands of people in North America, Europe and India since 1975. He is the spiritual son of the beggar-saint, Yogi Ramsuratkumar. Lee founded three ashrams and retreat sanctuaries (in US, France and India), and wrote twenty books, including: *Conscious Parenting* and *The Alchemy of Transformation;* and has been translated and published in French, German, Spanish, Portuguese and other languages. He was also a poet, a lyricist, and the lead singer for both an American blues group, *SHRI*, and a European band, *The Lee Lozowick Project.*

Karuna Fedorschak trained as an archeologist in New Jersey. She met Lee Lozowick in the mid-1970s. Moving with her husband, Vijaya, to Arizona in 1980 with Lee's earliest students, she dedicated herself to the support of the community and teaching as a practitioner, bookkeeper, cook, indexer and editor. Karuna had an evocative singing voice and was a vocalist in *liars, gods and beggars*, the first band founded by Lee. She later formed a duo band, *Small Change*, which produced two albums (*Small Change* and *No Regrets*) in which she arranged music, played guitar, and sang. She had two children with Vijaya and is author of *Parenting: A Sacred Task*. Karuna died gracefully before this book went to press.

Vijaya (VJ) Fedorschak was a city planner in the mid-1970s when he encountered the spiritual path and the teaching work of Lee Lozowick in New York/New Jersey. After moving to Arizona with his wife Karuna, he got jobs in landscaping and sales and became involved in theater projects and in organizing conferences. He has been a therapist for youth and families with histories of trauma for over twenty years. VJ is author of *The Shadow on the Path: Clearing Psychological Blocks to Spiritual Development*, and *Father and Son* in which the visits between Lee and Yogi Ramsuratkumar in India are recounted. He is the organizer of the Western Baul Podcast Series. VJ has two adult children and lives in Prescott, Arizona.

Contact: If you are interested in activities, podcasts, or further information about Lee Lozowick or the Hohm Community, visit westernbaul.org and hohmsahajmandir.org.

Hohm Press is committed to publishing books that provide readers with alternatives to the materialistic values of the current culture, and promote self-awareness, the recognition of interdependence, and compassion. Our subject areas include parenting, transpersonal psychology, religious studies, women's studies, the arts and poetry.

Contact Information: Hohm Press, PO Box 4410, Chino Valley, Arizona, 86323, USA; 800-381-2700, or 928-636-3331; email: publisher@hohmpress.com

Visit our website at www.hohmpress.com